Advance praise for

BEHIND THE WAR ON TERROR

As the United States serves notice that it plans to
dominate world affairs by force, this finely researched book
offers a timely and powerful warning to us all.

— JOHN PILGER, Author of *The New Rulers of the World*

Yes, yes, I know he [Nafeez Mosaddeq Ahmed] is one of Them.
But they often know things that we don't – particularly about
what we are up to.

— GORE VIDAL, Author of *Dreaming War: Blood for Oil and the
Cheney-Bush Junta* and *Perpetual War for Perpetual Peace*

I wish every American who still believes in the good intentions
of our government would read this book. Drawing upon
his impressive research into recent history, Nafeez Ahmed
skillfully exposes the real motives behind the "war on terrorism"
and the invasions of Afghanistan and Iraq.

— HOWARD ZINN, Author of *A People's History of the United States*

If anyone craves irrefutable evidence of the U.S.'s aspirations
to empire since World War II, read this book.
If anyone wants to comprehend the mechanisms whereby
classical imperialism was restyled into corporate globalization,
read this book. And be shaken.

— CHELLIS GLENDINNING, Ph.D., Author of *Off the Map:
An Expedition Deep into Empire and the Global Economy*

Nafeez Mosaddeq Ahmed gives us an incisive,
longer-term view of U.S. and Western foreign policy
intentions in Iraq — well worth reading.

— PROFESSOR RICARDO RENE LAREMONT, Chair of Department
of Sociology; Associate Director of Institute for Global Cultural
Studies, State University of New York, Binghamton

In a worthy sequel to the author's path-breaking expose of 9/11,
this book exposes the real reasons for the War Against Iraq.
Ahmed recounts the untold history of how the orchestration
of conflict and the conduct of military operations by Anglo-
American power in the Middle East since Lawrence of Arabia
has led today to a form of worldwide surrogate-imperialism.

— ANDRE GUNDER FRANK, Senior Fellow, World History Center,
Northeastern University in Boston, and Professor of World
History, University of Nebraska in Lincoln

Why did we (really) go to war? The Bush administration, whose
answers don't exactly add up, wishes the question would go away.
This book will, crucially, help to make sure that it doesn't.

— MIRIAM PEMBERTON, Research Fellow, Peace and Security
Program, Institute for Policy Studies, Washington DC,
and Military Affairs Editor of *Foreign Policy In Focus*

Nafeez exposes the buried truths, the real dangers, and double
standards of U.S. policy toward Iraq in a timely work all
Americans should carefully read. A clearly written work that
makes the complexity and hypocrisy of U.S. foreign policy
understandable to all. This powerful and prescient book is a
must-read for those who want to know why 'they' hate the
US government and what causes terrorism.

— ELSON BOLES, Professor at Department of Sociology,
Saginaw Valley State University, Michigan

The second U.S. war against Iraq has already unveiled itself
as the most nonsensical war in American history.
The American public will eventually have her fair share of
'shock and awe' discovering the subversive, yet spineless,
influence of a neo-conservative cadre in trying to shape the
Middle East. This book will range among the foremost
contributions to the final account with the 'velociraptors'.

— PETER SPENGLER, Editor of *Contemporary Studies*
(Studien von Zeitfragen)

Americans have never been known for paying attention to the
uglier side of U.S. history, but never has such history been so
important. Nafeez Ahmed provides a valuable service by clearly
laying out the facts and analysis people need to make sense of the
U.S. attack on Iraq. The reality of U.S. policy in the Middle East
isn't pretty, which makes it all the more important to confront.
Thanks to Ahmed for taking on the challenge.

— ROBERT W. JENSEN, Professor at the School of Journalism and
Director of College of Communication Senior Fellows Program,
University of Texas, Austin

… an invaluable source work on a much repressed topic.
It proves beyond a reasonable doubt the systematic war crimes
and crimes against humanity by the U.S. and British states in the
Middle East over decades. Most horrifically, it provides compelling
evidence for deliberate and long-term U.S.-led policies of genocide
against the once advanced Iraqi society, with Saddam Hussein
himself employed by the U.S. as a tool in the violent dismember-
ment of the Arab world's most successful social economy.
A must-read for all who seek the facts behind the propaganda
of the "U.S. coalition of the willing to liberate Iraq".

— JOHN MCMURTRY, PhD, FRSC, Professor of Philosophy,
University of Guelph, Author of *Value Wars: The Global Market
versus the Life Economy*

This is an important, perhaps controversial, but always well-informed book which will become a standard item for the 'new peace movement' and also for students across the globe.

— ARNO TAUSCH, Professor, Department of Political Science at Innsbruck University, and Ministerial Counselor, Department of European and International Affairs, Republic of Austria

BEHIND
THE
Western Secret Strategy and the Struggle for Iraq
WAR ON TERROR

NAFEEZ MOSADDEQ AHMED

To my precious wife, Akeela, and our wonderful daughter,
Amina, because I value them higher than anything; because
without them, the value of this book would be nothing.

Cataloguing in Publication Data:
A catalog record for this publication is available from the National Library of Canada.

Cover design by Diane McIntosh; cover photo by Michael Liphitz, used by permission of Associated Press.

Printed in Canada.

New Society Publishers acknowledges the support of the Government of Canada through the Book Publishing Industry Development Program (BPIDP) for our publishing activities.

Paperback ISBN: 0-86571-506-8

Inquiries regarding requests to reprint all or part of *Behind the War on Terror* should be addressed to New Society Publishers at the address below.

To order directly from the publishers, please add $4.50 shipping to the price of the first copy, and $1.00 for each additional copy (plus GST in Canada). Send check or money order to:

New Society Publishers
P.O. Box 189, Gabriola Island, BC V0R 1X0, Canada
1-800-567-6772

New Society Publishers' mission is to publish books that contribute in fundamental ways to building an ecologically sustainable and just society, and to do so with the least possible impact on the environment, in a manner that models this vision. We are committed to doing this not just through education, but through action. We are acting on our commitment to the world's remaining ancient forests by phasing out our paper supply from ancient forests worldwide. This book is one step towards ending global deforestation and climate change. It is printed on acid-free paper that is **100% old growth forest-free** (100% post-consumer recycled), processed chlorine free, and printed with vegetable based, low VOC inks. For further information, or to browse our full list of books and purchase securely, visit our website at: www.newsociety.com

NEW SOCIETY PUBLISHERS   www.newsociety.com

Contents

Acknowledgments

Beyond the sources cited directly in this work, I benefited greatly from reading the following authors whose works provide an invaluable repository of inspiration, general information and some data that is not exclusive to them, or did not seem specific enough to cite or ascribe to them directly.

Andre Gunder Frank's *Third World War: A Political Economy of the Gulf War and the New World Order* pulled together a vast amount of material on the entire history of US involvement in Iraq, which was extremely helpful in locating important sources. Ramsey Clark's *The Fire This Time* was, to my mind, the first book to thoroughly expose the realities of that crisis as well as document the thesis that it had been a direct product of US regional policy. Mark Curtis' *The Ambiguities of Power* and *The Great Deception* were extremely useful for locating some declassified documents with respect to the special relationship between Britain and the US, and their policies in the Middle East and the Persian Gulf. Noam Chomsky's *Towards a New Cold War*, *Deterring Democracy* and *World Orders, Old and New* were the first texts that brought my attention to the pattern and grand strategy of US foreign policy in the postwar period, including with respect to Iraq and the Middle East. William Blum's *Killing Hope* was instrumental in the same regard, but mainly in garnering evidence that the US government manufactured the 1991 Gulf crisis. Several of Milan Rai's ARROW Briefings, later published in his *War Plan Iraq*, provided useful data on the US manipulation of the United Nations inspection process from 2001 onwards.

Preface

The 2003 war against Iraq, led principally by the United States and the United Kingdom, reached its final stages towards the end of April, heralding the beginning of a dangerous new era in international relations. Just how dangerous this new era is likely to be is discussed in detail in this book.

Of course, no attempt to properly understand the 2003 war on Iraq can avoid grappling with the complex historical developments in the region vis-à-vis Western interventionism in the Middle East and the Persian Gulf. The bulk of this study, originally written before the outbreak of war in 2003, attempts to analyse the war in its historical context, with the view to discern its real character and motives – which most often are completely at odds with the official story propagated by our political leaders.

The picture that emerges is frightening indeed, replete with bloodshed, repression and profiteering – and all the more frightening because those primarily responsible for this grim record of atrocities in the region belong to our very own Western institutions of power.

Most significantly, we discover that little has really changed since the British and Europeans began to carve-up the Arab world in the early 1900s. An in-depth and impartial analysis of the documentary record demonstrates that President Bush and Prime Minister Blair have faithfully followed in the footsteps of their governmental predecessors both in motives and in methods, however brutal those may be.

This has many crucial implications for our understanding of world affairs and their future course, as well as of solutions to threats and problems such as terrorism, weapons of mass destruction, and repressive regimes. These implications, which point to the necessity of fundamental change, are also considered in this book, and I hope that the overall results are sufficient to contribute to developing a more informed public awareness of the realities of conflict in the Middle East, as well as subsequently a more informed approach to policy-making.

I would like to thank my editor, Sevak Edward Gulbekian, and everyone else at Clairview Books, for everything they have done to prepare and release this book with such speed and professionalism. Thanks also to my agent, Jonathan Pegg, for bringing us together in the first place, and for being so supportive of the entire project. My Italian editor and agent, Vincenzo Ostuni, deserves my thanks for his unfailing, continuing support and counsel, through some of the most dubious experiences. I cannot omit my father-in-law, Shabbir Gheewalla, for his voluntary research assistance, which often involved burning the midnight oil (far beyond midnight!). Most of all, I must thank Akeela Gheewalla for being by my side through everything, and Amina Ahmed, for keeping me alive.

Nafeez Mosaddeq Ahmed
Brighton
15 July, 2003

Introduction

The terrorist attacks of 11 September 2001 opened the eyes of many to the turbulence and turmoil of political events in the Arab and Muslim world. Those attacks to some extent signalled the beginning of a new age – both in terms of the new dangers to world order from amorphous, fluid, non-state terror structures such as Al-Qaeda, and in terms of the response to these dangers on the part of Western governments, under United States leadership, in the new 'War on Terror'.

President George W. Bush, and along with him many respected political commentators, characterized the 9/11 atrocity as an attack on freedom and civilization by people who hate both. Indeed, many opinion-makers deride the idea that the 11 September terrorist attacks could have been somehow linked to American foreign policy. To seek such connections may be seen as adding insult to injury or unpatriotic. At the same time, it is clear that such an outrage could not appear simply out of the blue.

No attempt to understand the new 'War on Terror' and the terrorist attacks that preceded it can succeed without attempting to analyse the context of both. Such an analysis, of course, is not an attempt to justify such appalling terrorism – but simply to scientifically discover the political, economic and historic policies on the part of the United States and the West that may have cultivated the extreme psychological grievances that inspire terror.

The conventional wisdom portrays the 9/11 attacks and previous such terrorist atrocities against US and Western targets in a false ahistorical light that isolates such events from the wider context of Western policy in the non-Western world. The general idea is that the terrorists responsible for such atrocities, due to their inexplicably and intrinsically evil nature, possess an unfathomable hatred against Western civilization and the values it supposedly holds most dear. This idea is integral to legitimizing the new 'War on Terror' that has commenced in the aftermath of 9/11.

Harvard political scientist Professor Samuel Huntington is well known for establishing a theoretical context for this idea in the form of an academically acceptable theory of international relations. His 'clash of civilizations' thesis is a particularly stark example of how many elements of Western academia attempt to justify the concept of an unfathomable Islam-West divide and a new, inevitable cold war with Islam.[1] The thesis is also highly influential in US policy-making circles. Tim Hames, a leading politician in the Republican Party who is very close to the Bush administration, claimed only one day after the attacks that Huntington's thesis was dominating the US political scene.[2] Huntington has most recently presented a summary of his work in an article titled 'The Age of Muslim Wars' for *Newsweek* magazine. The article's introductory synopsis asserts that:

> Contemporary global politics is the age of Muslim wars. Muslims fight each other and fight non-Muslims far more often than do peoples of other civilizations. Muslim wars have replaced the cold war as the principal form of international conflict. These wars include wars of terrorism, guerrilla wars, civil wars and interstate conflicts. These instances of Muslim violence could congeal into one major clash of civilizations between Islam and the West or between Islam and the Rest.[3]

Huntington's thesis builds upon a long tradition of Western political animosity – motivated by geostrategic interests – in the Middle East, since the end of the cold war. Such animosity, it seems, is justified by repeated reference to the intrinsically violent character of the 'Other', in this case, of 'Islam'. This ideological duality between the intrinsically superior civilization of the West and the intrinsically bestial civilization of the 'Other' is not a new phenomenon in international relations, but rather builds upon a longstanding tradition of warmongering.

Indeed, the new 'War on Terror' being led by the United States in the aftermath of the 11 September terrorist attacks is an extension of the same fundamental plans and principles that have motivated and directed US foreign policy since the Second World War. On the pretext of fighting against international terrorism, the US Government is in reality attempting to expand and consolidate its global pre-eminence in accordance with longstanding strategies that have been contemplated and elaborated over a period of decades. The roots of the new 'War on Terror' go all the way back to the international political climate that resulted in the cold war with the Soviet Union. In order to clearly grasp the continuity between these successive periods in the development of world order, we need to go back to the foundations of that order under US direction.

Post-War Planning for World Control

The essential structure of world order envisaged by the US Government in the post-Second World War period was candidly described in a now declassified top-secret planning report produced by the US State Department's policy planning staff, headed at the time by George Kennan. The secret memo, produced in February 1948, states as follows:

> We have about 50 per cent of the world's wealth, but only 6.3 per cent of its population ... In this situation, we cannot fail to be the object of envy and resentment. Our real task in the coming period

is to devise a pattern of relationships which will permit us to maintain this position of disparity without positive detriment to our national security. To do so we will have to dispense with all sentimentality and day-dreaming; and our attention will have to be concentrated everywhere on our immediate national objectives ... We need not deceive ourselves that we can afford the luxury of altruism and world-benefaction ... We should cease to talk about vague and ... unreal objectives such as human rights, the raising of living standards, and democratization. The day is not far off when we will have to deal in straight power concepts. The less we are then hampered by idealistic slogans, the better.[4]

This document affirms that primary US goals are oriented towards securing economic domination, or in other words, control over world resources. This domination must be institutionalized by establishing a global pattern of political relationships throughout the world, in which such US domination can be maintained. Altruism and world-benefaction are therefore not relevant to US goals. In fact, the very ideals that have always been traditionally associated with the United States are here being dismissed as 'vague' and 'unreal objectives'. US monopoly over world resources will inevitably create a global economic disparity, at the expense of the human rights, living standards and decisions of the populations of the non-Western world.

It comes as no surprise then that the process of decolonization initiated by the British Empire was, in reality, an attempt to reconfigure that Empire in order to allow colonial control to continue to survive in the face of increasing problems. Decolonization therefore constituted a front for covert colonialism – or rather, neo-colonialism.

As historian Professor Cranford Pratt of the University of Toronto observes in his study of decolonization, 'all that Hailey, Cohen and other colleagues [the British planners who drew up the plans for decolonization] advocated can be interpreted as shrewdly designed to protect and advance British economic and political interests in these changing circumstances.'[5] In fact, the planners even admitted that the essence of the so-called process of decolonization 'was a plan to convert (or reconvert) formal into informal empire as the need arose' in order that 'such colonial reform would extend the life of colonial control'.[6] Thus, regarding the process of decolonization in the Middle East, British Prime Minister Clement Attlee observed in 1947 that 'we shall constantly appear to be supporting vested interests and reaction against reform and revolution in the interests of the poor' − in other words, maintaining the entrenched domestic social, economic and political structures under colonial rule favouring colonial interests, despite the withdrawal of colonial forces.[7] The form of imperialism that resulted from this strategy was described well by Kwame Nkrumah, Ghana's first post-colonial president. Nkrumah, as part of a growing awareness among the elite in post-colonial Africa, saw first hand that the granting of formal independence and national sovereignty to African states by the colonial powers was a purely token gesture that failed to substantially alter relations between the former and the latter. The term he coined to describe this stage of imperialism was 'neo-colonialism':

> Neo-colonialism is ... the worst form of imperialism. For those who practise it, it means power without responsibility, and for those who suffer from it, it means exploitation without redress. In the days of old-fashioned colonialism, the imperial power had at least to explain and justify at home the actions it was taking abroad. In the colony those who served the ruling imperial power could at least look to its protection against any violent move by their opponents. With neo-colonialism neither is the case.[8]

But as British global power steadily declined, the US gladly took its place, taking Britain in particular under its wing as a 'junior partner in an orbit of power predominantly under the American aegis', as described in a declassified British document.[9] A series of other documents produced during the Second World War by the War and Peace Studies Project of the Council on Foreign Relations, which enlisted the participation of top government planners, confirms that 'the British Empire as it existed in the past will never reappear ... the United States may have to takes its place'.[10] Policy planners set out to fulfil the 'requirement[s] of the United States in a world in which it proposes to hold unquestioned power' (1940). This implied the implementation of 'an integrated policy to achieve military and economic supremacy for the United States', including the plan 'to secure the limitation of any exercise of sovereignty by foreign nations that constitutes a threat to the world area essential for the security and economic prosperity of the United States and the Western Hemisphere'.

The documents further state that the United States 'must cultivate a mental view toward world settlement after this war which will enable us to impose our own terms, amounting perhaps to a pax-Americana'. Accordingly, it was decided that the definition of the 'security interests' of the United States be extended to include regions of the world that are 'strategically necessary for world control'. A State Department memorandum of April 1944 clarified the philosophy behind this concept of Western 'access to resources'.[11] The philosophy was: equal access for American companies to world resources, but not for others;[12] the US domination of Western Hemispheric production while US holdings are diversified elsewhere;[13] and in summary, 'the preservation of the absolute position presently obtaining, and therefore vigilant protection of existing concessions in United States hands coupled with insistence upon the Open Door principle of equal opportunity for the United States companies in new areas'.[14]

It was well understood that these policies, if expressed honestly, would be highly unpalatable to the general public around the world. For example, Council on Foreign Relations documents from mid-1941 recognized that a 'formulation of a statement of war aims for propaganda purposes is very different from a formulation of one defining the true national interest'. It was further noted: 'If war aims are stated, which seem to be concerned solely with Anglo-American imperialism, they will offer little to people in the rest of the world ... Such aims would also strengthen the most reactionary elements in the United States and the British Empire. The interests of other peoples should be stressed, not only those of Europe, but also of Asia, Africa and Latin America. This would have a better propaganda effect.'[15]

Propaganda and the Necessity of a Permanent Threat to 'Civilization'

In accordance with the need to establish ideological legitimacy for Anglo-American imperialism, it was essential – as part and parcel of war propaganda – to manufacture a global threat that would provide justification for military interventions designed to expand the US empire.

By fabricating a malignant global threat to the very existence of Western civilization, the great powers could legitimize the illegitimate use of force. And this is how the cold war, the apparently noble defence against global Communist aggression, escalated. Former US statesman and noted scholar George Kennan, who had originally proposed the aggressive US strategy of Russian containment, admits that the threat of Russian military expansion that justified US policy during the cold war did not exist:

I ... went to great lengths to disclaim the view, imputed to me by implication ... that containment was a matter of stationing mili-

tary forces around the Soviet borders and preventing any outbreak of Soviet military aggressiveness. I protested ... against the
implication that the Russians were aspiring to invade other areas
and that the task of American policy was to prevent them from
doing so. 'The Russians don't want,' I insisted, 'to invade anyone.
It is not their tradition ... They don't want war of any kind.'[16]

Kennan also noted that 'the image of a Stalinist Russia poised
and yearning to attack the West, and deterred only by [US]
possession of atomic weapons, was largely a creation of Western
imagination'.[17]

The Soviet/Communist threat was therefore certainly exaggerated far beyond reality to legitimize Anglo-American imperialism. This has been further documented in detail by British
historian Mark Curtis, a former Research Fellow at the Royal
Institute of International Affairs, in his book *The Ambiguities of
Power*. Curtis digs deep into newly declassified British documents, proving country-by-country that the real motivation
behind US military interventions during the cold war was not
Soviet deterrence but the crushing of popular, indigenous
nationalist movements for independence, and the establishment
of US control over strategic regions.

On 1 January 1999, *The Guardian* reported on some such
documents from 1968. Among them was one based on an
analysis by the Foreign Office Joint Intelligence Committee,
summarized by *The Guardian* as follows:

> The Soviet Union had no intention of launching a military attack
> on the West at the height of the cold war, British military and
> intelligence chiefs privately believed, in stark contrast to what
> Western politicians and military leaders were saying in public
> about the 'Soviet threat'. 'The Soviet Union will not deliberately
> start general war or even limited war in Europe,' a briefing for the
> British chiefs of staff — marked Top Secret, UK Eyes Only, and

headed The Threat: Soviet Aims and Intentions – declared in June 1968. 'Soviet foreign policy had been cautious and realistic,' the department argued, and despite the Vietnam War, the Russians and their allies had 'continued to make contacts in all fields with the West and to maintain a limited but increasing political dialogue with Nato powers ...'

National Security Council Directive – NSC68 – clearly affirms that US military interventions during the cold war would have been pursued whether or not the Soviet Union constituted a threat. 'Our overall policy at the present time may be described as one designed to foster a world environment in which the American system can survive and flourish ... This broad intention embraces two subsidiary positions. One is a policy which we would probably pursue even if there were no Soviet threat.'

But as Kennan confirmed, there was no such 'monolithic and ruthless conspiracy' emanating from the Soviet Union, as it had been described by President John F. Kennedy. That did not stop British and American government officials from pretending that there was, in order to justify imperialism. Former Under-Secretary of State and future Deputy Secretary of Defense Robert Lovett said pointedly about the international Communist threat, 'if we can sell every useless article known to man in large quantities, we should be able to sell our very fine story in larger quantities'.[18]

During the cold war, as noted by historian Howard Zinn, Professor Emeritus at Boston University, the US administrations of the time 'worked to create an atmosphere of crisis and cold war'. Even though 'the rivalry with the Soviet Union was real', the United States 'presented the Soviet Union as not just a rival but an immediate threat. In a series of moves abroad and at home, it established a climate of fear – a hysteria about Communism – which would steeply escalate the military budget, stimulate the economy with war-related orders. This combination of policies would permit more aggressive actions abroad, more repressive actions at home ... Revolutionary movements in Europe and Asia,' that were in fact 'nationalist' in orientation, 'were described to the American public as examples of Soviet expansionism'.[19]

The process of empire-building that occurred during this period has been extensively analysed by Professor Andrew Bacevich, Director of the Center for International Relations at Boston University, in his seminal study *American Empire*. Professor Bacevich's well-documented thesis is that the emergence of the American empire was the meticulously planned product of a concerted design. Building upon the works of the American historians Charles Beard and William Appleman Williams, Bacevich observes that during the cold war the US was consciously attempting to expand its empire using every excuse possible resulting from the bipolar division of global power. Prior to the cold war period, the US exploited the two World Wars in the same manner. The basic policy was: to conduct pre-emptive strikes often without justification, when considered necessary (for instance, when annexing the Spanish empire); delay entry into world conflicts until potential competitors were suitably weakened; intervene to stabilize the situation and collect the spoils. The US was thus able to establish its global leadership unchallenged.[20]

Thus, as former State Department official William Blum observes, between 1945 and 1999 the US had conducted extremely serious military interventions against over 70 nations to secure the following basic imperatives:

- making the world safe for American corporations;
- enhancing the financial statements of defence contractors at

home who have contributed generously to members of Congress;
- preventing the rise of any society that might serve as a successful example of an alternative to the capitalist model;
- extending political and economic hegemony over as wide an area as possible, as befits a 'great power.'[21]

As Bacevich concludes:

> The question that urgently demands attention – the question that Americans can no longer afford to dodge – is not whether the United States has become an imperial power. The question is what sort of empire they intend theirs to be. For policy makers to persist in pretending otherwise – to indulge in myths of American innocence or fantasies about unlocking the secrets of history – is to increase the likelihood that the answers they come up with will be wrong. That way lies not just the demise of the American empire but great danger for what used to be known as the American republic.[22]

Post-Cold War Propaganda

After the collapse of the Soviet Union, US plans and strategies for the expansion and consolidation of the American empire required a new threat, and a new pretext, to provide humanitarian legitimacy to those plans and strategies. Successive US administrations thus began working incessantly on new threats and pretexts with which to replace the dead threat of Communism. Several spectres of doom came to the fore: rogue states, weapons of mass destruction and, most dangerous of all, Islamic terror.

Former bureau chief of the *Jerusalem Post* and adjunct scholar of the Cato Institute, Leon T. Hadar, documented in the early 1990s how terrorism with an Islamic face became the most prominent new threat: 'Now that the cold war is becoming a memory, America's foreign policy establishment has begun searching for new enemies. Possible new villains include "instability" in Europe – ranging from German resurgence to new Russian imperialism – the "vanishing" ozone layer, nuclear proliferation, and narco-terrorism. Topping the list of potential new global bogeymen, however, are the Yellow Peril, the alleged threat to American economic security emanating from East Asia, and the so-called Green Peril (green is the color of Islam). That peril is symbolized by the Middle Eastern Moslem fundamentalist – the "Fundie", to use a term coined by *The Economist*.'[23] In 1995, then NATO Secretary-General Willy Claes described Islam as 'at least as dangerous as Communism was'. He added: 'NATO is much more than a military alliance. It has committed itself to defending basic principles of civilization that bind North American and Western Europe.'[24]

Mamoun Fandy of the Center for Contemporary Arab Studies at Georgetown University reports: 'The US has placed counter-terrorism at the top of its international and domestic agendas, and much of the political mobilization to win support for anti-terrorism measures has been focused on the need to confront and overcome "Muslim fundamentalism" or "Islamic terror". Domestically, the US Government won support for sweeping new anti-terrorism legislation through repeated references, both veiled and overt, to the threat posed by Islamic terrorists ... The US identifies all political activities that mobilize using Islamic symbols as "terrorism" aimed at undermining Washington's grand strategy in the Middle East ... US policymakers continue to use "Islamic terror" as the replacement for "the Communist menace" or the "Evil Empire", as the ideological enemy against which all US policy should be aimed. The US is still thinking in state-based, cold war terms.'[25]

And that, of course, brings us back to the controversial 'clash of civilizations' thesis of Samuel Huntington, a thesis which projects the probability of a future cataclysmic war between Western and Islamic civilizations.

11 September and the Function of Terror

The 'clash of civilizations' thesis provides a stunningly convenient ideological framework in which to situate the new threat posed by Osama bin Laden and Al-Qaeda. Al-Qaeda is a fluid non-state international network of terrorist cells which has tentacles all over the world, and yet due to its fluidity remains as elusive as ever. And such international Islamic terrorism, the reach of which is indefinite and the defeat of which is indeterminable, provides a permanent spectre of imminent doom that is highly convenient for a US government which plans to conduct worldwide operations to expand and consolidate its hegemony.

The new 'War on Terror' undoubtedly builds upon this pre-9/11 policy in the Middle East, a policy motivated less by the reality of an all-pervading terrorist threat, and more by a longstanding regional 'grand strategy' designed to consolidate and expand US global power. Indeed, the series of interventions and the essential strategy deployed in the new 'War on Terror' were extensively planned prior to the 11 September terrorist attacks, in order to target key strategic regions heavily laden with energy reserves, particularly oil. Scotland's *Sunday Herald* refers to 'a secret blueprint for US global domination' revealing extensive military plans endorsed by 'President Bush and his cabinet ... even before he took power in January 2001 ...'

> The blueprint, uncovered by the *Sunday Herald*, for the creation of a 'global Pax Americana' was drawn up for Dick Cheney (now Vice-President), Donald Rumsfeld (Defense Secretary), Paul

Wolfowitz (Rumsfeld's deputy), George W. Bush's younger brother Jeb and Lewis Libby (Cheney's Chief of Staff). The document, entitled Rebuilding America's Defenses: Strategies, Forces and Resources for a New Century, was written in September 2000 by the neo-conservative think-tank Project for the New American Century (PNAC).[26]

Other members of the Bush administration who contributed to the report include: John Bolton, Under-Secretary of State; Stephen Cambone, head of the Pentagon's Office of Program, Analysis and Evaluation; Eliot Cohen and Devon Cross, members of the Defense Policy Board, the powerful Pentagon advisory group; and Dov Zakheim; Defense Department Controller.[27] The plan outlined in the PNAC document, representing the essential sentiments of Bush's cabinet, is therefore worth exploring here in some detail. Principally, the document supports a 'blueprint for maintaining global US pre-eminence, precluding the rise of a great power rival, and shaping the international security order in line with American principles and interests'. It also cites approvingly an earlier 1992 Pentagon document authored by Wolfowitz and Libby advocating that the US must 'discourage advanced industrial nations from challenging our leadership or even aspiring to a larger regional or global role'.

In this vein, US armed forces operating abroad are described as 'the cavalry on the new American frontier'. A 'core mission' for the 'cavalry' is to 'fight and decisively win multiple, simultaneous major theatre wars'. To thus preserve the 'global Pax Americana', the report concludes that US forces must perform 'constabulary duties' – in other words, act as policeman of the world thus undermining the United Nations. Peacekeeping missions, for instance, 'demand American political leadership rather than that of the United Nations'. Instead of the UN, the United Kingdom is pinpointed as a convenient instrument of the

American empire, or, in the words of the PNAC, 'the most effective and efficient means of exercising American global leadership'. Moreover, this overall imperial blueprint amounts to an 'American grand strategy' that must be advanced for 'as far into the future as possible'.

To secure this state of affairs and to prevent any state from challenging the US, a much larger US military presence must be spread throughout the world in addition to the approximately 130 nations where US forces are already stationed. To that end, permanent military bases must be installed in the Middle East, in southeast Europe, in Latin America and in southeast Asia, where no such bases previously existed. Even further, the report endorses the creation of 'US Space Forces' to dominate space, as well as absolute control of cyberspace to counter 'enemies' attempting to use the internet to thwart US interests.

Most pertinent to this study, the PNAC blueprint shows that Bush's cabinet had planned to establish military control over the Persian Gulf regardless of Saddam Hussein and any threat his regime may or may not have posed to the world or to his own people. 'The United States has for decades sought to play a more permanent role in Gulf regional security,' the document notes. 'While the unresolved conflict with Iraq provides the immediate justification, the need for a substantial American force presence in the Gulf transcends the issue of the regime of Saddam Hussein.' In one fell-swoop, the document dispels the myth that the Bush plan to invade Iraq was fundamentally motivated by concerns regarding Saddam's regime such as weapons of mass destruction and so on. Such 'unresolved' issues were only useful in providing 'immediate justification' for an intervention designed to expand 'the new American frontier' in order to maintain 'global US pre-eminence'.

But Iraq is only the beginning. Among the other pertinent points raised by the PNAC report is the fact that 'even should

Saddam pass from the scene', the US intends to maintain bases in Saudi Arabia and Kuwait permanently, despite domestic opposition. The document further lists several other states as dangerous rogues representing a threat to US designs, namely, North Korea, Libya, Syria and Iran. The existence of such regimes requires the establishment of a 'world-wide command-and-control system' under US tutelage. Iran in particular, the report observes 'may well prove as large a threat to US interests as Iraq has', raising the spectre of another US intervention. Worse still, the document advocates 'regime change' in China, to be supported by increasing 'the presence of American forces in southeast Asia' in order that 'American and allied power' provide 'the spur to the process of democratization in China'. Europe is also targeted as potentially rivalling the US.[28]

Labour MP Tam Dalyell, the highly regarded father of the House of Commons, described the PNAC report as 'a blueprint for US world domination – a new world order of their making. These are the thought processes of fantasist Americans who want to control the world. I am appalled that a British Labour Prime Minister should have got into bed with a crew which has this moral standing.'[29]

The 'American grand strategy' outlined by the PNAC in 2000, however, was in the making for at least almost a decade. As noted by David Armstrong, an investigative reporter for the Washington DC-based National Security News Service, unclassified documents from the Office of the Secretary of Defense, authored principally by current Vice-President Dick Cheney as well as by other key government officials such as Paul Wolfowitz, Colin Powell and Donald Rumsfeld, reveal continually updated planning 'for global dominance'.[30] The series of documents outlines a consistent direction for US foreign policy that Armstrong characterizes as 'the Plan'. The Plan was published in unclassified form most recently as *Defense Strategy for the 1990s*, when Cheney was ending his term as Secretary of Defense under the presidency of George Bush, Sr., in 1993. The Plan, 'a perpetually evolving work', again surfaced in June 2002 as 'a presidential lecture in the form of a commencement address at West Point', and was 'leaked to the press as yet another *Defense Planning Guidance* . . .'

> It will take its ultimate form, though, as America's new national security strategy . . . The Plan is for the United States to rule the world. The overt theme is unilateralism, but it is ultimately a story of domination. It calls for the United States to maintain its overwhelming superiority and prevent new rivals from rising up to challenge it on the world stage. It calls for dominion over friends and enemies alike. It says not that the United States must be more powerful, or most powerful, but that it must be absolutely powerful.[31]

The international terrorist threat, following on from the 11 September terrorist attacks, is being used to justify the US drive 'to rule the world', implementing plans and strategies that were formulated quite independently (i.e., long before those attacks). Under the guise of fighting international terrorism on a crusade for justice, the US-led 'War on Terror' in reality continues a far more familiar tradition of Western crusading for the expansion of power and profit. International terrorism thus plays a functional role in world order under US hegemony. President Bush needs terrorist Osama. Without bin Laden, Bush would have no permanent world-wide target, and thus no legitimacy for the new 'Pax Americana'. Other bogeymen such as Saddam Hussein – who are alleged (without evidence) to be linked to Al-Qaeda – play a similar role in the strategic and highly lucrative Persian Gulf region, which appears to be one of the first stepping-stones by which the Bush administration intends to consolidate its empire-building strategy in the Middle East and beyond.

Although this book does not specifically argue against Huntington, whose theory is in many ways a product of a rising trend within the Western political establishment, it is intended in part to be a thorough – if indirect – rebuttal of his essential thesis. The study attempts to uncover the thrust of Western policy in the Middle East by contextualizing current events in the light of the historic pattern of that policy. Focusing on the history of Western policy in the Persian Gulf, specifically in Iraq, the work begins by analysing the impact of colonial policy on the Middle East in the early twentieth century. I then discuss how this imperial policy of direct regional control evolved into a more sophisticated system of indirect control in the period after the Second World War, whereby joint Anglo-American power in particular manipulated the political fabric of the region in accordance with Western interests consisting primarily of access to oil and gas.

As a matter of necessity, this consistently involved creating and supporting pliant pro-Western dictators and their corrupt regimes. In order to protect and maintain the stability of this system of indirect control – what might be characterized as 'surrogate imperialism' – Anglo-American power has routinely conducted military interventions and orchestrated conflicts in the region. The end-goal of such brutal overt and covert military policies has been simply to secure and protect regional Western interests, normally at the expense of the rights and wishes of indigenous populations.

I study the cases of Iran; the installation of the Shah; the Iran-Iraq War; the installation of Saddam Hussein; the 1991 Gulf War; the UN sanctions regime; the Western record *vis-à-vis* weapons of mass destruction; the apparent renewal of the Anglo-American war on Iraq in 1998; and the Anglo-American drive to invade and occupy Iraq in 2003 as outstanding examples of the historic operation of this regional system of Western (primarily Anglo-American) control.

My thesis, ultimately, is that this record of Western policy in the Middle East, specifically in the Persian Gulf, is unambiguous evidence of a system of surrogate imperialism that has been quite deliberately developed by the Western powers in order to protect and secure their regional interests which have remained fundamentally the same since the colonial era. The significant difference between the new stage of surrogate imperialism and the colonial system from which the former has developed is the more sophisticated and subtle structure of nation-states co-opted, manipulated and to a high degree effectively controlled by Anglo-American power. When that system of control shows signs of collapsing – for instance, by the rise of indigenous nationalism – the necessity of Western military intervention is invoked to protect that system, and brutal military force is utilized to impose Western will. The hysterical Anglo-American drive for war in the Persian Gulf since 11 September 2001 is a late example of this, manifesting at once the imminent collapse of this system of control due to a variety of factors (especially depletion of world energy resources and regional political developments) and the consequent urgent desire on the part of the Anglo-American elite to immediately intervene to protect, consolidate and expand that system. Consolidation and expansion is hoped to be achieved by the military invasion and permanent occupation of the Persian Gulf, converting the Anglo-American alliance – under US leadership – into a direct regional power with the capacity to restructure the entire Middle East.

By unveiling the little-understood record of Western policy in the Persian Gulf and its implications with regards to the fundamentally imperial structure of the international system, this study aims to clarify the roots and probable trajectory of current conflict in the Middle East. In doing so, I also hope that this work will contribute to generating a more balanced understanding of conflict and terrorism in the Middle East, thus reinvigorating the

Western approach to security, and perhaps helping to pave the way towards establishing a genuinely peaceful, just and democratic world for all.

Part One

THE 1991 GULF MASSACRE

The Historical and Strategic Context of Western State Terrorism in the Persian Gulf

Any attempt to properly understand and conceptualize current events in the Middle East, particularly in terms of Western policy in the region, must be based on an understanding of the broad direction of regional Western policy and the matrix of strategic, political and economic interests instrumental in the formulation of policy. In the Introduction, I presented a concise overview of the general principles of Western foreign policy under US leadership. The Middle East provides us with a pertinent illustration of these principles in action. In particular, Western policy in the Persian Gulf, including Iraq, to this day remains part of a wider historic pattern of regional interference designed to secure essentially hegemonic interests.

We therefore begin our study by analysing the historical and strategic context of Western policy in the Middle East in general, investigating the objective and direction of European power in the region during the colonial era, and examining the development of this power into a sphere of primarily American influence. Focusing on modern turmoil in the Persian Gulf, namely, Iran and Iraq, we then move on to discover how the imperial system constituted under European (primarily British) power in the colonial era developed during the twentieth century under US power, leading us to a clear understanding of the basic principles and strategies underlying the international system and the role of Western foreign policy within this system. On that basis, we are equipped to examine one of the most significant modern conflicts of the twentieth century, the 1991 Gulf War, and to unveil how that war arose from the convergence of longstanding patterns and interests vis-à-vis the Western relationship with the Middle East.

1

The Manipulation of the Middle East

The general tenor of Western interests in the Middle East can be gleaned from various declassified secret documents. In 1945, the United States had explicitly confirmed its desire to maintain control over the Middle East in joint coordination with its partner, the United Kingdom:

> [O]ur petroleum policy towards the United Kingdom is predicated on a mutual recognition of a very extensive joint interest and upon control, at least for the moment, of the great bulk of the free petroleum resources of the world ... US-UK agreement upon the broad, forward-looking pattern for the development and utilization of petroleum resources under the control of nationals of the two countries is of the highest strategic and commercial importance.[32]

The long-term implications of such leverage over the Middle East were understood. For instance, two years later, Britain expressly noted that the Middle East was 'a vital prize for any power interested in world influence or domination', since control of the world's oil reserves also means control of the world economy.[33] Accordingly, a 1953 internal US document articulates American aims in the Middle East without ambiguity: 'United States policy is to keep the sources of oil in the Middle East in American hands.'[34]

Clearly then, the United States aimed to dominate and control Middle East affairs to ensure its monopoly over regional resources, namely, oil. Within this US scheme, it was envisaged that the United Kingdom would play the role of 'junior partner in an orbit of power predominantly under the American aegis',[35] while the other Western European powers would be brought in as collaborators in this process: '[I]t is essential that we should increase our strength in not only the diplomatic but also the economic and military spheres. This can best be done by enrolling France and the lesser Western European powers and, of course, also the Dominions, as collaborators with us.'[36] This would be achieved by opposing any movement threatening Western domination of the region, particularly what is referred to as 'Arab nationalism', a term indicating the desire of the indigenous populations to determine their own political and economic destinies, particularly the utilization of their own resources. Thus, in 1958, a secret British document described the principal objectives of Western policy in the Middle East:

> The major British and other Western interests in the Persian Gulf [are] (a) to ensure free access for Britain and other Western countries to oil produced in states bordering the Gulf; (b) to ensure the continued availability of that oil on favourable terms and for sterling; and to maintain suitable arrangements for the investment of the surplus revenues of Kuwait; (c) to bar the spread of Communism and pseudo-Communism in the area and subsequently beyond; and, as a pre-condition of this, to defend the area against the brand of Arab nationalism.[37]

Thus, shortly after the First World War, turning their eyes towards the Middle East, the Western powers aimed to dismantle Ottoman Turkey, which had been the Muslim caliphate for four centuries. The region encompassed by the Ottoman caliphate included and integrated the areas of Syria, Iraq, Lebanon, Palestine, Jordan and much of Saudi Arabia. Islam was naturally the basis of unity of the caliphate, and to counteract this unity the Western powers perpetuated local divisions among the Arabs. This was achieved by relying on pro-West Arab leaders with local tribal or religious followings to promote the division of the Ottoman Empire. None of these leaders, however, had a claim to popular leadership.[38] In particular, Britain invaded southern Iraq as soon as war with the Ottomans had been declared, taking Baghdad in 1917, and Mosul in November 1918.

The plans of how to sponsor uprisings were improvised by British officers in the Arab Bureau in Cairo. According to Sir Arthur Hirtzel of the India Office, British aims were to divide Arabs not unify them. Thus, despite the essential publicized pretences of supporting Arab unity and independence, the British secretly signed the 1916 Sykes-Pikot Agreement with France, thus making official the task of manufacturing small impotent states in the Middle East, and sharing in their control — Iraq in particular was to be carved up between the two colonial powers. The contents of the Sykes-Pikot Agreement were revealed in 1921 when the Bolsheviks retrieved a copy. Oil was, of course, a major determinant in the West's creation, division, control and support of Middle East regimes, and this factor was officially recognized in the 1920 San Remo Treaty, and in the illegal 1928 Red Line Agreement, involving the British and French sharing of the oil wealth of former Turkish territories originally under Ottoman rule. Here, percentages of future oil production were allocated to British, French and American oil companies.[39]

In the aftermath of the war, what remained of the Ottoman Empire was divided among the colonial powers under the mandate system established under the League of Nations (the United Nations' predecessor), by which formerly Ottoman territories were to be governed by the European powers supposedly in the interest of guiding them towards self-government. Britain managed to obtain the mandate for Iraq, even threatening war to keep the oil-rich Mosul province in the country. The announcement of British mandate rule in Iraq in 1920 led to a widespread indigenous revolt, which was ruthlessly suppressed by British forces. That year, then Secretary of State for War and Air, Winston Churchill, proposed that Mesopotamia 'could be cheaply policed by aircraft armed with gas bombs, supported by as few as 4000 British and 10,000 Indian troops'. His proposal was formally adopted the next year at the Cairo conference, and Iraqi villages were bombed from the air.[40]

Subsequently, emir Faysal I – who belonged to the Hashemite family of Mecca – was appointed by the British High Commissioner as the King of Iraq. Faysal immediately signed a treaty of alliance with Britain that virtually reinstated the British mandate. To counter the widespread nationalist indigenous protests to this continuation of colonial rule by proxy, the British High Commissioner forcefully deported nationalist leaders, while establishing an Iraqi constitution granting King Faysal dictatorial powers over parliament. Indigenous unrest, however, was intolerable enough to make this state of affairs increasingly unsustainable, forcing Britain to grant Iraq 'independence' in 1932 as part of the process of decolonization. The gesture, however, was only token in practice. Britain had already signed a new treaty with Iraq establishing a 'close alliance' between the two countries and a 'common defence position'. With King Faysal still in charge and British bases remaining in Basra and west of the Euphrates, British rule was rehabilitated in an indirect form. However, the Western powers reserved the right to military intervention in order to maintain the regional framework of order established to meet their respective interests. Thus when elements of the Iraqi army and political parties toppled Britain's puppet King Faysal in 1941, Britain invaded and occupied Iraq again to reinstall Faysal.

This policy in Iraq – which included both the colonial phase of direct rule and the transition to effective indirect rule under decolonization – was candidly described by Lord George Curzon, then British Foreign Secretary, who noted that what the UK and other Western powers desired in the Middle East was an:

> Arab facade ruled and administered under British guidance and controlled by a native Mohammedan and, as far as possible, by an Arab staff ... There should be no actual incorporation of the conquered territory in the dominions of the conqueror, but the absorption may be veiled by such constitutional fictions as a protectorate, a sphere of influence, a buffer state and so on.[41]

Curzon had defined in explicit terms the network of surrogate client-regimes – the basic framework of order – constituting the end-goal of decolonization in the Middle East. The Western powers thus succeeded in breaking up the Arab world into several impotent client regimes, an exceedingly chaotic and bloody program that included the literal creation of twelve previously non-existent nations. The arbitrary creation of borders within what was formerly a single empire successfully carved the region into several divided and fragmented nation-states. Iraq was just one of these. In all of these fictional national entities, pro-West leaders were forcefully installed to execute Western instructions. Since the objective of this program included unimpeded access to regional resources (oil) in opposition to the wishes of the populations, it necessarily involved the provocation of force to manipulate the political environment and ensure the establishment of impotent client-regimes whose social and economic administration was subservient to Western interests. This inevitably resulted in the impoverishment and repression of the Arab people under their newly formed illegitimate governments. Due to this program, which involved a series of political, economic and cultural manipulations, these regimes became dependent on the West for their sheer survival in all significant respects. Policy was unequivocally directed at maintaining the resultant status quo consisting of these surrogate regimes. As one US State Department official stated in 1958: 'Western efforts should be directed at ... the gradual development and modernization of the Persian Gulf sheikhdoms without imperilling internal stability or the fundamental authority of the ruling groups.'[42]

This imperial program has been summarized well by the Committee On the Middle East (COME), a Washington DC-based academic body of Middle East experts directed by former Washington representative of the World Jewish Congress Mark Bruzonsky. 'Throughout this century Western countries, primarily the United States and Great Britain, have continually interfered in and manipulated events in the Middle East,' observes COME. The origins of the Iraq/Kuwait conflict can be found ultimately in the historic impact of this interference during the colonial era, namely, 'the unilateral British decision during the early years of this century to essentially cut off a piece of Iraq to suit British Empire desires of that now faded era'. That decision was merely one aspect of a regional policy by which the American and European powers, rather than 'agreeing to Arab self-determination at the end of World War I and the collapse of the Ottoman Empire ...

> ... conspired to divide the Arab world into a number of artificial and barely viable entities; to install Arab 'client regimes' throughout the region, to make these regimes dependent on Western economic and military power for survival; and then to impose an ongoing series of economic, cultural, and political arrangements seriously detrimental to the people of the area. This is the historical legacy that we live with today.
>
> Throughout the 1930s and the 1940s the West further manipulated the affairs of the Middle East in order to control the resources of the region and then to create a Jewish homeland in an

area long considered central to Arab nationalism and Muslim concerns. Playing off one regime against the other and one geopolitical interest against another became a major preoccupation for Western politicians and their closely associated business interests.[43]

By thus creating fictional divisions and utilizing existing ones, the West manufactured false states and nationalities, and set them off against each other – meanwhile exploiting all of them. After the Second World War, Britain's global role was on the decline, soon to be replaced by the United States. COME has again described the process aptly: 'After World War II, and from these policy origins, the United States became the main Western power in the region, supplanting the key roles formerly played by Britain and France ...

> In the 1960s Gamel Abdel Nasser was the target of Western condemnation for his attempt to reintegrate the Arab world and to pursue independent 'non-aligned' policies. By the 1970s the CIA had established close working relationships with key Arab client regimes from Morocco and Jordan to Saudi Arabia and Iran – regimes that even then were among the most repressive and undemocratic in the world – in order to further American domination and to secure an ever-growing supply of inexpensive oil and the resultant flow of petrodollars.[44]

The pattern of interference and manipulation thus continued under regional US domination. To this day, the Western powers under the leadership of the United States continue to prop up the same illegitimate regimes created in the twentieth century in contradiction to basic humanitarian and democratic principles, to fulfil strategic and economic interests. As the US National Security Council noted in 1958: 'Our economic and cultural interests in the area have led not unnaturally to close US relations with elements in the Arab world whose primary interest lies in the maintenance of relations with the West and the status quo in their countries.'[45] Middle East specialist Mamoun Fandy of Georgetown University's Center of Contemporary Arab Studies elaborates that this attitude is prevalent in the US policy of 'dual containment' with respect to two key countries of the Persian Gulf, Iran and Iraq:

> Securing the flow of affordable oil is a cornerstone of US Middle East policy. The US strategy of dual containment of Iran and Iraq, designed to ensure that neither Iraq nor Iran is capable of threatening neighboring Gulf countries, is inextricably linked to Washington's oil policy ... Uncritical US support for autocratic Gulf monarchies and their human rights abuses have weakened both US policy and the oil regimes. It undermines US policy by demonstrating the hypocrisy in American rhetoric about democracy and human rights and weakens the regimes by creating the perception among Gulf subjects that their countries are being ruled in the interests of an outside power.[46]

US policy in the region is, in other words, formulated on the basis of essentially the same interests that were instrumental during the colonial era: access to regional resources by the manipulation of local actors in accordance with Western designs. Indeed, the dire implications of this policy have been harshly criticized by the American academy of Middle East scholars COME:

> US policies in the Middle East have for too long been determined by the power and money of special interest groups, as well as by narrow nationalist economic exploitation. This has led to a grossly hypocritical situation in American foreign policy, in dealing with the nations and peoples of the Middle East. While the US Government constantly professes a strong belief and commitment to democracy, human rights, and national self-determination, far too often the same US Government actually

supports tyranny, repression, massive arms sales, despotism, and ongoing subjugation.[47]

Dr J. W. Smith, Research Director of the California-based Institute for Economic Democracy, describes how this strategy was employed systematically not only during the colonial era but all the way through to the post-Second World War period: 'Once small weak countries are established, it is very difficult to persuade their rulers to give up power and form those many dependent states into one economically viable nation. Conversely, it is easy for outside power brokers to support an exploitative faction to maintain or regain power.'[48] In doing exactly this in the Middle East, the West established a framework of regional policemen, 'powers who, for their own interests, will support the regional order preferred by the Western states', as noted by British historian Mark Curtis. Former US Defense Secretary Melvin Laird described this strategy as follows: 'America will no longer play policeman to the world. Instead we will expect other nations to provide more cops on the beat in their own neighborhood.'[49]

While Western foreign policy in the late twentieth century is conventionally assumed to have been benevolent in nature, on the contrary, the record of policy in the Persian Gulf illustrates exactly the harsh realities bluntly noted by COME and other experts. The Persian Gulf provides an unambiguous representative case study of this doctrine of establishing surrogate regimes that police the region on behalf of US and Western interests, to effectively extend and rehabilitate the system of imperialism.

Although the ultimate focus of our study is Western policy in Iraq, in the interests of developing a proper understanding of that policy it is essential to situate it in its regional and historical context. This takes us to the preceding crisis in Iran, which was inextricably linked to the later development of a Western-Iraq alliance. Indeed, in the ensuing analysis we shall find that Western policy in the Persian Gulf, from interference in Iran to intervention in Iraq, has operated consistently to secure strategic and economic interests at the expense of the most elementary principles of human rights and democracy.

2

Defending Western Values in Iran

The Shah

The case of Iran supplies a clear illustration of the profit-oriented nature of Western foreign policy and its consistent opposition to basic humanitarian principles, primarily because during the era in which the West retained close ties to the country it was governed by a brutal dictator. During this period in the 1970s, Iran was under the reign of a monarchy ruled by the renowned Shah of Iran, Mohammad Reza Pahlevi. The Shah had been directly installed by the Western powers in a covert operation masterminded by the American CIA and British MI6 through a military coup.[50]

The Shah's installation had replaced the democratically elected Iranian leader, Mussadeq, whose policies were unfavourable to Western interests (Mussadeq had, for instance, planned on nationalizing oil operations in Iran, i.e., employing the domestic resources for the benefit of the indigenous population, rather than the control and benefit of foreign investors). The Federation of American Scientists provides a lucid description of this process: 'Shah-an-Shah [King of Kings] Mohammad Reza Pahlevi was restored to the Peacock Throne of Iran with the assistance of the Central Intelligence Agency in 1953' as well as British intelligence. 'The CIA mounted a coup against the left-leaning government of Dr Mohammad Mussadeq, which had planned to nationalize Iran's oil industry' and 'subsequently provided organizational and training assistance for the establishment of an intelligence organization for the Shah. With training focused on domestic security and inter-rogation, the primary purpose of the intelligence unit, headed by General Teymur Bakhtiar, was to eliminate threats to the Shah' from the indigenous population.[51]

This entire episode took place during the cold war. Accord-ingly, it was legitimized under the guise of the fight against Communism, supposedly to prevent Communist elements within Iran from taking power.[52] The fact of the matter, how-ever, was that there was negligible danger of a Communist takeover. Indeed, this was privately recognized by the United States and the United Kingdom as is clear from now declassified secret documents unearthed by Mark Curtis. For example, the UK ambassador had observed in September 1952 that: '... [T]he Communists have ... played a largely passive role, content to let matters take their course with only general encouragement from the sidelines ... they have not been a major factor in the devel-opment of the Mussadeq brand of nationalism.'[53] Similarly, the US embassy noted in March 1953 that 'there was little evidence that in recent months the Tudeh [the Communist Party of Iran, which had close contacts with the Soviet Union] had gained in popular strength'.[54] As for the possibility of a successful Tudeh-sponsored Communist coup that the West could have feared, the US State Department itself dismissed this idea, noting in a January 1953 intelligence report that 'an open Tudeh move for power ... would probably unite independents and non-Communists of all political leanings and would result ... in energetic efforts to destroy the Tudeh by force'.[55]

Thus, the Western-sponsored coup was actually a bid to eliminate 'the Mussadeq brand of nationalism' that had included the plan to nationalize Iranian oil, bringing it and the rest of Iran's resources out of the grip of Western, particularly British and American, investors. Once the Shah — a pliant Western puppet — was installed, the normal policies of plundering Iranian resources could resume. In a candid report, the *New York Times* revealed the US/Western elite sentiments towards the Shah's violent restoration: 'Underdeveloped countries with rich resources now have an object lesson in the heavy cost that must be paid by one of their number which goes berserk with fanatical nationalism' with the view to bring 'rich resources' out of Western control, so that the general population may benefit. 'It is perhaps too much to hope that Iran's experience will prevent the rise of Mussadeqs in other countries,' who may similarly wish to eliminate massive poverty, 'but that experience may at least strengthen the hands of more reasonable and more far-seeing leaders', who will henceforth keep to their subservient role of repressing their people, while providing cheap labour and resources to the Western powers.[56]

The Shah implemented economic policies in accordance with the interests of Western investors, thus ensuring that political repression resulted in the siphoning of the country's wealth to a minority elite. Astute observers note that the Shah's reforms 'favoured the rich, concentrated on city dwellers, and ignored peasantry. The profits derived from oil and natural gas were not used efficiently but were spent on showy projects and the latest in military technology.' The result was that 'an even greater gulf yawned between the Westernized rich and the traditional poor'.[57] Mark Curtis, a former Research Fellow at London's Royal Institute for International Affairs, reports that an agreement was signed the year following the coup establishing a new oil consortium in which the US and the UK both had a 40 per cent interest. The consortium controlled the production, pricing and export of Iranian oil. Though Britain's share was reduced from the level of complete control it had prior to Mussadeq, it was nevertheless far greater than it would have been under the latter's nationalization plans. However, the US had achieved the greater substantial economic stake and political influence in the country, including a significant share in oil.[58]

American investors and the Iranian elite alike both profited immensely from the Shah's 'White Revolution'. Yet while Western investors thus enriched themselves on Iranian resources, the country's own population suffered horrendously. As the state had grown richer, the people had grown poorer. British historian and religious affairs commentator Karen Armstrong reports that:

> There was rampant consumerism in the upper echelons of society, and corruption and deprivation among the petty bourgeoisie and the urban poor. After the oil price increase in 1973–4, there was tremendous inflation, owing to lack of investment opportunity for all but the very wealthy. A million people were unemployed, many of the smaller merchants had been ruined by the influx of foreign goods, and by 1977 inflation had even begun to affect the rich ... During these years the Shah's regime became more tyrannical and autocratic than ever.[59]

Twenty years after the Western-backed coup the top 20 per cent of households accounted for nearly half of all consumption expenditure, whilst the bottom 40 per cent accounted for 15 per cent of consumption expenditure and less than 12 per cent of total income. Mark Curtis comments: 'Some of those who failed to benefit from the "extreme concentration of wealth" in Iran — for example, the poor migrants and squatters in Tehran — were forced to engage regularly in a "desperate contest for shelter and land", in a system that was in large part the result of the considered actions and priorities of Anglo-American power.'[60]

John Foran, assistant Professor of Sociology at the University of California, similarly elaborates in his award-winning study *Fragile Resistance*:

The system was replete with officially sanctioned corruption, bribe-taking, and greed, from the Shah to his sister Ashraf to the minister of court Assadullah 'Alam on down through the officer corps and economic elite, with each maintaining a mini-court of his or her own, surrounding themselves with clients and attaching a portion of all major contracts in the economy.[61]

The extent of the deepening poverty within Iran as a result of the Shah's regime, propped up by the Western powers, can be discerned from the heartfelt observation of a young Iranian peasant:

> Yes, we need schools and doctors, but they are just for the rich. I wish I didn't even know doctors existed. Before, we were ignorant, but now we know that pills and shots can help us. But we can't buy them, so we watch our children die from sickness as well as hunger. Before, the elders said if a child died, it was from the will of God (*dasti khudda*), but now I think it is the fault of the government (*dasti-dowlat*).[62]

Naturally then, the Shah's socio-economic policies were deeply unpopular among the Iranian population. For the Shah to maintain power, he had to control an increasingly agitated and resentful populace, and this implied pursuing policies of brutal repression — policies that were supported and, indeed, directed by the American and British governments. According to Amnesty International (AI), the Shah's regime succeeded in slaughtering over 10,000 Iranians, estimating that there were between 25–100,000 political prisoners in 1976. AI thus observed that: '[The] Shah of Iran retains his benevolent image despite the highest rate of death penalties in the world, no valid system of civilian courts and a history of torture which is beyond belief. No country in the world has a worse record in human rights than Iran.'[63] Barry Rubin noted that 'prisoners were subjected to horrendous torture, equal to the worst ever devised', in a system in which 'the entire population was subjected to a constant, all-pervasive terror'.[64] Not only did this fail to cause any concern to the Western powers, it in fact became a cause of closeness between the Shah and the West. As US Iran specialist Eric Hooglund reports: 'The more dictatorial his [the Shah's] regime became, the closer the US-Iran relationship became.'[65]

The United States and United Kingdom, however, were directly responsible for the repression committed under the Shah's regime – not merely for establishing his power while encouraging and consenting to his policies, but also for creating and guiding the SAVAK secret police under the Shah's command which perpetrated the aforementioned atrocities. SAVAK, created by the United States and trained primarily by Israel with significant British input, was even instructed in torture techniques by the CIA. The British SAS was also responsible for training the Shah's Special Forces.[66] The Federation of American Scientists reports that SAVAK, formed 'under the guidance of United States and Israeli intelligence officers in 1957', 'developed into an effective secret agency', its job being to ensure the effective subjugation of the Iranian population to the rule of the Shah.

> An elaborate system was created to monitor all facets of political life. For example, a censorship office was established to monitor journalists, literary figures, and academics throughout the country; it took appropriate measures against those who fell out of line. Universities, labour unions, and peasant organizations, among others, were all subjected to intense surveillance by SAVAK agents and paid informants. The agency was also active abroad, especially in monitoring Iranian students who publicly opposed Pahlavi rule.

The agency's 'torture methods' passed on to it from its US, Israeli and British masters, 'included electric shock, whipping, beating,

inserting broken glass and pouring boiling water into the rec-
tum, tying weight to the testicles, and the extraction of teeth and
nails'. The extent of its terrorization of the indigenous population is clear from the fact that it even had 'at least 13 full-time
case officers running a network of informers and infiltration
covering 30,000 Iranian students on United States college
campuses ... The head of the SAVAK agents in the United States
operated under the cover of an attaché at the Iranian Mission to
the United Nations, with the FBI, CIA, and State Department
fully aware of these activities.'[67] Iranian scholar Reza Baraheni
observes that SAVAK's aim was to 'spread a deep sense of fear,
suspicion, disbelief and apathy throughout the country'.[68] This
objective was successfully attained. The Shah's regime of 'torture
and intimidation, made people feel that they were held prisoner
in their own country, with the connivance of Israel and the
United States'.[69]

The Western powers were very pleased with their
creation's brutal activities. Former US Secretary of State
Henry Kissinger, for instance, referred to the Shah as 'that
rarest of leaders, an unconditional ally'.[70] Kissinger also
described the tyrant as 'a pillar of stability in a turbulent
and vital region', a 'dedicated reformer' with the most 'noble
aspirations'. 'The least we owe him is not retrospectively to
vilify the actions that eight American Presidents – including
the present incumbent – gratefully welcomed', namely, the
institutionalization of mass poverty, torture, murder and corruption.[71] At a ceremonial dinner hosting the Shah in November 1973 President Jimmy Carter delivered a moving
address in which he described the Iranian regime as 'an
island of stability in a turbulent corner of the world'.[72] In a
report submitted to President Eisenhower's National Security
Council in 1953, US policymakers summed up their
approval of the dictatorship:

> Over the long run, the most effective instrument for maintaining Iran's orientation towards the West is the [Shah's] monarchy, which in turn has the army as its only real source of power. US military aid serves to improve army morale, cement army loyalty to the Shah, and thus consolidate the present regime and provide some assurance that Iran's current orientation towards the West will be perpetual.[73]

In 1958, the US National Security Council reiterated its approval of the Shah's regime. 'Since 1953,' it noted, 'Iran has been regarded in the area as the symbol of US influence' in the Middle East, particularly due to its 'strategic location between the USSR and the Persian Gulf' and 'its great oil reserves', all of which made the regime 'critically important to the United States'.[74]

The Western powers exploit other countries in the Middle East, and other areas of the world, in much the same way, developing close political ties and using those to secure economic relations that are favourable to the West and to the Eastern dictators with whom they are working – relations which also happen to be highly detrimental to the masses who live under the grip of these regimes (most of which are creatures of the colonial empire). Countries that have been regularly subject to such counter-democratic Western procedures include Saudi Arabia, Jordan, Lebanon, Egypt, Iraq, Syria and Bahrain, among numerous others.[75] Their goal, as we have seen for instance from the official declassified documentary record, is to further Anglo-American/Western domination of the Middle East and to secure control over the price and flow of oil, which inevitably results in huge profits as well as effective control of the world economy. 'Mutual Anglo-American support,' Curtis explains, 'in ordering the affairs of key nations and regions, often with violence, to their design has been a consistent feature of the era that followed the Second World War.'[76]

It is clear that the purpose of such policies lies in the fact that the main Western interest in the Middle East is to ensure that there is no development of what the West describes as 'radical nationalism' – a technical term meaning nationalist forces that refuse to obey Western orders – with the view to protect the major Western interest in the region: control of the Middle East's energy resources which are currently the largest and cheapest in the world. As Noam Chomsky has astutely noted, in earlier years the West was able to intervene directly to ensure such control. However, as the world has become more complex and Western capacity to intervene directly has reduced, the West has turned to surrogates. This strategy of utilizing regional surrogate regimes to play a subservient role within a wider matrix of Western interests was formalized in the Nixon-Kissinger doctrine. According to this doctrine, the United States, now leading the Western powers, would be committed to maintaining what US statesman Henry Kissinger called the 'overall framework of order'. Regional powers would pursue particular goals within this overall framework. With regard to the extremely crucial Middle East region – primarily the Persian Gulf and the Arabian Peninsula, where most of the oil is – the broad plan was that Israel and Iran under the Shah would play the role of 'guardians of the Gulf,' i.e., the principal surrogates appointed to guard regional US interests.

Indeed, the essential components of this strategy were explicitly confirmed in May 1973 by the late Senator Henry Jackson, an acknowledged expert on national security and energy who was Chairman of the Senate Committee on Energy and Natural Resources, member of the Select Committee on Intelligence and the Governmental Affairs Committee, as well as ranking member of the Armed Services Committee. Jackson stressed the necessity of 'the strength and Western orientation of Israel on the Mediterranean and Iran [under the Shah] on the

Persian Gulf'. Israel and Iran were 'reliable friends of the United States' who, along with Saudi Arabia, 'have served to inhibit and contain those irresponsible and radical elements in certain Arab states ... who, were they free to do so, would pose a grave threat indeed to our principle sources of petroleum in the Persian Gulf,' which are needed primarily as a reserve and a lever for control of the global economy.[77]

The Iranian Revolution

In the 1960s, open opposition to the Shah's regime began to grow tremendously. More and more students were attending the course in Islamic ethics by the late Ayatollah Khomeini at the Fayziyah Madrasah in Qum. He would often sit on the floor beside his students and openly criticize the government. In 1963, Khomeini spoke from his pulpit in his official capacity against the Shah's regime. Karen Armstrong records that:

> At a time when nobody else dared to speak out against the regime, Khomeini protested against the cruelty and injustice of the Shah's rule, his unconstitutional dismissal of the Majlis, the torture, the wicked suppression of all opposition, the Shah's craven sub-servience to the United States, and his support of Israel, which had deprived Palestinians of their homes. He was particularly concerned about the plight of the poor: the Shah should leave his splendid palace and go and look at the shanty towns in south Tehran ... Reprisals were swift and inevitable. On 22 March 1963 ... SAVAK forces surrounded the madrasah, and attacked it, killing a number of students. Khomeini was arrested and taken into custody.[78]

Some naive commentators attribute the unfolding Islamic movement within Iran spearheaded by Ayatollah Khomeini as well as many other religious scholars, intellectuals and writers to an insincere desire to gain power and establish an autocratic

Islamic regime. This view arises from a failure to account for the complex developments within Iran at that time, particularly the new ideas and visions of political Islam being explored even by Western-educated Iranian philosophers such as Dr Ali Shariati (1933–77).[79] Of course, there is little doubt that many elements of the unfolding revolution – including elements of its leadership – were keen to exploit its momentum to secure their own power for its own sake. However, while this may go some way in explaining the social and political turmoil within Iran in the aftermath of the revolution – accompanied as it is by the regime's often repressive policies – this does not explain the essential causes and character of the revolution and its main early pioneers. Indeed, Khomeini's outspoken opposition to the Shah's regime almost led to his death. He only narrowly escaped execution because a senior mujtahid, Ayatollah Muhammad Kazim Shariatmadari (1904–85), saved him from this fate by promoting him to the rank of Grand Ayatollah, making it too risky for the regime to kill him without provoking massive protests.[80] His radical and controversial thesis on Islamic government was thus not written to legitimize his own rise to power, but rather to provide an Islamic political alternative that was relevant and meaningful to the Muslim masses of Iran. When he first wrote his landmark book *Hokomat-e-eslami* (Islamic government), he had not anticipated an imminent revolution. On the contrary, he thought that it would be another two hundred years before Iran would be capable of implementing such a system.[81]

In fact, the revolution occurred much earlier, entering a new stage on 9 January 1978, when four thousand students poured onto the streets of Qum, demanding a return to the 1906 constitution, freedom of speech, the release of political prisoners, the reopening of Fayziyyah Madrasah, and permission for Khomeini, who had been exiled since 1964, to return to Iran.

The Shah's police opened fire into the crowds of unarmed pro-testors, killing 70 students.[82] For the Shah, this was the begin-ning of the end. Millions of Iranians responded to the massacre with outrage, and the uprising against his regime escalated. In different subsequent marches hundreds of demonstrators were killed in the following months as the Iranian people protested against his reign. In one gathering at Jaleh Square of around 20,000 people on Friday, 8 September, martial law was declared and all large gatherings were banned. The demonstrators had no knowledge of the ban which was declared at 6 a.m. that day. The Shah's soldiers responded to their refusal to disperse with rifle-fire, resulting in the killing of as many as 900 civilians. The massacre only inflamed the anger of the Iranian people further as crowds began raging through the streets in protest while the Shah's forces continued to fire at them from tanks.[83]

The US response to such events is instructive. At 8 a.m. on 10 September, President Jimmy Carter called the Shah from Camp David to reassure him of US support. Several hours later, the White House officially confirmed the conversation and affirmed the ongoing 'special relationship' between the US and Iran. The White House added that despite the President's regret for the loss of life, he had expressed hope that the campaign of political liberalization just begun by the Shah would continue.[84] A clearer statement of support for state terrorism can barely be imagined. Highly relevant in regard to the US role is an astute series of *Washington Post* reports by American journalist Scott Armstrong, which is based in part on government documents. According to Armstrong, US National Security Adviser Zbigniew Brzezinski continually urged the Shah to employ military force to crush the mounting popular opposition against his dictatorship. US State Department sources indicate that Brzezinski even drafted a letter to the Shah 'which unambiguously urged him to use force to put down the demonstrations', despite the fact that State Department officials recognized that this would lead to the deaths of tens of thousands of Iranians. After the September 1978 massacre of demonstrators on 'Black Friday', 'American policymakers viewed the Shah's willingness to use force as a good sign', reports Armstrong. US admiration for the sort of brutal, dictatorial and anti-humanitarian policies habitually employed by military juntas to enforce regional US hegemony was reconfirmed by then US Ambassador William H. Sullivan who objected when the Shah's forces reduced the repression of the Iranian people. He found that 'the Shah's new directives to his security forces, such as instructions to desist from torture ... are disorienting' – clearly because the practice of torture by US client-regimes serves well to subjugate the masses and is therefore 'orienting'. Sullivan resented the command to refrain from torture, because it meant that the Shah's security forces were 'being prevented from using the time-honored methods of arrest, long imprisonment and manhandling – if not worse – to get at the threat' (report of 1 June 1978). Indeed, the US clearly played a role that was unequivocally supportive of human rights abuses. US General Robert Huyser, for instance, was dispatched to Tehran to urge Iranian generals 'that the military should be pushed into action', and should employ military force to capture the oilfields.[85]

By mid-January, the revolution had succeeded. The Shah had fled and his appointed prime minister Shahpour Bhaktiar was forced by the massive protests to allow Khomeini to return. From here onwards, a complex new process of political development and turmoil began, and Khomeini was voted in as Iran's new leader almost unanimously by the Iranian population in democratic elections whose authenticity, like the entire revolution, shocked the Western powers. As Karen Armstrong observes, 'Western people were also forced to note that Khomeini never lost the love of the masses of Iranians, especially the bazaaris, the madrasah students, the less-eminent ulema, and the poor.'[86]

Indeed, for this reason the economic hardships suffered by the new regime in the early years were embarrassing, especially since 'for religious reasons', the government had 'put social welfare at the top of its original agenda on coming to power ...'

> Khomeini did his best for the poor. He set up the Foundation for the Downtrodden to relieve the distress of those who had suffered most under the Pahlavis. Islamic associations in the factories and workshops provided workers with interest-free loans. In the rural areas, Construction Jihad employed young people in building new houses for the peasants, and in agricultural, public health, and welfare projects, especially in the war zones ... In 1981, the Majlis had proposed some important land reforms, which would ensure a fairer distribution of resources.

Unfortunately, these socio-economic efforts made during the regime's early years had been 'offset by the war with Iraq, which had not been of Khomeini's own making'.[87] During and after that war, internal political turmoil affecting the regime's leadership – and consequently policies – further circumvented such early efforts; nevertheless the Iran-Iraq War had a particularly devastating economic impact on Iran. That war had been to a significant extent created by the US Government. The context of doing so undoubtedly lay in the policy reiterated by then President Carter in January 1980, apparently influenced by the huge oil spikes resulting from the regional political unrest throughout that decade (particularly in 1973, 74 and 79), where an oil embargo by OPEC members in October 1973 disrupted oil supplies and elevated prices to unprecedented levels: 'Let our position be absolutely clear. An attempt by any outside force to gain control of the Persian Gulf region will be regarded as an assault on the vital interests of the United States of America, and such an assault will be repelled by any means necessary, including military force."[88] This policy, later known as the Carter Doctrine, was supported by the creation of the Rapid Deployment Force, a military unit able to rush several thousand US troops to the Persian Gulf in a crisis.

3

The Iran-Iraq War: Still Defending Western Values

The Western powers were horrified by the 1979 revolution regardless of its domestic popularity. It implicated their expulsion from Iranian territory and the subsequent insecurity of elite interests in that region, including America's strategic designation of Iran as a 'guardian of the Gulf' subordinate to US orders. The Islamic character adopted by the revolution gave the West further reason to fear. The Western powers anticipated that the events in Iran might pose a model for other Muslim nations in the region whose people suffered similarly under Western-backed dictatorships. In this respect, the Iranian revolution bore the potential to severely damage US hegemony in the Middle East. As noted by John Keane, Professor of Politics and founder of the Centre for the Study of Democracy at the University of Westminster:

> To the surprise of most observers Islam did the unthinkable. It showed that a late twentieth-century tyrant, armed to the teeth and backed by Western investors and governments, could be toppled by popular pressure, and that the new Islamic regime installed by such pressure could stand politically between the two superpowers without being committed to either.[89]

The solution was to crush the Iranian revolution before it bore fruit in order to illustrate to other countries in the region what is liable to happen to those who attempt to pursue an independent course. The very same Iraqi regime that is ruthlessly condemned today was built up and pushed into a devastating confrontation with Iran that would cripple the newly formed Islamic republic. With the fall of the Shah's repressive US-friendly regime, a 'pillar' of US policy was lost. Therefore, a new 'guardian of the Gulf' was required to keep Middle East oil 'in American hands'. Iraq represented many possibilities in this regard. There was the possibility of infiltrating Iraq; of overthrowing the new government of Iran; of Iraq becoming a replacement for the former Iranian 'guardian of the Gulf'; and of course the lucrative opportunities for investment. Once Saddam's Iraq was removed from the terrorism list, the new US plan could begin actualization. Throughout this period, the disregard for human rights, democracy and peace consistently manifested itself in the traditional manner. *The Guardian* reports that the war 'which Saddam Hussein started' continued with 'encouragement from the Americans, who wanted him to destroy their great foe, Ayatollah Khomeini. When it was over, at least a million lives had been lost in the cause of nothing, fuelled by the arms industries of Britain and the rest of Europe, the Soviet Union and the United States.'[90]

Befriending Tyranny

Before the inception of the Iran-Iraq war, the US Government had extended the hand of friendly relations to the Iraqi regime under the rule of Saddam Hussein. In a television interview, then National Security Advisor Zbigniew Brzezinski stated: 'We see no fundamental incompatibility of interests between the United States and Iraq.' He emphasized that: 'We do not feel that American-Iraqi relations need to be frozen in antagonism.'[91] On 22 September 1980, Saddam Hussein initiated his offensive against Iran with US consent. Referring to the tacit US influence in this connection, former National Security Council aide Gary

Sick reports that there was a strategy of 'letting Saddam assume there was a US green light because there was no explicit red light'.[92] Other reports are even more revealing, referring to US involvement in a covert operation for a 'blitzkrieg' against Iran, launched from Iraq. This was to be led by several of the Shah's ex-generals 'to form a provisional government [in Iran] under Iraqi tutelage'.[93] On 26 February 1982, the US-Iraq special relationship was officially sealed – Iraq was removed from the US terrorism list. As was later admitted by the leading Defense Department counter-terrorism official, 'no one had any doubts about his [Saddam's] continued involvement with terrorism ... The real reason [for taking Iraq off the terrorism list] was to help them succeed in the war against Iran.'[94]

This was followed by intensive support of Iraq during its devastating war with Iran, including the use of chemical and biological – and other – weapons of mass destruction, military training and instruction, and the provision of intelligence. According to the *Los Angeles Times*, 'the United States turned a blind eye when Iraq used American intelligence for operations against Iran that made rampant use of chemical weapons and ballistic missiles, according to senior administration and former intelligence officials', while the 'combination of Iraq's weapons of mass destruction and American intelligence eventually helped turn the tide of the eight-year war in Baghdad's favour'. A former US intelligence official familiar with the American role admitted US awareness that Iraq 'used chemicals in any major campaign ... Although we publicly opposed the use of chemical weapons anywhere in the world we knew the intelligence we gave the Iraqis would be used to develop their own operational plans for chemical weapons.' Another administration official stated: 'They [the Americans] built this guy up and let him do whatever it took to win. And that included the use of chemical weapons and ballistic missiles.' US intelligence sources went so far as to provide data to Iraq on Iran's equipment and troop strength. Former intelligence officials have stated clearly that Washington was well aware that Iraq began using chemical weapons in 1983 and intensified their use in 1986. By 1988, Iraq's use of gases had also repeatedly been documented by UN specialists.[95]

According to another former US intelligence official: 'It was all done with a wink and a nod ... We knew exactly where this stuff was going, although we bent over backwards to look the other way.' Washington knew Iraq was 'dumping boatloads' of chemical weapons on Iranian positions, he added. Policy at the time, according to another former Reagan official, recognized that: 'Hussein is a bastard. But at the time, he was our bastard.' In 1986, as the Iran-Iraq War began to turn decisively in Iran's favour the pace of US intelligence information to Iraq escalated as part of a bid to restore Iraq's edge. The United States was not alone in this endeavour. In advance of the Faw counter offensive, France, Egypt and Jordan provided help in reorganizing and retraining the Iraqi military.[96]

The United Kingdom was also heavily involved. Throughout the devastating eight-year war, the British Government assured its public that it was not selling 'lethal equipment' to either side. However, evidence given to the inquiry by Lord Justice Scott into arms sales to Iraq has revealed that this alleged policy was for the purpose of public deception only. In reality, Britain was one of the 26 countries – including the United States, France and other Western nations along with their Middle East client-regimes – which sold the greater bulk of arms to Saddam's genocidal regime.[97] American arms specialist William D. Hartung, Senior Fellow at the World Policy Institute, observes that despite recent efforts by the US defence industry and the Clinton administration to argue that the United States did not arm Iraq in the period leading up to the 1991 Persian Gulf War, there is ample documentation (some of which shall be discussed here)

demonstrating that the Reagan and Bush administrations supplied critical military technologies that were put directly to use
in the construction of the Iraqi war machine. Further strong
evidence discussed by Hartung indicates that the 'executive
branch's failure to crack down on illegal weapons traffickers or
keep track of third party transfers of US weaponry allowed a
substantial flow of US-origin military equipment and military
components to make their way to Iraq'.[98]

Arming Iraq

Leading American analyst Bruce Jentleson, Director of the Terry
Sanford Institute of Public Policy, Professor of Public Policy and
Political Science, and formerly of the US State Department Policy
Planning Staff as Special Assistant to the Director, reports that
huge amounts of military aid were poured into Iraq.[99] With Iraq
off the terrorism list and export controls on dual-use technologies (i.e., with both civilian and military applications) therefore
less restrictive, 60 Hughes MD-500 'Defender' helicopters, and
then ten Bell Helicopters – models which were widely employed
in the invasion of Vietnam – were sold to Saddam's regime.
Other helicopter sales followed, such as 48 that were said to be
for 'recreation' purposes. These were subsequently employed to
bomb and gas Kurdish civilians.[100]

A total of 241 licences were approved for dual-use exports to
Iraq in the last two years of Reagan's administration; only six
were denied. The nature of these exports was conspicuously
such that they could be put to military use. Bruce Jentleson
notes, for instance, that precision tools for 'general military
repair' ended up being used to upgrade SCUD missiles for
longer-range firing. Quartz crystals and frequency synthesizers
as 'components in a ground radar system' were used for missile
guidance systems. Fuel air explosive technology was exported,

although it was capable of producing bombs ten times more lethal than conventional bombs. Indeed, exports 'were knowingly sent to Iraqi nuclear installations', according to a former White House official.[101]

The Iraqi Ministry of Industry and Military Industrialization (MIMI) was a notorious example of this. Having been created in April 1988 to bring together civilian and military projects, the United States was fully aware that MIMI was linked to nuclear, chemical and biological weapons programs. Yet it was regularly inundated with dozens of dual-use technologies, licensed for export by the US.[102] Another typical example was NASSR (Nassr State Establishment for Mechanical Industries), which from the 1970s onwards was well known to be an important military installation. By 1987, the United States knew of a ballistic missiles program in operation there. Yet the Department of Commerce continued to license exports for dual-use technologies to this installation.[103] Dual-use technologies supplied to military installations such as MIMI, Sa'ad 16, and others, as well as directly to the Iraqi military, included: equipment for the Arab Company for Detergent Chemicals (a front for chemical weapons); bacteria samples to the Iraqi Atomic Energy Commission and University of Baghdad (both linked to 'biological warfare support and numerous other military activities' by the CIA); communications and tracking agreement for Sa'ad 16; helicopter guidance, helicopters, engines and flight equipment for the Iraqi airforce; computers to the Iraqi navy; and so on.[104]

Douglas Frantz and Murray Waas of the *Los Angeles Times* report that in 410 of 526 cases with potential nuclear applications, export licences were approved. According to US Congressman Henry Gonzalez, two of every seven US non-agricultural exports to Iraq between 1985 and 1990 accrued to its expanding military-industrial complex.[105] The United Nations Special Commission (UNSCOM) on Iraq and International Atomic Energy Agency (IAEA) inspection teams confirmed that US technology was used by Iraq in its weapons program – not a surprise considering that dual-use US technologies were being systematically and knowingly licensed to military installations undertaking exactly these kinds of programs. According to the head UN/IAEA inspector: 'The simple answer to the question of whether US-produced equipment and technology has been found to be part of the Iraqi nuclear weapons program is *yes*.'[106] Examples of this include the equipment discovered by UNSCOM from 11 American companies in Iraqi missiles and chemical weapons plants. Some of the 17 bacterial and viral cultures licensed by the US were also found at the Salman Pak site that was party to 'a major military research program … concentrating on anthrax and botulism'.[107]

As the torrent of military and financial assistance continued to pour into Iraq, Saddam was busy applying this aid – which came to him not only from the US, but from France, Germany, Britain, among others – in systematic human rights abuses. According to former US Secretary of State Shultz, the first reports of Iraq's use of chemical weapons against Iran 'drifted in'.[108] As was the case with Saddam's other flagrant violations of the 1925 Geneva Protocol Banning the Use of Chemical Weapons in War, his use of chemical weapons against Iran was extensively documented by the UN.[109] The UN found evidence that Saddam had used chemical weapons four times during the Iran-Iraq War. The other three were in April 1985, February–March 1986 and April–May 1987. Saddam was also busy violently oppressing his own people, cracking down particularly on the Kurds of northern Iraq – including, for instance, according to Amnesty International, the abduction and torture of about three hundred children from Kurdish families.[110] In 1987, a US Senate staff delegation to Kurdistan discovered the ravaging effects of Saddam's policy towards the Kurds in Iraq, reporting 'hundreds of villages levelled'; the countryside was described as having 'an eerie quality to it. Fruit trees, graveyards and cemeteries stand as reminders of the absent people and livestock.'[111]

In February 1988, Saddam instigated an even more massive campaign against the Kurds. His troops employed the traditional methods of destruction. By 16 March 1988, the Iraqi air force was strafing Halabja with mustard gas and nerve toxins. 'Entire families were wiped out and the streets were littered with the corpses of men, women and children,' reported the *Washington Post*. 'Other forms of life in and around the city – horses, house cats, cattle – perished as well.'[112] An estimated 5000 people were massacred. As Professor Jentleson observes, this death toll is proportionate to over a half million deaths in a city the size of New York. The US response to all the above is instructive. Such atrocities did not suffice for the United States and its Western allies to cease military assistance to the Ba'athist regime. Even the Halabja atrocities only led to the token tightening of a few export controls related to chemical weapons manufacture and the production of what amounted to an effectively meaningless condemnatory resolution in the UN Security Council. These gestures were apparently propagandistic in purpose, since they unfortunately did not amount to any significant reduction in US/Western military assistance to Saddam's regime.[113]

Indeed, the possibility of sanctions being imposed on Iraq due to the massacres was deliberately blocked by the US administration, because they would 'undermine relations and reduce US influence on a country that has emerged from the Persian Gulf War as one of the most powerful Arab nations'.[114] Rather than impose sanctions, the very opposite was done. Bruce Jentleson observes that after the Halabja massacres, the US was granting new licences for dual-use technology exports at a rate *more than 50 per cent greater* than before Saddam's gassing of the Kurds. Between September and December 1988, 65 licences were granted for dual-use technology exports, this averages out as an annual rate of 260 licences, more than double the rate between January and August 1988 (which involved the granting of 85 licences, amounting as Jentleson notes to a 128 annual rate).[115] The tremendous escalation of exports occurred in spite of the fact that inspectors of the US Customs Service had 'detected a marked increase in the activity levels of Iraq's procurement networks. These increased levels of activity were particularly noticeable in the areas of missile technology, chemical-biological warfare and fuse technology.'[116]

In January 1988, reports of Iraqi germ warfare capabilities in the specialized press emerged. According to a respected American analyst, 'there were growing indications in late 1988 that Iraq was producing a botulin toxin in military quantities, or some similar agent'. A US government official was more forthcoming: 'Everybody knows the Iraqis are trying to develop biological weapons.'[117] Nevertheless, during 1985–9, 17 licences were approved for exports of bacterial and fungal cultures to Iraqi government agencies.[118] This occurred in spite of a human rights appeal to the UN Subcommission on Prevention of Discrimination and Protection of Minorities, issued by Amnesty International, pointing clearly to the 'grave fears that in the aftermath of the [Iran-Iraq] War a further significant deterioration in human rights could occur in Iraq'. Amnesty noted that Saddam's regime was conducting 'a systematic and deliberate policy … to eliminate large numbers of Kurdish civilians'.[119] This AI report was issued just three days before the Iran-Iraq cease-fire of 20 August 1988. Further domestic chemical attacks on an unprecedented scale were initiated by Saddam only a few days later. Yet as noted above, the aftermath of these attacks did not result in a reduction in US licensed exports of dual-use technologies, but on the contrary resulted in their *increase*.

Friendly Relations

The US not only provided Saddam's regime with military aid, but also with financial aid, huge investment and abundant trade. For example, American CCC credits had grown to exceed $1 billion per year.[120] The US had become a major customer for Iraqi oil, importing by 1987 30 million barrels. This was still minimal in comparison to later imports. In 1988 – the year of the most conspicuous domestic atrocities instigated by Saddam's forces – US imports of Iraqi oil had rocketed to 126 million barrels. This figure should be compared to the 1981 figures when the US had not imported even a single barrel of Iraqi oil. The disparity constituted a momentous increase of over 400 per cent, with US purchases bringing in $1.6 billion. The US was essentially purchasing one out of every four barrels of Iraqi oil exports.[121] Jentleson points out that American oil companies also began receiving a discount of $1 per barrel below the prices being charged to European oil companies. This amounted to approximately $37 million in the last quarter of 1988 and another $123 million through the first three-quarters of 1989. The per-barrel discount was later increased to $1.24 in January 1990, resulting in savings of another hefty $241 million on imports (the US was so enthusiastic about these that they continued for over a month after Iraq's invasion of Kuwait).[122]

Iraq became the twelfth largest market for American agricultural exports in the 1980s; for some crops (e.g. rice) the country became the number one export market. Iraq was, in fact, second only to Mexico as a beneficiary of CCC export credit guarantees. In addition to the $1.1 billion the previous year and $3.4 billion cumulative since fiscal year 1983, another $1.1 billion in guarantees were scheduled for the fiscal year about to begin. The US Agricultural Department was unsurprisingly optimistic about 'Iraq's enormous market potential for US agricultural exports'.[123] As has already been seen, business was also flourishing on the manufacturing and dual-use technology export front. Jentleson reports that in sectors such as petroleum, electricity generation, petrochemicals, steel and transportation, billions of dollars in contracts were being fervently signed.[124]

One of the groups which was particularly active in ensuring that the US did not impose sanctions on Iraq was the US-Iraq Business Forum, established in 1985, whose president Marshall Wiley was a lawyer and former US Ambassador to Oman as well as former ranking US diplomat in Baghdad.[125] According to Bruce Jentleson, companies that were members of this group whose influence was crucial in preventing sanctions (providing yet another example of the preference of Western governments for elite interests as opposed to human rights) included those involved in importing discounted Iraqi oil (Amoco, Mobil, Exxon, Texaco, Occidental), defence contractors (Lockheed, Bell Helicopter-Textron, United Technologies) and others (AT&T, General Motors, Bechtel, Caterpillar).[126] This clearly illustrates that the United States is influenced most significantly in its policies by the interests of corporate elites – the military-industrial complex and multinational corporations – at the expense of the human rights and decisions of the masses throughout the world. These elite sectors possess the most powerful leverage over policy; and the results, as is now quite evident, are globally catastrophic.

Fellow at the Institute for Policy Studies, Phyllis Bennis, a Middle East expert based in Washington DC, describes the anti-humanitarian nature of the US-Iraq alliance while Saddam Hussein was in power, an alliance based solely on strategic and economic interests:

Long before the invasion of Kuwait, one might have wondered about the US-Iraq alliance. Certainly it was partly tactical, aimed at preventing outright victory for the ascendant Islamic Republic of Iran in the Iran-Iraq War. Certainly it reflected the three long-standing goals of US policy in the Middle East: protection of Israel, control of access to oil, and stability. One might have wondered why US officials willingly, if not eagerly, turned a blind eye to the Iraqi regime's crimes. It wasn't as if they didn't know of Iraq's repressive rule, its Anfal campaign to depopulate Kurdish villages and its use of internationally outlawed poison gas against both civilians and Iranian soldiers. Human rights violations are common throughout the region – arbitrary arrests and detention, torture, house demolitions, repression of dissidents, persecution of Communists – and Iraq's government was right up there with the best. Washington knew of Iraq's violations, but expressed little official concern.[127]

During the period of the Iran-Iraq War, apart from the flagrant manipulation of both sides to secure US interests, the US attempted to increase its military occupation of the region. Carter's Rapid Deployment Force was transformed into a new US military command authority, the US Central Command, overseeing not only the Persian Gulf but also the surrounding region from eastern Africa to Afghanistan. Under an anti-Soviet 'strategic consensus', the US sold billions of dollars' worth of arms to regional surrogates including Turkey, Israel and Saudi Arabia. In 1987, operation Joint Task Force-Middle East, consisting of over 40 aircraft carriers, battleships and cruisers, was established by the US Navy to protect Gulf oil tankers.[128]

US/Western policy then is simply not premised on concern for human rights or democracy. On the contrary, Western strategic and economic interests are the driving force of foreign policies that are systematically anti-humanitarian and counter-democratic, consisting of support for terrorism, conflict and repression. This explains why US military intelligence was instrumental in violently installing the Ba'athist regime to be later led by Saddam Hussein despite the devastating ramifications of such an operation for the Iraqi people.

4

Protecting Order in the Gulf

The Creation of Saddam Hussein

London-based historian and journalist Said K. Aburish, one of the world's leading authorities on Arab affairs, has documented in his study of Western-Middle East relations how the CIA masterminded the 8 February 1963 military coup that brought the Ba'athist regime – and eventually Saddam Hussein – to power. Then Iraqi president Abdul Karim Kassim, who was overthrown in the 1963 coup, had been a prime target for US intervention. After taking power in 1958, he ensured that Iraq pulled out of the Baghdad Pact, the US-backed anti-Soviet alliance in the Middle East. By 1961, he challenged US-led Western interests again by nationalizing part of the concession of the British-controlled Iraq Petroleum company. He also declared that Iraq had a legitimate historical claim to the oil-rich Western client-regime Kuwait.[129]

These multiple policies, which threatened Western control over Iraqi resources, made President Kassim an extremely unsavoury character as far as Western interests in the Middle East were concerned. The change in attitude on the part of the US regarding Kassim has been candidly described by the *New York Times*:

> From 1958 to 1960, despite Kassim's harsh repression, the Eisenhower administration abided him as a counter to Washington's Arab nemesis of the era, Gamal Abdel Nasser of Egypt – much as Ronald Reagan and George H. W. Bush would

aid Saddam Hussein in the 1980s against the common foe of Iran
... By 1961, the Kassim regime had grown more assertive. Seeking
new arms rivalling Israel's arsenal, threatening Western oil
interests, resuming his country's old quarrel with Kuwait, talking
openly of challenging the dominance of America in the Middle
East – all steps Saddam Hussein was to repeat in some form –
Kassem was regarded by Washington as a dangerous leader who
must be removed.[130]

Consequently, plans were laid to overthrow him enlisting
the assistance of Iraqi elements hostile to Kassim's administration, with the CIA at the helm. 'In Cairo, Damascus, Tehran
and Baghdad, American agents marshalled opponents of the
Iraqi regime,' notes the *New York Times*. 'Washington set up
a base of operations in Kuwait, intercepting Iraqi communications and radioing orders to rebels. The United States armed
Kurdish insurgents.' Former Ba'athist leader Hani Fkaiki has
confirmed that Saddam Hussein – then a 25-year-old who
had fled to Cairo after attempting to assassinate Kassim in
1958 – was colluding with the CIA at this time.[131] Aburish
collects together official documents and testimony showing
that the CIA had even supplied the lists of people to be eliminated once power was secured. Approximately 5000 people
were killed in the 1963 coup, including doctors, teachers, lawyers and professors, resulting in the decimation of much of
the country's educated class. Iraqi exiles such as Saddam
assisted in the compilation of the lists in CIA stations throughout the Middle East. The longest list, however, was produced
by an American intelligence agent, William McHale. None
were spared from the subsequent butchery, including pregnant women and elderly men. Some were tortured in front
of their children. Saddam himself 'had rushed back to Iraq
from exile in Cairo to join the victors [and] was personally
involved in the torture of leftists in the separate detention

centres for fellaheen [peasants] and the Muthaqafeen or educated classes'.[132]

US intelligence was integrally involved in planning the details of the operation. According to the CIA's royal collaborator: 'Many meetings were held between the Ba'ath party and American intelligence – the most critical ones in Kuwait.' Although Saddam's Ba'ath party was then only a minor nationalist movement, the party was chosen by the CIA due to the group's close relations with the Iraqi army. Aburish reports that the Ba'ath party leaders had agreed to 'undertake a cleansing program to get rid of the Communists and their leftist allies' in return for CIA support. He cites one Ba'ath party leader, Hani Fkaiki, confessing that the principal orchestrator of the coup was William Lakeland, the US assistant military attaché in Baghdad.[133]

In 1968, another coup granted Ba'athist general Ahmed Hassan al-Bakr control of Iraq, bringing to the threshold of power his kinsman, Saddam Hussein. The violent coup was also supported by the CIA. Roger Morris, formerly of the US National Security Council under Lyndon Johnson and Richard Nixon in the late 1960s, recalls that he had 'often heard CIA officers – including Archibald Roosevelt, grandson of Theodore Roosevelt and a ranking CIA official for the Near East and Africa at the time – speak openly about their close relations with the Iraqi Baathists'.[134] Thus, two gruesome CIA military coups brought the genocidal Ba'ath party, and with it Saddam Hussein, to power, in order to protect US strategic and economic interests.

A declassified National Security directive issued by then President Bush Snr in October 1989 prioritized the provision of funds and technology to Saddam's regime, described as the 'West's policeman in the region'.[135] This, of course, was part and parcel of a decades-long special relationship between the brutal Iraqi dictatorship and the United States. This state of affairs, however, was destined to reverse: in order to protect the very same array of regional interests in maintaining 'order' – unimpeded access to oil and other resources – in the Persian Gulf.

The Domestic Scene in the US

Contrary to conventional opinion, there exists considerable evidence to indicate that the first Gulf War had not only been anticipated by the United States, but fell well within its political, strategic and economic interests. A variety of factors, both within the US and the Middle East, appear to support the conclusion that Iraq's invasion of Kuwait was deliberately engineered by the US to provide a pretext for a much-needed war.[136]

Prior to the Gulf War, the United States was facing massive cutbacks in military expenditure. With the collapse of the Soviet Union, the US had lost its old cold war foe, leaving its military institutions such as NATO with nothing left to do – or at least no credible pretext on which to do it. Consequently, a political conflict had begun within the US over the issue of the necessity of defence spending. As William Blum has documented, with the cold war over, many outside the US military establishment naturally called for the reduction of military expenditure. In February 1990, the *Washington Post* reported that 'the administration and Congress are expecting the most acrimonious, hard-fought defence budget battle in recent history'.[137] By June, the *Post* reported that 'tensions have escalated' between the Congress and the Pentagon, 'as Congress prepares to draft one of the most pivotal defence budgets in the past two decades'.[138] By July, due to the vote of a Senate Armed Services subcommittee calling for cuts in military manpower almost three times that of Bush's recommendations, it appeared that the Pentagon was losing the battle for military spending. The *Los Angeles Times* reported: 'The size and direction of the [military] cuts indicate that President Bush is losing his battle on how to manage reductions in military spending.'[139] Being Commander-in-Chief of the Armed Forces, former CIA Director, and a former investor in Texas oil, then President Bush Snr was instrumental in fighting against such reductions. Yet while he was drastically failing to secure high US military spending, his domestic popularity was also drastically decreasing. Although in January 1990 he had an approval rating of 80 per cent having emerged victorious from the US war in Panama, towards the end of July his ratings had steadily dropped to 60, and were set to drop further.[140] Thus, President Bush and the corporate-military interests he was supporting were searching for a way to boost military spending and generate renewed public popularity.

The background for Bush Snr's campaign to maintain high levels of military spending was rooted in the prospects for a US military presence in the Middle East, particularly the Persian Gulf region. When the Iran-Iraq War ended in 1988, US contingency plans for war in the Gulf region posed Iraq as the enemy.[141] In January 1990, CIA Director William Webster acknowledged the West's increasing dependency on Middle East oil in testimony before the Senate Armed Services Committee.[142] One month later, General Schwarzkopf advised the Committee to increase the US military presence in the Middle East, describing new plans to intervene in a regional conflict. The principal vehicle of this operation would be the US Central Command (CENTCOM), formerly the Rapid Deployment Joint Task Force, which had been covertly expanding a network of US military-intelligence bases in Saudi Arabia.[143] Notably, CENTCOM's War Plan 1002, which was designed during the inception of the Reagan administration to implement the Carter Doctrine of confronting any challenge to US access to Middle East oil by military force, was revised in 1989 and renamed War Plan 1002–90, the last two digits, of course, standing for 1990.

In the updated plan, Iraq replaced the Soviet Union as the principal enemy.[144]

Blum reveals that it is in this crucial context that CEN-TCOM, under the direction of General Schwarzkopf, began devising war simulations directed at Iraq. At least four such simulations were conducted in 1990, some of which hypothesized an Iraqi invasion of Kuwait long before the actual invasion occurred. One of the first of these, dubbed 'Internal Look', occurred in January. In May 1990, the Center for Strategic and International Studies (CSIS), a Washington-based think-tank affiliated to Georgetown University, completed a two-year study predicting the outcome of a US war with Iraq. The study explored the future of conventional warfare, and concluded that the war most likely to occur requiring US military intervention was between Iraq and Kuwait or Saudi Arabia. The study was widely circulated among Pentagon officials, members of Congress, and military contractors.[145] By July, the Pentagon's computerized command post exercise (CPX), initiated in late 1989 to explore possible responses to 'the Iraqi threat', was in full swing, focusing on simulations of an Iraqi invasion of Kuwait or Saudi Arabia or both.[146] The Naval War College in Newport, RI, ran programs in which participants were asked to determine effective US responses to a hypothetical invasion of Kuwait by Iraq.[147]

Indeed, according to Professor of International Law at the University of Illinois, Francis Boyle — who is on the Board of Directors of Amnesty International USA, and who worked with the International Commission of Inquiry into United States war crimes committed during the Persian Gulf War headed by former US Attorney-General Ramsey Clark — the US had been planning an assault on Iraq for some time. Reviewing the year-by-year process of intensification of war plans, Professor Boyle records that:

Sometime after the termination of the Iraq-Iran War in the summer of 1988, the Pentagon proceeded to revise its outstanding war
plans for US military intervention into the Persian Gulf region in
order to destroy Iraq. Schwarzkopf was put in charge of this
revision. For example, in early 1990, Schwarzkopf informed the
Senate Armed Services Committee of this new military strategy in
the Gulf allegedly designed to protect US access to and control
over Gulf oil in the event of regional conflicts. In October 1990,
[General] Powell referred to the new military plan developed in
1989. After the war, Schwarzkopf referred to 18 months of
planning for the campaign.

Boyle reports that in late 1989 or early 1990, these war plans for
'destroying Iraq and stealing Persian Gulf oilfields were put into
motion'. Accordingly, General Schwarzkopf 'was named the
Commander of the so-called US Central Command – which was
the renamed version of the Rapid Deployment Force – for the
purpose of carrying out the war plan that he had personally
developed and supervised. During January of 1990, massive
quantities of United States weapons, equipment, and supplies
were sent to Saudi Arabia in order to prepare for the war against
Iraq.'[148] The US, it thus seems, had begun conducting intense
planning for a possible war with Iraq as early as 1988 through to
1990.[149]

The International Scene

By the end of the 1980s, the United States was facing significant
obstacles to its domination of the Persian Gulf, which had
effectively reached an impasse. In general, the Gulf States
refused to allow a permanent US presence on their soil. Specifically, although Saudi Arabia – a crucial US client-regime –
continued to maintain a close relationship with the US, it
nevertheless had begun diversifying its commercial and military

ties. As former US Ambassador to Saudi Arabia Chas Freeman observed, by the end of the 1980s: 'The United States was being supplanted even in commercial terms by the British, the French, even the Chinese.' In this vein, the US had fallen as far as fourth place among arms suppliers. Thus, US domination of the region had not only reached an impasse, it was being steadily challenged by other powers.[150]

It is against this backdrop of a gradual waning of US regional influence that conflict began to brew between Iraq and Kuwait. The historical context of Iraq-Kuwait conflict lies in the fact that Kuwait was once a district of Iraq during Ottoman rule, before the British carved it off to form an independent state. This had never been accepted by Iraq as a legitimate division, thus establishing a context of political tension between the two entities. Yet the main cause of Iraq-Kuwait tension just prior to the Persian Gulf War was far more contemporary, originating in the policies of Kuwait. Iraq was incensed at Kuwait for three reasons: during the Iran-Iraq War, Kuwait was apparently stealing $2.4 billion worth of oil from the Rumaila oilfield beneath the Iraq-Kuwait border; Kuwait had built various structures, including military structures, on Iraqi territory; after the Iran-Iraq War, Kuwait had been colluding with the United Arab Emirates to exceed the production quotas fixed by the Organization of Petroleum Exporting Countries (OPEC), resulting in the reduction of oil prices.

Kuwait decided to drastically increase oil production on 8 August 1988, only one day after Iran agreed to a cease-fire with Iraq.[151] Stable oil prices were essential to finance post-war reconstruction at this critical time. Yet Kuwait's violation of OPEC agreements sent crude oil prices plummeting from $21 to $11 a barrel. Consequently Iraq was losing $14 billion a year.[152] This was only the beginning. In March 1989, Kuwait demanded a 50 per cent increase in the OPEC quotas it was already flagrantly violating. Although OPEC rejected the demand in a June 1989 conference, Kuwait's oil minister declared that Kuwait would not be bound by any quota at all. Kuwait then went on to double production to over a million barrels per day.[153]

Furthermore, as Pierre Salinger recorded, Kuwait 'intended to extract more from the oilfields at Rumaila', which lie on the disputed Iraq-Kuwait border.[154] During the Iran-Iraq War, Kuwait had illegally extended its border northward, thus grabbing hold of 900 square miles of the Rumaila oilfield. US-supplied slant drilling technology allowed Kuwait to steal oil from the part of Rumaila that was clearly within Iraq's borders. Additionally, Kuwait's rulers had lent Iraq $30 billion during its war with Iran, and were now demanding that Iraq recompense them. Yet Kuwait's own behaviour towards Iraq had made this impossible. The Iran-Iraq War had already cost Iraq over $80 billion. With oil prices plummeting thanks to Kuwaiti intransigence, it became impossible for Iraq to generate the necessary funds to recompense Kuwait. Iraq's response between 1988 and 1990 was to endeavour to resolve these problems through diplomatic means. Yet all attempts at negotiation were rebuffed.[155] One senior US official in Bush's administration remarked: 'Kuwait was overproducing, and when the Iraqis came and said, 'Can't you do something about it?' the Kuwaitis said, 'Sit on it.' And they didn't even say it nicely. They were nasty about it. They were stupid. They were arrogant. They were terrible.'[156]

Director of the Center for Strategic and International Studies (CSIS) Henry M. Schuler described these policies as 'economic warfare' against Iraq.[157] Iraq complained that Kuwait's policies were 'tantamount to military aggression'.[158] By now Iraq was losing a billion dollars a year for each reduction of one dollar in the oil price. By 1990, these policies had decimated Iraq's economy to such an extent that it was in worse condition than during its war with Iran, with inflation at 40 per cent and its currency plummeting.[159] Considering that Iraq had always espoused a historical claim to Kuwait, Saddam's reaction to Kuwait's policies is notable. Rather than immediately utilizing the crisis as a pretext for acquiring Kuwaiti territory by force, Iraq appeared to be anxious to resolve the situation swiftly and peacefully. The late King Hussein of Jordan, a friend of the Western powers particularly admired by the United States and Israel, found Kuwait's response perplexing. He testified to the *San Francisco Chronicle*:

> He [Saddam Hussein] told me how anxious he was to ensure that the situation be resolved as soon as possible. So he initiated contact with the Kuwaitis ... this didn't work from the beginning. There were meetings but nothing happened ... this was really puzzling. It was in the Kuwaitis' interest to solve the problem. I know how there wasn't a definite border, how there was a feeling that Kuwait was part of Iraq.[160]

Indeed, after having fought for eight devastating years with Iran, war was the last thing on Saddam's mind. A study by the Strategic Studies Institute of the US Army War College, issued in early 1990, found that:

> Baghdad should not be expected to deliberately provoke military confrontations with anyone. Its interests are best served now and in the immediate future by peace ... Revenues from oil sales could put it in the front ranks of nations economically. A stable Middle East is conducive to selling oil; disruption has a long-range adverse effect on the oil market which would hurt Iraq ... Force is only likely if the Iraqis feel seriously threatened. It is our belief that Iraq is basically committed to a nonaggressive strategy, and that it will, over the course of the next few years, considerably reduce the size of its military. Economic conditions practically

mandate such action ... There seems no doubt that Iraq would like to demobilize now that the war has ended.[161]

Yet Kuwait's provocative – and for Iraq devastating – behaviour, continued to generate increasing tension between the two countries. The international community ignored the growing tension. By July 1990, Kuwait had continued to ignore Iraq's territorial and economic demands – including its OPEC-assigned quota. Subsequently, Iraq prepared for a military venture, amassing large numbers of troops along the border. A significant indication of the US role in this can be discerned from a crucial discovery that occurred after the invasion, when the Iraqis found a confidential memorandum in a Kuwaiti intelligence file. The document (dated 22 November 1989) was a top secret report to the Kuwaiti Minister of the Interior by his Director General of State Security, informing him of a meeting with the Director of the CIA in Washington, William Webster. The document stated:

> We agreed with the American side that it was important to take advantage of the deteriorating economic situation in Iraq in order to put pressure on that country's government to delineate our common border. The Central Intelligence Agency gave us its view of appropriate means of pressure, saying that broad cooperation should be initiated between us on condition that such activities be coordinated at a high level.[162]

In response, the CIA accused Iraq of forging the memo. Yet the *Los Angeles Times* disagrees with the CIA allegation, pointing out that: 'The memo is not an obvious forgery, particularly since if Iraqi officials had written it themselves, they almost certainly would have made it far more damaging to US and Kuwaiti credibility.'[163] There is convincing circumstantial evidence demonstrating the memo's authenticity. When the Iraqi foreign minister confronted his Kuwaiti counterpart with the document at an Arab summit meeting in mid-August, his Kuwaiti colleague found it so sufficiently authentic – and indeed damaging – that he fainted.[164] And as noted by Ramsey Clark, former US Attorney-General under the Lyndon Johnson administration, 'many experts affirm that it is genuine. It is telling evidence, documenting the economic warfare waged against Iraq by Kuwait and the United States.'[165]

There are further reasons to believe that the US encouraged Kuwait not to come to a peaceful compromise with Iraq. Indeed, this is what has been asserted by the head of the Palestine Authority, Yasser Arafat, in relation to the events at an Arab summit in May. Arafat stated that the US pressured Kuwait to refuse any deal when Saddam offered to negotiate a mutually acceptable border with Kuwait at the summit to resolve the issue. 'The US was encouraging Kuwait not to offer any compromise which meant that there could be no negotiated solution to avoid the Persian Gulf crisis.'[166] Astute observers have noted that Kuwait's behaviour was plainly irrational and could not have been conducted without external encouragement from a more powerful ally. Dr Mussama al-Mubarak, Professor in Political Science at Kuwait University, for instance, commented: 'I don't know what the [Kuwaiti] Government was thinking, but it adopted an extremely hard line, which makes me think that the decisions were not Kuwait's alone. It is my assumption that, as a matter of course, Kuwait would have consulted on such matters with Saudi Arabia and Britain, as well as the United States.'[167]

The testimony of King Hussein of Jordan, who had been an intermediary in negotiations between Iraq, Kuwait and other Arab states at that time, confirms the US role. American investigative journalist Dr Michael Emery, using King Hussein as his pre-eminent source, found that:

Parties to the Arab negotiations say the Kuwaitis ... had enthusiastically participated in a behind-the-scenes economic campaign inspired by Western intelligence agencies against Iraqi interests. The Kuwaities even went so far as to dump oil for less than the agreed upon OPEC price ... which undercut the oil revenues essential to cash hungry Baghdad. The evidence shows that President George Bush, British prime minister Margaret Thatcher, Egyptian president Hosni Mubarak, and other Arab leaders secretly cooperated on a number of occasions, beginning August 1988, to deny Saddam Hussein the economic help he demanded for the reconstruction of his nation ... However, Washington and London encouraged the Kuwaitis in their intransigent insistence.[168]

As a consequence, Kuwait adopted a hard-line policy of no-compromise with Iraq, refusing to negotiate and intransigent in the face of Iraq's threat of using military means to put a stop to Kuwait's policies. According to senior Kuwaiti officials, this was because the US had already promised to intervene in case of an Iraqi attack. The Kuwaiti foreign minister, who is also brother of the ruling Emir, declared just before the Iraqi invasion: 'We are not going to respond to [Iraq] ... if they don't like it, let them occupy our territory ... we are going to bring in the Americans.' According to King Hussein, the Kuwaiti Emir commanded his senior military officers to hold off the Iraqis for 24 hours in the event of an invasion, by which time 'American and foreign forces would land in Kuwait and expel them'.[169]

Middle East expert Milton Viorst interviewed both US and Kuwaiti officials for a report in the *New Yorker*. He was informed by Kuwaiti Foreign Minister Sheikh Salem al-Sabah that General Schwarzkopf was a regular visitor to Kuwait after the Iran-Iraq War: 'Schwarzkopf came here a few times and met with the Crown Prince and Minister of Defense. These became routine visits to discuss military cooperation, and by the time the crisis with Iraq began last year, we knew we could rely on the Americans.'[170] Schwarzkopf's role has been corroborated by other sources, particularly the testimony of a US official in Kuwait who stated: 'Schwarzkopf was here on visits before the war, maybe a few times a year. He was a political general, and that was unusual in itself. He kept a personally high profile and was on a first-name basis with all the ministers in Kuwait.'[171] The American-Kuwaiti plot was also confirmed after the Gulf War. The Kuwaiti Minister of Oil and Finance stated: 'But we knew that the United States would not let us be overrun. I spent too much time in Washington to make that mistake, and received a constant stream of visitors here. The American policy was clear. Only Saddam didn't understand it.'[172] As Professor Francis Boyle thus notes, reviewing this sequence of events, the United States encouraged Kuwait in 'violating OPEC oil production agreements to undercut the price of oil to debilitate Iraq's economy'; 'extracting excessive and illegal amounts of oil from pools it shared with Iraq'; 'demanding immediate repayment of loans Kuwait had made to Iraq during the Iraq-Iran War'; and 'breaking off negotiations with Iraq over these disputes'. In doing so, the US 'intended to provoke Iraq into aggressive military actions against Kuwait that they knew could be used to justify US military intervention into the Persian Gulf for the purpose of destroying Iraq and taking over Arab oilfields'.[173]

When Iraq began preparing for a military incursion into Kuwait, the US did not publicize its official position of willingness to intervene on behalf of Kuwait. Instead the United States presented a green light to Saddam Hussein by consistently asserting a position of neutrality on the issue, contrary to its actual policy. On 25 July, while Saddam's troops were amassed on Kuwait's border in preparation to attack, after hearing the Iraqi dictator inform her that Kuwait's borders were drawn in the colonial era April Glaspie, US Ambassador to Iraq, told Saddam:

> We studied history at school. They taught us to say freedom or death. I think you know well that we ... have our experience with the colonialists. We have no opinion on the Arab-Arab conflicts, like your border disagreement with Kuwait ... [Secretary of State] James Baker has directed our official spokesmen to emphasize this instruction.

On 24 July, Glaspie received a cable from the US State Department directing her to reiterate to Iraqi officials that the US had 'no position' on 'Arab-Arab' conflicts.[174] Leading authority on US foreign policy John Stockwell – the highest-ranking CIA official to dissent and go public – has conducted an important review of Glaspie's role and its context in a wider array of US policies.[175] With regard to the Gulf War, he observes that 'the United States and Kuwait and Saudi Arabia lured Saddam Hussein and Iraq' into attacking Kuwait. Saddam Hussein had been 'protesting ... formally to every public body' against Kuwait's US-sponsored policies of 'economic warfare' against Iraq. There was no response from the international community. In the summer of 1990 Saddam 'called in the US Ambassador, April Glaspie, and asked her what the US position was ... on the defence of Kuwait. She did not know she was being tape-recorded, and she told him ten times in the conversation that [the US] had no defence agreement with Kuwait,' adding that 'the Secretary of State [James Baker] had ordered her to emphasize this instruction', and moreover that 'she had conferred with the President about it'. Stockwell also points out the crucial fact that then US Congressman Lee Hamilton – member of the US House Committee on International Relations, Chair of the Joint Economic Committee, and now Director of the Woodrow Wilson International Center for Scholars – concluded that the United States had indeed intentionally goaded Iraq into invading Kuwait: 'Congressman Lee Hamilton concluded, from hearings on this, that [America] had deliberately given Saddam Hussein the green light to invade Kuwait.'[176]

On 31 July, John Kelly, Assistant Secretary of State for Near Eastern and South Asian Affairs, told Congress: 'We have no defence treaty relationship with any Gulf country. That is clear ... We have historically avoided taking a position on border disputes or on internal OPEC deliberations.' Representative Lee Harrison then asked that if Iraq 'charged across the border into Kuwait', would it be true to say that the United States did 'not have a treaty commitment which would obligate us to engage US forces' in the region. 'That is correct,' replied Kelly.[177] Numerous official statements of similar intent were issued by US officials, while indications to the contrary were almost immediately withdrawn and corrected. Indeed, not long before the Gulf War — just after Saddam's hanging of London-based *Observer* journalist Farzad Bazoft in 1990 — a group of American senators visited Saddam in Baghdad and assured him that 'democracy is a very confusing issue — I believe that your problems lie with the Western media and not with the US Government' (US Senator Alan Simpson). Senator Howard Metzenbaum told Saddam: 'I have been sitting here and listening to you for about an hour, and I am now aware that you are a strong and intelligent man and that you want peace.'[178] All these statements of neutrality — and indeed appeasement of Saddam's Ba'athist regime — were clearly a misrepresentation of the actual US position. While giving Saddam a green light to invade by carefully not showing him a red light, the US covertly assured its Kuwaiti ally that in the event of an invasion, US forces would intervene and expel the Iraqi army from Kuwaiti territory.

Even the mainstream press has been forced to acknowledge how US statements of neutrality were so frequent and noninterventionist in character that they led Saddam to believe he had a green light to invade Kuwait. The *Washington Post* reported:

> Since the invasion, highly classified US intelligence assessments have determined that Saddam took US statements of neutrality … as a green light from the Bush administration for an invasion. One senior Iraqi military official … has told the [CIA] agency that Saddam seemed to be sincerely surprised by the subsequent bellicose reaction.[179]

'State Department officials … led Saddam Hussein to think he could get away with grabbing Kuwait,' concluded the *New York Daily News*. 'Bush and Co. gave him no reason to think otherwise.'[180] This was clearly the desired outcome. The former French Foreign Minister Claude Cheysson has observed that: 'The Americans were determined to go to war from the start,' and Saddam Hussein 'walked into a trap.'[181] A major piece of evidence on how the US manufactured the war with Iraq is contained in an impeachment resolution and brief in support by US Representative Henry Gonzalez presented to US Congress and printed in full in the *Congressional Record*:

> As early as October 1989 the CIA representatives in Kuwait had agreed to take advantage of Iraq's deteriorating economic position to put pressure on Iraq to accede to Kuwait's demands with regard to the border dispute.
>
> … Encouraging Kuwait to refuse to negotiate its differences with Iraq as required by the United Nations Charter, including Kuwait's failure to abide by OPEC quotas, its pumping of Iraqi oil from the Rumaila oil field and its refusal to negotiate these and other matters with Iraq.
>
> Months prior to the Iraqi invasion of Kuwait, the United States administration prepared a plan and practised elaborate computer

war games pitting United States forces against Iraqi armoured divisions.

In testimony before Congress prior to the invasion, Assistant Secretary Kelly misleadingly assured Congress that the United States had no commitment to come to Kuwait's assistance in the event of war.

April Glaspie's reassurance to Iraq that the dispute was an 'Arab' matter and the US would not interfere.[182]

As leading scholar of international affairs and authority on international law, former US Attorney-General Ramsey Clark — who led the Commission of Inquiry for the International War Crimes Tribunal on the Gulf War — thus concludes:

> The evidence that this assault was planned for years before Iraq invaded Kuwait cannot be doubted. That a decision to provoke Iraq into an act that would justify the execution of those plans is clear beyond a reasonable doubt. It was not Iraq but powerful forces in the United States that wanted a new war in the Middle East: the Pentagon, to maintain its tremendous budget; the military-industrial complex, with its dependence on Middle East arms sales and domestic military contracts; the oil companies, which wanted more control over the price of crude oil and greater profits; and the Bush administration, which saw in the Soviet Union's disintegration its chance to establish a permanent military presence in the Middle East, securing the region and achieving vast geopolitical power into the next century through control of its oil resources.[183]

This of course leads us to the question as to why the US would wish to remove Saddam Hussein from power. The answer perhaps lies in Saddam Hussein's domestic policies combined with his emerging tendencies towards independence. Although his regime was a dictatorship whose policies were exceedingly brutal against any form of opposition to the Ba'athist establishment, 'in his pre-war period', Saddam Hussein 'did more than most rulers in that part of the world to meet the basic material needs of his people in terms of housing, health care, and education,' reports Middle East expert Stephen Zunes of the University of San Francisco.

> In fact, Iraq's impressive infrastructure and strongly nationalistic ideology led many Arabs to conclude that the overkill exhibited by American forces and the post-war sanctions was a deliberate effort to emphasize that any development strategy in that part of the world must be pursued solely on terms favourable to Western interests. Saddam Hussein was also able to articulate the frustrations of the Arab masses concerning the Palestinian question, sovereignty regarding natural resources, and resistance to foreign domination. He was certainly opportunistic and manipulative in doing so, but it worked.[184]

As similarly pointed out by Director of the Middle East Project at the Institute for Policy Studies in Washington DC, Phyllis Bennis, 'the majority of Iraqi civilians enjoyed an almost First World-level standard of living, with education and health care systems that remained free, accessible to every Iraqi and among the highest quality in the developing world'.[185] According to the Economist Intelligence Unit's *Country Report for Iraq*, prior to the imposition of sanctions the Iraqi welfare state was 'among the most comprehensive and generous in the Arab world'.[186] The International Committee of the Red Cross (ICRC) reported in December 1999 that: 'Just a decade ago, Iraq boasted one of the most modern infrastructures and highest standards of living in the Middle East,' furnishing a 'modern, complex health care system' along with 'sophisticated water-treatment and pumping facilities'.[187] The New York-based Center for Economic and Social Rights (CESR) provides detailed elaboration:

Over 90% of the population had access to primary health-care, including laboratory diagnosis and immunizations for childhood diseases such as polio and diphtheria. During the 1970s and 80s, British and Japanese companies built scores of large, modern hospitals throughout Iraq, with advanced technologies for diagnosis, operations and treatment. Secondary and tertiary services, including surgical care and laboratory investigative support, were available to most of the Iraqi population at nominal charges. Iraqi medical and nursing schools emphasized education of women and attracted students from throughout the Middle East. A majority of Iraqi physicians were trained in Europe or the United States, and one-quarter were board-certified specialists.[188]

This domestic development strategy was combined with a strongly nationalistic ideology that appeared to be intensifying with time. In February 1990, Saddam made a speech before an Arab summit that certainly seemed to show that his days of subservience to the West could be ending. Harshly condemning the ongoing US military presence in the Gulf, Saddam warned, 'If the Gulf people and the rest of the Arabs along with them fail to take heed, the Arab Gulf region will be ruled by American will,' and that the United States would dictate the production, distribution and price of oil, 'all on the basis of a special outlook which has to do solely with US interests and in which no consideration is given to the interests of others.'[189] Saddam, in other words, was openly advocating the expulsion of US influence and control in the Gulf region, particularly with regard to the flow of oil.

Saddam's demonstration of a developing propensity for independence, originating from the nationalist Ba'athist ideology, was almost certainly a crucial factor in the US decision to eventually attempt to eliminate him, or at least cut him down to size. Having developed weapons of mass destruction under US tutelage and being strategically located in the Persian Gulf, any significant moves towards independence from the West by Iraq would present a serious threat to US/Western domination of Gulf oil, and thereby a wider threat to general US hegemony in the region. When Saddam began manifesting this very propensity it was thus necessary to block that movement long before it could gain regional momentum. 'With the launch of the allied attacks, the primary showdown pitted one of the most articulate spokesmen for Arab nationalism against the West,' notes Professor Zunes. 'Thus, there was real concern, both in the Middle East and beyond, that the United States was using Iraq's invasion of Kuwait as an excuse to exert a long-desired military, political, and economic hegemony in the region.'[190]

This strategy has been confirmed by the Pentagon itself. A leaked Pentagon draft document stated:

> In the Middle East and south-west Asia, our overall objective is to remain the predominant outside power in the region and preserve US and Western access to the region's oil ... As demonstrated by Iraq's invasion of Kuwait, it remains fundamentally important to prevent a hegemon or alignment of powers from dominating the region.[191]

In other words, the Pentagon describes US policy as being designed to maintain US/Western control over the Persian Gulf, primarily to maintain energy security, by preventing any single state or group of states from challenging in any manner this control. Saddam had demonstrated his intent to do exactly this – and thus it became essential for the US to neutralize this potential, as per official Pentagon strategy.

US Warmongering

This pre-eminent drive to protect and consolidate US control over the Persian Gulf via military intervention explains the consistent US attempts to push for war. According to conventional opinion, Saddam Hussein had not demonstrated any desire to seek a peaceful solution to the conflict with Kuwait, and the impending conflict with the United States. The truth, however, is quite the contrary. While the US had played an instrumental role in engineering a regional war crisis between Iraq and Kuwait, it had also continued to eagerly fabricate further pretexts to justify US military intervention in the Persian Gulf.

The *Christian Science Monitor* records in detail how the first Bush administration lied repeatedly to generate support for the 1991 Persian Gulf War:

- When George H. W. Bush ordered American forces to the Persian Gulf – to reverse Iraq's August 1990 invasion of Kuwait – part of the administration case was that an Iraqi juggernaut was also threatening to roll into Saudi Arabia. Citing top-secret satellite images, Pentagon officials estimated in mid-September that up to 250,000 Iraqi troops and 1500 tanks stood on the border, threatening the key US oil supplier. But when the *St Petersburg Times* in Florida acquired two commercial Soviet satellite images of the same area, taken at the same time, no Iraqi troops were visible near the Saudi border – just empty desert.

  'It was a pretty serious fib,' says Jean Heller, the *Times* journalist who broke the story . . . Shortly before US strikes began in the Gulf War, for example, the *St Petersburg Times* asked two experts to examine the satellite images of the Kuwait and Saudi Arabia border area taken in mid-September 1990, a month and a half after the Iraqi invasion. The experts, including a former Defense Intelligence Agency analyst who specialized in desert warfare, pointed out the US build-up – jet fighters standing wing-tip to wing-tip at Saudi bases – but were surprised to see almost no sign of the Iraqis. 'That [Iraqi build-up] was the whole justification for Bush sending troops in there, and it just didn't exist,' Ms Heller says. Three times Heller contacted the office of Secretary of Defense Dick Cheney (now Vice-President) for evidence refuting the *Times* photos or analysis – offering to hold the story if proven wrong.

The official response: 'Trust us.' To this day, the Pentagon's photographs of the Iraqi troop build-up remain classified.[192]

This war-mongering attitude was accompanied by an adamant refusal to acknowledge the grievances that had led Iraq to implement its offensive in the first place. President Bush declared that the Iraqi invasion was 'without provocation' – an assertion that specifically denied the reality of Kuwait's US-inspired policies of 'economic warfare' against Iraq.[193] Despite this, Saddam had made several crucial offers of peace that were rejected outright by the international community under US leadership, without even a feeble attempt at negotiation. According to the *New York Times*, the US wanted to 'block the diplomatic track because it might defuse the crisis at the cost of a few token gains for Iraq'.[194] As Stephen Zunes notes: 'Unilateral demands are not negotiations. American specialists on the negotiation process felt that the United States wanted a war, given that Washington gave the Iraqis no opportunity to save face.'[195]

In early August 1990, and once again in October, Saddam made explicitly clear that he was willing to pull Iraqi forces out of Kuwait and allow foreigners to leave the country, in return for the following: control of the Rumaila oilfield; access to the Persian Gulf; the lifting of sanctions that had been subsequently imposed; and a resolution of the oil price problem with Kuwait.[196] There was nothing particularly unreasonable about these conditions. One Bush administration official who special-ized in the Middle East acknowledged that 'the terms of the proposal are serious', describing the package as 'negotiable'. *Newsday* reported that in response to the offer, 'some [US] government officials now say that they see some hope of a negotiated settlement'.[197] The offers were rejected. The 23 August offer, for instance, was simply dismissed by the US administration and virtually blacked out by the mass media. Indeed, at first the State Department 'categorically' denied that the offer had even been made; only later was the existence of Iraq's offer confirmed by the White House.[198]

On 2 January 1991, Iraq proposed another peace package, offering to withdraw from Kuwait on condition that the US did not attack Iraqi soldiers as they pulled out; foreign troops left the region; there would be agreement on the Palestine issue and on the banning of weapons of mass destruction in the region. The proposal was described as 'a serious pre-negotiation position' by a State Department Middle East expert. Other US officials observed that the prospects of the offer were 'interesting'.[199] The proposal illustrated a clear willingness to compromise — Saddam had now dropped the previous Iraqi claims to two Kuwaiti islands and control of the Rumaila oilfield. Yet this was barely reported in the mass media.[200] Instead, Western leaders continued to categorically dismiss the possibility of negotiations, pushing eagerly for a full-scale offensive.[201]

US political analyst and CIA specialist William Blum, a former State Department official, chastises the blanket US dismissal of all possible peaceful solutions: 'The US military and President Bush would have their massive show of power, their super-hi-tech real war games, and no signals from Iraq or any peacenik would be allowed to spoil it.'[202] As a consequence, the United States, with support from its Western allies, attacked Iraq and imposed a massive military presence in the Gulf region.

The whole process, notes Blum, allowed Bush Snr to maintain both US military spending and his domestic popularity.[203] The Senate was led as the war proceeded to acknowledge that the Iraqi attack 'demonstrates the continuing risk of war and the need for advanced weapons'. Concerning the need for continued high military spending demonstrated by Iraqi aggression, Senator Dole remarked: 'If we needed Saddam Hussein to give us a wake-up call at least we can thank him for that.'[204] The *Washington Post* recorded the legitimacy the war gave to the expansion of the US military-industrial complex:

> Less than a year after political changes in Eastern Europe and the Soviet Union sent the defence industry reeling under the threat of dramatic cutbacks, executives and analysts say the crisis in the Persian Gulf has provided military companies with a tiny glimmer of hope ... The possible beneficiaries of the crisis cover the spectrum of companies in the defence industry.[205]

By early October 1990 this 'tiny glimmer of hope' was transformed into a massive boost:

> The political backdrop of the US military deployment in Saudi Arabia [in response to Iraq's invasion] played a significant role in limiting defence cuts in Sunday's budget agreement, halting the military spending 'free fall' that some analysts had predicted two months ago, budget aides said. Capitol Hill strategists said that Operation Desert Shield forged a major change in the political climate of the negotiations, forcing lawmakers who had been advocating deep cuts on the defensive. The defence budget compromise ... would leave not only funding for Operation Desert Shield intact but would spare much of the funding that has been spent each year to prepare for a major Soviet onslaught on Western Europe.[206]

Meanwhile, Bush Snr's approval rating had been boosted to a successful 73 per cent in October 1990. When Bush continued to contradict himself about the actual purpose of the Gulf War, this soon dropped to a meagre 56 per cent.[207] But once the actual military onslaught against Iraq had begun, by January 1991 Bush's popularity was again soaring at 82 per cent – the highest ever during his presidency.[208] Yet in spite of his success in duping the American public, beneath Bush Snr's popularity there was an uneasy awareness that the war was merely an excuse to legitimize US military expansion. James Webb, former Assistant Secretary of Defense and Secretary of the Navy, observed that:

> The President should be aware that, while most Americans are labouring very hard to support him, a mood of cynicism is just beneath the veneer of respect. Many are claiming that the build-up is little more than a 'Pentagon budget drill', designed to preclude cutbacks of an Army searching for a mission as bases in NATO begin to disappear.[209]

The process during the 1980s by which the United States was in some respects being supplanted by other powers was also crushed, with the US able to reinsert itself as the dominant hegemon in the region. The Persian Gulf states, including Saudi Arabia, no longer opposed a direct US military presence, which was rushed in immediately. As former US Ambassador Chas Freeman observes: 'The Gulf War put Saudi Arabia back on the map and revived a relationship that had been severely attrited.' Thus, in the ensuing decade the US sold $43 billion worth of military assistance to Saudi Arabia, and another $16 billion to Kuwait, Qatar, Bahrain and the United Arab Emirates. Whereas prior to 1991 the US could only 'pre-position' military supplies in Oman, the Gulf War allowed the US to conduct joint military exercises, pre-position military supplies, and place naval units and Air Force squadrons with nearly every country in the region. The US military presence in the Persian Gulf in other words increased dramatically.[210]

US War Crimes and Crimes Against Humanity

The US-led attack on Iraq enthusiastically employed a policy of wholesale destruction, which intentionally targeted not only

Iraq's military, but also the entire civilian infrastructure. A report by the US General Accounting Office, for instance, explicitly affirms that the Desert Storm air campaign of 1991 was aimed at: 'Five basic categories of targets – command and control, industrial production, infrastructure, population will, and fielded forces.' The bombing of civilian infrastructure, including electricity, water, sanitation and other life-sustaining essentials, was intended, according to the report, to 'degrade the will of the civilian population'.[211]

These facts, contrary to the mainstream myth of Western 'smart' bombs hitting solely military targets, have been exhaustively documented by Middle East Watch (MEW), affiliated to the international US-based rights monitor Human Rights Watch (HRW). MEW has documented numerous cases of the intentional mass destruction of civilian buildings and areas, such as the bombing of residential areas; crowded markets; bridges while they were brimming with pedestrians and their vehicles; a busy central bus station, all of which occurred largely in broad daylight with no governmental or military structures in the vicinity.[212]

According to its principal report on the Persian Gulf War, MEW records that 'allied attacks appear to have been indiscriminate, in that they failed to distinguish between military and civilian objects ...'

> [N]umerous witnesses described incidents in which civilian structures, most typically houses in residential areas they lived in or knew well, were destroyed or damaged in areas where they believed there were no conceivable military installations or facilities nearby, including anti-aircraft artillery ... [These] accounts suggest that some civilian casualties during the war were not the product of inaccurate bombing – mere misses – but of attacks that, pending convincing justification from the allies, appear to have been indiscriminate.

A typical example of these policies is the targeting of Basra, 'which was largely off-limits to foreign reporters during the air wars, [and] appears to have suffered considerably more damage to civilian structures than Baghdad, where a small international press force was present'. MEW also dissects the pretexts for the targeting of Iraqi civilian infrastructure. Referring to the destruction of Iraq's nationwide electrical system, MEW reports:

> The apparent justification for attacking almost the entire electrical system in Iraq was that the system functioned as an integrated grid, meaning that power could be shifted countrywide, including to military functions such as command-and-control centres and weapons-manufacturing facilities. But these key military targets were attacked in the opening days of the war. The direct attacks by the allies on these military targets should have obviated the need simultaneously to destroy the fixed power sources thought to have formerly supplied them. If these and other purely military targets could be attacked at will, then arguably the principle of humanity would make the wholesale destruction of Iraq's elec-trical-generating capability superfluous to the accomplishment of legitimate military objectives.[213]

Indeed, the Allies embarked on purposeful destruction of almost the entirety of Iraq's civilian infrastructure. Eric Hoskins, a Canadian doctor and coordinator of a Harvard study team on Iraq, observed that the bombing 'effectively terminated every-thing vital to human survival in Iraq – electricity, water, sewage systems, agriculture, industry, health care. Food, warehouses, hospitals and markets were bombed. Power stations were repeatedly attacked until electricity supplies were at only 4 per cent of pre-war levels.'[214] Hoskin's team further recorded that:

> The children strive to understand what they saw: planes bombing, houses collapsing, soldiers fighting, blood, mutilated and crushed bodies. The children fight to forget what they heard: people

screaming, desperate voices, planes, explosions, crying people. They are haunted by the smell of gunfire, fires and burned flesh.[215]

Many Iraqi civilians tried to escape the bombing by fleeing to Jordan, only to be bombarded by air attacks on the highway between Baghdad and Jordan's border. This included assaults on buses, taxis and private cars with Western cluster bombs, rockets and machine guns. The violence occurred in broad daylight, with no military structures or vehicles in sight, and with targets clearly being civilians. Busloads of passengers were literally incinerated, while civilians evacuating their vehicles fled for their lives; they too were subsequently fired at by tailing Allied planes.[216]

Probably it was 13 February 1991 when the Allies first escalated their bombing strategy to terrorize the Iraqi people. Two missiles launched from a US stealth bomber hit a civilian establishment — an air raid shelter — killing 1500 civilians, many of them women and children. In response to international concern and outrage, the US claimed that the shelter was a cover for a military outpost. Yet neighborhood residents insistently pointed out the existence of constant Western aerial surveillance overhead which clearly would have observed the daily flow of women and children into the shelter,[217] and Western reporters at the site admitted that absolutely no signs of military use could be discovered.[218] People living in the vicinity informed researchers that it was simply 'unbelievable' that the US was unaware that the shelter was used primarily by women and children coming and going twice a day. Abu Kulud, who lost his wife and two daughters in the bombing, testified: 'It was impossible for them not to know there were only civilians in the shelter. Their air [communications] were everywhere.' Similar testimony came from a woman who lost her mother and two sisters: 'How could they not know? They had to know. They had the satellite over our heads 24 hours a day, as well as photographs the planes took before they bombed.'[219]

US officials also failed to answer a reporter's key question at a military briefing, and prevented any form of independent inquiry from taking place:

> Why did they not show the video that showed military personnel going in and out of the bomb shelter? The US military refused to produce the pictures or allow an independent investigation of the incident. Within the space of 24 hours the Pentagon announced that its own internal investigation, conducted in secret, of course, was over and the case closed.[220]

However, the later testimony of a Pentagon official revealed the duplicity of a US cover-up. The US had known the site was a civilian shelter, but had targeted it to intentionally terrorize the Iraqi people. Brian Becker, Co-director of the Washington-based International Action Center (IAC) – the anti-war organization founded and headed by former US Attorney-General Ramsey Clark – calls attention to the official's crucial testimony:

> The US has deliberately targeted Iraqi civilians in the past. During the Persian Gulf War, for instance, the US used two precision or 'smart' bombs to destroy the Al-Amariyah bomb shelter in downtown Baghdad ... The Pentagon spokesman went on TV in February 1991 to announce that the attack on Al-Amariyah was not an accident. The US was trying to terrorize the population.[221]

This was only one representative example of a bombing campaign that can only be described as terrorism. Francis Boyle provides an accurate summary of the campaign:

> Systematic aerial and missile bombardment of Iraq was ordered to begin at 6:30 p.m. EST January 16, 1991, in order to be reported on prime time TV. The bombing continued for 42 days.

It met no resistance from Iraqi aircraft and no effective anti-aircraft or anti-missile ground fire. Iraq was basically defenceless. Most of the targets were civilian facilities. The United States intentionally bombed and destroyed centres for civilian life, commercial and business districts, schools, hospitals, mosques, churches, shelters, residential areas, historical sites, private vehicles and civilian government offices. In aerial attacks, including strafing, over cities, towns, the countryside and highways, United States aircraft bombed and strafed indiscriminately. The purpose of these attacks was to destroy life and property, and generally to terrorize the civilian population of Iraq. The net effect was the summary execution and corporal punishment indiscriminately of men, women and children, young and old, rich and poor, of all nationalities and religions. As a direct result of this bombing campaign against civilian life, at least 25,000 men, women and children were killed. The Red Crescent Society of Jordan estimated 113,000 civilian dead, 60% of them children, the week before the end of the war. According to the Nuremberg Charter, this 'wanton destruction of cities, towns, or villages' is a Nuremberg War Crime.[222]

Other experts agree, including the authoritative Commission for Inquiry of the International War Crimes Tribunal initiated by former US Attorney-General Ramsey Clark, which elaborates on these horrendous war crimes and crimes against humanity:

> The destruction of civilian facilities left the entire civilian population without heat, cooking fuel, refrigeration, potable water, telephones, power for radio or TV reception, public transportation and fuel for private automobiles. It also limited food supplies, closed schools, created massive unemployment, severely limited economic activity and caused hospitals and medical services to shut down. In addition, residential areas of every major city and most towns and villages were targeted and destroyed. Isolated Bedouin camps were attacked by US aircraft. In addition to deaths and injuries, the aerial assault destroyed 10–20,000 homes,

apartments and other dwellings. Commercial centres with shops, retail stores, offices, hotels, restaurants and other public accommodations were targeted and thousands were destroyed. Scores of schools, hospitals, mosques and churches were damaged or destroyed. Thousands of civilian vehicles on highways, roads and parked on streets and in garages were targeted and destroyed. These included public buses, private vans and mini-buses, trucks, tractor trailers, lorries, taxi cabs and private cars. The purpose of this bombing was to terrorize the entire country, kill people, destroy property, prevent movement, demoralize the people and force the overthrow of the government.[223]

According to a United Nations inspection team in the aftermath of the war, the Western offensive had 'a near apocalyptic impact' on Iraq. The country, which 'had been until January a rather highly urbanized and mechanized society', had been bombed into a 'pre-industrial age nation'.[224] It is reasonable to believe that one of the motivations for ruthlessly targeting the civilian population was to encourage desperate citizens to overthrow Saddam Hussein, and institute a new subservient regime. A US Air Force planner declared: 'Big picture, we wanted to let people know, "Get rid of this guy and we'll be more than happy to assist in rebuilding. We're not going to tolerate Saddam Hussein or his regime." Fix that and we'll fix your electricity.'[225]

This did not mean that the US preferred a popular democratic government to take power. On the contrary, when a popular Shi'ite and Kurdish uprising erupted in Iraq during the Gulf War after President Bush Snr had urged Iraqis to rebel against Saddam's regime, the revolt was put down by Saddam's forces with US complicity, as was revealed by a report by Peter Galbraith of the Senate Foreign Relations Committee in light of a March 1991 fact-finding mission. Galbraith reported that the US administration withheld support of the uprising against Saddam Hussein. Noam Chomsky describes the revealing account provided by Galbraith and other sources on the matter:

> Galbraith reported that the administration did not even respond to Saudi proposals to assist Shiite and Kurdish rebels, and that the Iraqi military did not attack until it had 'clear indication that the United States did not want the popular rebellion to succeed'. A BBC investigation found that 'several Iraqi generals made contact with the United States to sound out the likely response if they moved against Saddam', but received no support, concluding that 'Washington had no interest in supporting revolution; that it would prefer Saddam Hussein to continue his office …' An Iraqi general who escaped to Saudi Arabia told the BBC that 'he and his men had repeatedly asked the American forces for weapons, ammunition and food to help carry on the fight against Saddam's forces', only to be refused each time. As his men fell back towards US-UK positions, the Americans blew up an Iraqi arms dump to prevent them from obtaining arms, and then 'disarmed the rebels'. Reporting from northern Iraq, ABC correspondent Charles Glass described how 'Republican Guards [Saddam's army], supported by regular army brigades, mercilessly shelled Kurdish-held areas with Katyusha multiple rocket launchers, helicopter gunships and heavy artillery', while journalists observing the slaughter listened to General Schwarzkopf boasting to his radio audience that 'we have destroyed the Republican Guard as a militarily effective force' and eliminated the military use of helicopters. Such truths are not quite the stuff of which heroes are fashioned, so the story was finessed at home, though it could not be totally ignored, particularly the attack on the Kurds, with their Aryan features and origins; the Shi'ites who appear to have suffered even worse atrocities right under the gaze of Stormin' Norman, raised fewer problems, being mere Arabs.[226]

Western aversion to the removal of Saddam in this case appears to have been associated with the problem of how to ensure that the Kurdish/Shi'ite rebellion would result in the installation of an appropriately subservient government. There was no guarantee in this regard – the US certainly did not want the Shi'ite Muslims to take power, as had happened in Iran. Hence, the revolt went unsupported – not because the first Bush administration wanted Saddam Hussein to remain in power, but because it was clear that an indigenous rebellion would replace Saddam only with another nationalist leadership likely to be opposed to US/Western domination of the Persian Gulf.

Western indifference to the plight of the Kurds, rooted in strategic and economic interests, has a long record worth recounting here. The contradiction between the West's professed concern for the rights of Kurds in Iraq, and Western policy towards Turkey, is one contemporary example. Human Rights Watch (HRW), for instance, reports that it 'is particularly troubled that throughout Turkey's scorched-earth campaign, US troops, aircraft and intelligence personnel have remained at their posts throughout Turkey, mingling with Turkish counterinsurgency troops and aircrews in southeastern bases such as Incirlik and Diyarbakir ...'

> Some US troops are in Turkey on NATO-related duties, while others operate within the framework of Operation Provide Comfort, a no-fly zone in northern Iraq designed to defend Iraqi Kurds from Saddam Hussein's Air Force ... US military and diplomatic personnel have studiously ignored the abusive actions of their Turkish allies. It appears that in return for Turkey's support for Operation Provide Comfort, the US has agreed not to publicly criticize what Turkey does with its own Kurdish citizens, located directly across the Iraqi border from the zone protected by US warplanes ... [E]lements within the US Government possess detailed knowledge of the full scope of Turkish abuses as well as the key role played by US weapons.[227]

This combination of hypocrisy and complicity can be located in 'Turkey's status as an important NATO ally and as a major base for US troops, including US intelligence units, as well as US nuclear weapons'. In other words, strategic interests far outweigh alleged humanitarian concerns.[228]

All this is nothing novel and remains consistent with traditional policies. For example, in the early 1970s there was a Kurdish revolt supported by Iran — then ruled by the Shah. The purpose of the revolt as far as Iran and its American masters were concerned was simply to cause trouble for Iraq in accordance with strategic considerations — Iraq was not a US ally at this time. In order to further its strategic interests the US decided to help. The Pike Committee report has made clear that both the US and its Iranian stooge of the time did not want the Kurds to win, and that the uprising was given limited support only to pressurize Iraq to settle a border issue concerning access to the Persian Gulf. Consequently, as soon as Iraq accepted Iranian demands, both Iran and the United States cancelled their support of the Kurdish uprising. A classified report by the House Select Committee on Intelligence that was leaked to the press clarified this matter, stating that US officials:

> ... hoped that our clients [the Kurds] would not prevail. They preferred instead that the insurgents simply continue a level of hostilities sufficient to sap [Iraqi] resources ... This policy was not imparted to our clients, who were encouraged to continue fighting. Even in the context of covert action, ours was a cynical enterprise.[229]

It was in 1975 that aid to the Kurds was suddenly cut off, allowing Saddam to begin slaughtering them immediately. One thousand *pesh merga* fighters who had surrendered were shot down 'in cold blood', while another five thousand Kurdish women, children and elderly men were slaughtered as they attempted to flee the country.[230]

Western indifference to the slaughter of Kurds and people of other ethnicities in the non-Western world is therefore a long-standing reality that continues to this day, because policy is driven not by benevolence, but by elite interests in the maximization of power and profit. The massive military presence in the Persian Gulf today, legitimized by the no-fly zones over Iraq purportedly established to monitor Saddam's treatment of his people and ensure their protection, in fact plays the role of continuing the war against the Iraqi people. As IAC Coordinator Brian Becker pointedly remarks:

> The US says it is 'concerned' about the Kurds in northern Iraq and the Shi'ite population in the south. That's hogwash. Those are the people who are being killed and maimed by US bombs and missiles. The real reason is that the US wants control over these two regions because that is where Iraq's oil reserves are located. This oil constitutes 10% of the world's known reserves.[231]

It is clear then that a fundamental purpose of attacking the civilian society of Iraq during the 1991 Gulf War was politically motivated, and performed with the view to induce a population that could be appropriately subdued into recognizing Western superiority, to support the removal of the overly independent Saddam and bring Iraq back under US sphere of influence.[232] Western objectives in Iraq were candidly outlined by Thomas Friedman, then Chief Diplomatic Correspondent of the *New York Times*. Friedman reported that the West's hope was for Iraqi generals to topple Saddam Hussein, 'and then Washington would have the best of all worlds: an iron-fisted Iraqi junta without Saddam Hussein'. In this way, the United States – civilized leader of the 'free world' – hoped to recreate the days when Saddam's pro-West 'iron-fist ... held Iraq together, much to the satisfaction of the American allies Turkey and Saudi Arabia', as well as their Western masters.[233]

This record of Western policy in the Middle East illustrates not only that the concept of Western humanitarian intervention is redundant, but also that the conventional assumptions of mainstream political discourse — in which Western benevolence, concern for human rights and promotion of democracy are integral aspects of Western foreign policy — are without genuine empirical foundation. Indeed, these assumptions are entirely at odds with the systematically brutal and anti-democratic nature of Western foreign policy under US leadership in the Middle East, specifically in the Persian Gulf. This has broad implications for the basic terms and foundations of our understanding of international relations. In particular, it brings into question the relevance of the concept of a global 'civil society' in understanding the structure of the current world order, which is clearly dominated by imperial values. Indeed, as we shall see, the record of Western policy in Iraq in the aftermath of the 1991 Gulf War only serves to clarify this stark and unsavoury reality.

Part Two

BLEEDING THE GULF

*The United Nations Sanctions on Iraq
and the Corruption of Human Rights
Discourse*

Perhaps the most shocking element of Western policy in Iraq in the aftermath of the 1991 Gulf War is the United Nations sanctions regime established at that time, which served the purpose of extending the Western war on Iraq into a protracted system of civilian decimation. Using official reports, we document the escalation of the humanitarian crisis in Iraq under the UN sanctions regime, exposing the international community's unconscionable complicity in an ongoing tide of genocide. To that end, we conduct a detailed assessment of the sanctions on Iraq, their history, their effects, and the objectives behind them. The sanctions regime, furthermore, cannot be understood without grasping the context in which it has existed, namely, an escalating Anglo-American military strategy of invasion and occupation of Iraq.

As we demonstrate in detail, the Western-imposed humanitarian catastrophe in Iraq reaches atrocious proportions, but is nevertheless veiled from public understanding by a variety of successfully propagated Orwellian myths. The extent of the crisis clarifies the utter failure of the contemporary world order to genuinely implement ethical values, to protect human rights, to foster self-determination, and to create a just world community. It also illustrates with clarity how the political, military and economic pre-eminence of US power is capable of acting through international institutions such as the United Nations – as well as in complete disregard of them – in order to satisfy strategic objectives to maintain and impose the imperial structure of world order.

5

The US-UN Sanctions on Iraq

US Foreknowledge of Humanitarian Crisis Due to Sanctions Policy

The economic sanctions regime was imposed against Iraq on 2 August 1990 by the United Nations Security Council in response to the invasion of Kuwait, with a key purported aim being to prevent Iraq from securing the materials and technologies necessary to manufacture weapons of mass destruction. The sanctions prohibited all imports into Iraq and all exports from Iraq, unless the Security Council permitted exceptions. A Select Committee of the UK House of Commons described the sanctions regime as 'unprecedented in terms of longevity and its comprehensive nature'.[234] A spokesman from the US State Department similarly described these sanctions as 'the toughest, most comprehensive sanctions in history'.

The United States and United Kingdom bear primary responsibility for the UN sanctions regime on Iraq – as they do for many Security Council policies. In his historical study of the Anglo-American special relationship, journalist John Dickie finds that:

> One aspect of British expertise which came to be highly regarded in the last two years of the Reagan-Thatcher era was Tea Party diplomacy at the United Nations. It enabled the Americans to get action taken at the Security Council which otherwise might have been blocked as a superpower's bid to bulldoze the rest of the Council. Britain's status as being friendly with, but being seen as

not unwilling to disagree with, the United States provided the Americans with a means of securing results without appearing to be directly involved.[235]

Indeed, the UN has for long been used 'as an instrument of Anglo-American foreign policy', as a 1952 British Foreign Office memo reveals.[236] The UN sanctions regime against Iraq remains an outstanding example of a specifically Anglo-American policy being effectively imposed on a supposedly democratic international institution to the direct detriment of human rights. Extensive evidence shows that, in violation of international law, the United States was fully aware that the combined impact of the bombing campaign against Iraqi civilian infrastructure and the UN sanctions regime would be devastating. Recently released internal US Defense Intelligence Agency (DIA) documents reveal that the United States anticipated the dire civilian health consequences of destroying Iraq's drinking water and sanitation systems in the Gulf War. The documents also illustrate US awareness that sanctions would prevent the Iraqi Government from repairing the degraded facilities, and lead to the inevitable destruction of the Iraqi water system, resulting in a devastating humanitarian crisis for the Iraqi people.

The primary document on the subject, dated January 1991, outlines explicitly how sanctions will block Iraq's citizens from access to clean water, leading to dire health consequences:

> Iraq depends on importing specialized equipment and some chemicals to purify its water supply, most of which is heavily mineralized and frequently brackish to saline. With no domestic sources of both water treatment replacement parts and some essential chemicals, Iraq will continue attempts to circumvent United Nations sanctions to import these vital commodities. Failing to secure supplies will result in a shortage of pure drinking

water for much of the population. This could lead to increased incidences, if not epidemics, of disease.

The document goes on to note that the quality of untreated water in Iraq 'generally is poor', and that the consumption of such water 'could result in diarrhoea'. Iraq's rivers 'contain biological materials, pollutants, and are laden with bacteria. Unless the water is purified with chlorine, epidemics of such diseases as cholera, hepatitis and typhoid could occur.' Yet as the document points out, under the UN sanctions regime the importation of chlorine 'has been embargoed ... Recent reports indicate the chlorine supply is critically low.' Not only water, but food and medicine will inevitably be affected: 'Food processing, electronic, and, particularly, pharmaceutical plants require extremely pure water that is free from biological contaminants.'

Addressing potential counter-measures to obtain drinkable water that could be adopted by the Iraqi Government during the sanctions regime, the document finds that they cannot be effective:

> Iraq conceivably could truck water from the mountain reservoirs to urban areas. But the capability to gain significant quantities is extremely limited. The amount of pipe on hand and the lack of pumping stations would limit laying pipelines to these reservoirs. Moreover, without chlorine purification, the water still would contain biological pollutants. Some affluent Iraqis could obtain their own minimally adequate supply of good quality water from northern Iraqi sources. If boiled, the water could be safely consumed. Poorer Iraqis and industries requiring large quantities of pure water would not be able to meet their needs.

The use of rainwater is also out of the question:

> Precipitation occurs in Iraq during the winter and spring, but it falls primarily in the northern mountains ... Sporadic rains, sometimes heavy, fall over the lower plains. But Iraq could not

rely on rain to provide adequate pure water. Iraq could try convincing the United Nations or individual countries to exempt water treatment supplies from sanctions for humanitarian reasons. It probably also is attempting to purchase supplies by using some sympathetic countries as fronts. If such attempts fail, Iraqi alternatives are not adequate for their national requirements.

The ultimate effect of the UN sanctions regime therefore constitutes a humanitarian disaster. The US document admits that the lack of clean water will lead to dangerous health problems, including potential epidemics, until the entire water system will be effectively destroyed under the internationally imposed sanctions regime:

> Iraq will suffer increasing shortages of purified water because of the lack of required chemicals and desalination membranes. Incidences of disease, including possible epidemics, will become probable unless the population were careful to boil water ... Iraq's overall water treatment capability will suffer a slow decline, rather than a precipitous halt. Although Iraq is already experiencing a loss of water treatment capability, it probably will take at least six months (to June 1991) before the system is fully degraded.[237]

These and other DIA documents highlighting the impact of the sanctions have been unearthed and discussed at length by Professor Thomas J. Nagy, of the School of Business and Public Management at George Washington University. For instance, another January 1991 document, dealing with 'Effects of Bombing on Disease Occurrence in Baghdad', admits that: 'Increased incidence of diseases will be attributable to degradation of normal preventive medicine, waste disposal, water purification/distribution, electricity, and decreased ability to control disease outbreaks. Any urban area in Iraq that has received infrastructure damage will have similar problems.' The probable outbreaks include typhoid, cholera and 'acute diarrhoea' due to bacteria such as *E. coli*, shigella and salmonella, or by protozoa such as giardia, or by rotavirus, all of which will affect 'particularly children'.[238]

A February 1991 DIA document elaborates that under the sanctions regime:

> Conditions are favourable for communicable disease outbreaks, particularly in major urban areas affected by coalition bombing ... Infectious disease prevalence in major Iraqi urban areas targeted by coalition bombing (Baghdad, Basra) undoubtedly has increased since the beginning of Desert Storm ... Current public health problems are attributable to the reduction of normal preventive medicine, waste disposal, water purification and distribution, electricity, and the decreased ability to control disease outbreaks.

The most likely diseases during 'the next 69 days (descending order)' are 'diarrhoeal diseases (particularly children); acute respiratory illnesses (colds and influenza); typhoid; hepatitis A (particularly children); measles, diphtheria, and pertussis (particularly children); meningitis, including meningococcal (particularly children); cholera (possible, but less likely)'.[239]

A March 1991 document similarly finds that:

> Communicable diseases in Baghdad are more widespread than usually observed during this time of the year and are linked to the poor sanitary conditions (contaminated water supplies and improper sewage disposal) resulting from the war. According to a United Nations Children's Fund (UNICEF)/World Health Organization report, the quantity of potable water is less than 5 per cent of the original supply, there are no operational water and sewage treatment plants, and the reported incidence of diarrhoea is four times above normal levels. Additionally, respiratory infections are on the rise. Children particularly have been affected by these

diseases ... Conditions in Baghdad remain favourable for com-
municable disease outbreaks.[240]

A March document describes the impact of the sanctions regime
on Iraqi refugee camps:

> Cholera and measles have emerged at refugee camps. Further
> infectious diseases will spread due to inadequate water treatment
> and poor sanitation ... The main causes of infectious diseases,
> particularly diarrhoea, dysentery, and upper respiratory pro-
> blems, are poor sanitation and unclean water. These diseases
> primarily afflict the old and young children.[241]

A heavily censored June document reveals that a DIA official was
sent 'to assess health conditions and determine the most critical
medical needs of Iraq. The source observed that the Iraqi medical
system was in considerable disarray, medical facilities had been
extensively looted, and almost all medicines were in critically
short supply'. In one refugee camp named Cukurca, the source
found that 'at least 80 per cent of the population' has diarrhoea,
and that 'cholera, hepatitis type B, and measles have broken out'.
The document further observes that the protein deficiency disease kwashiorkor was found to be active in Iraq 'for the first time
... Gastroenteritis was killing children ... In the south, 80 per
cent of the deaths were children (with the exception of Al
Amarah, where 60 per cent of deaths were children).'[242]

As Nagy thus concludes, the United States was clearly aware
that sanctions would degrade the water treatment system of Iraq,
resulting in increased outbreaks of disease and high rates of
child mortality. According to the 1979 protocol, Article 54 of the
Geneva Convention:

> It is prohibited to attack, destroy, remove, or render useless
> objects indispensable to the survival of the civilian population,
> such as foodstuffs, crops, livestock, drinking water installations

and supplies, and irrigation works, for the specific purpose of denying them for their sustenance value to the civilian population or to the adverse Party, whatever the motive, whether in order to starve out civilians, to cause them to move away, or for any other motive.

Yet this is exactly what the United Nations did under US leadership, through an illegal sanctions regime depriving the Iraqi people of the basic necessities for survival. As Professor Thomas Nagy thus notes:

> The sanctions, imposed for a decade largely at the insistence of the United States, constitute a violation of the Geneva Convention. They amount to a systematic effort to, in the DIA's own words, 'fully degrade' Iraq's water sources ... For more than ten years the United States has deliberately pursued a policy of destroying the water treatment system of Iraq, knowing full well the cost in Iraqi lives.[243]

Experts on the Impact of the Sanctions Regime

Of course the role of the Iraqi Government in exacerbating the devastating impact of sanctions cannot be denied. As Middle East specialist Sarah Graham-Brown of Christian Aid reports in a briefing for the London-based Council for the Advancement of Arab-British Understanding (CAABU):

> By the late 1980s after eight years of war with Iran, the centralized economic structure of Iraq was already in difficulties. Its problems were greatly exacerbated by imposition of economic sanctions in 1990, but the Iraqi Government has continued to manage – or mismanage – economic and fiscal policy, deploying increasingly scarce resources to its own advantage and that of favoured groups. The government took some steps to provide a safety net in the form of basic rations, often meagre and of low protein content, but nonetheless preventing mass starvation. It has evidently used

this system politically as a means to increase the dependence of the population and as a form of control.[244]

Yet this in no way absolves the Western powers under US leadership of their principal responsibility for the humanitarian catastrophe which plagued Iraq under the UN sanctions regime. The sanctions regime essentially magnified the impact of the Iraqi Government's mismanagement and corruption, while also contributing directly to the devastation of civilian life in Iraq. This devastation has been inflicted by the sanctions regime to an extent that goes far beyond what the Iraqi Government would have been capable of alone. As Graham-Brown observes:

> The steep rise in morbidity and mortality rates in Iraq, especially among young children, is clearly a matter of great concern ... A critical factor in the impact of sanctions has been the impoverishment of large sections of the population. This has been combined with the erosion, and in some cases virtual collapse, of services on which most people depend, including water and sanitation services, healthcare and education. The living standards of the middle class have been seriously undermined, while those who were already poor live on the edge of survival.
>
> Unemployment and the falling purchasing power of salaries have deepened social divisions and social inequalities. The economic embargo has had an uneven impact on different regions and sections of Iraqi society. This discriminatory economic impact, combined with the Iraqi leadership's tendency to distribute largesse to favoured individuals and groups, creates a struggle for scarce resources which has probably exacerbated preexisting ethnic religious and tribal rivalries.[245]

There is no doubt that Saddam Hussein's regime would routinely compromise the humanitarian needs of the Iraqi people to maintain its own survival, directing as much as possible the worst effects of the sanctions against the civilian population and away from itself. But this is hardly surprising. Indeed, Western understanding of this elementary fact only illustrates that the international community expected UN sanctions, combined with internal corruption, to devastate Iraq, yet went ahead with them regardless. As a British House of Commons International Development Select Committee points out:

> The reasons sanctions were imposed in the first place were precisely the untrustworthiness of Saddam Hussein, his well-documented willingness to oppress his own people and neighbors, his contempt for humanitarian law. The international community cannot condemn Saddam Hussein for such behaviour and then complain that he is not allowing humanitarian exemptions to relieve suffering. What else could be expected? A sanctions regime which relies on the good will of Saddam Hussein is fundamentally flawed.[246]

Indeed, 'with or without the good will of Saddam Hussein', the sanctions regime would inevitably have resulted in the devastation of civilian life. As Graham-Brown noted:

> The often-repeated statement that the intention of international sanctions is to target 'the regime and not the people' is at best disingenuous. This does not in any way absolve the Iraqi Government of its responsibilities but several pertinent issues need to be addressed. The application of this type of 'blanket' economic sanctions inevitably leads to some measure of civilian hardship, since they affect the whole spectrum of civilian life — even when the infrastructure is not damaged or disrupted by war, as it was in Iraq. Allowing food and medicine through does not solve this problem. Certainly in the aftermath of a war, it has been the experience of aid agencies in Iraq that humanitarian aid alone cannot solve the infrastructural problems of a whole country, nor can the piecemeal and short-term approach adopted by the current oil for food program ... The hardship created by the economic embargo has been misdirected [by the very nature of that

embargo] to the civilian population rather than to the regime. As a result, the economic and social rights of the population – their right to life, health, a basic livelihood and education – have been seriously infringed by the outcomes of the embargo. For this the international community, having taken the decision to impose and maintain the embargo, must take its share of responsibility.[247]

There can be no surprise then that the United Nations itself has consistently attributed the suffering in Iraq *not* principally to the Iraqi Government of Saddam Hussein, but *principally* to the sanctions regime imposed by the Western powers through the UN under US leadership since 1991. In 1997, the UN Human Rights Committee found that: '[T]he effect of sanctions and blockades has been to cause suffering and death in Iraq, especially to children.'[248] In 1998, the UN Committee on the Rights of the Child reported that: '[T]he embargo imposed by the Security Council has adversely affected the economy and many aspects of daily life, thereby impeding the full enjoyment by the ... population, particularly children, of their rights to survival, health and education.'[249] The Humanitarian Panel of the Security Council similarly confirmed in 1999 that: 'Even if not all suffering in Iraq can be imputed to external factors, especially sanctions, the Iraqi people would not be undergoing such deprivations in the absence of prolonged measures imposed by the Security Council and the effects of the war.'[250] Towards the end of 2000, the Office of the United Nations High Commissioner for Human Rights reported that it 'believes that the current sanctions regime is having a disproportionately negative impact on the enjoyment of human rights by the Iraqi population. OHCHR considers that the time has come for the extent and nature of the sanctions regime on Iraq to be re-examined.'[251] The United Nations Sub-Commission on the Promotion and Protection of Human Rights further issued a Resolution in August 2000 outlining the direct link between sanctions and the Iraqi civilian population's suffering, and affirmed that it was 'considering any embargo that condemned an innocent people to hunger, disease, ignorance and even death to be a flagrant violation of the economic, social and cultural rights and the right to life of the people concerned and of international law'. The UN human rights body further referred to the 1949 Geneva Conventions which 'prohibit the starving of civilian populations and the destruction of what is indispensable to their survival', and accordingly 'decided, without a vote, to appeal again to the international community, and to the Security Council in particular, for the embargo provisions affecting the humanitarian situation of the population of Iraq to be lifted'.[252]

Independent experts have come to similar conclusions about the devastating impact of the sanctions on Iraqi civilian life throughout their period of operation. Save The Children Fund UK, for example, describes the economic sanctions regime as 'a silent war against Iraq's children'. The Catholic Relief Agency (CAFOD) depicts the sanctions regime as 'humanly catastrophic [and] morally indefensible'. Human Rights Watch in August 2000 reported that 'the continued imposition of comprehensive economic sanctions is undermining the basic rights of children and the civilian population generally' and further that 'the [Security] Council must recognize that the sanctions have contributed in a major way to persistent life-threatening conditions in the country'.[253] In 1999, 70 members of the US Congress signed a letter to President Clinton urging him to lift the embargo and put an end to what they called 'infanticide masquerading as policy'.[254]

6

The Impact of the Sanctions

Genocide Through Economic Warfare

Rick McDowell of the Chicago-based organization Voices in the Wilderness (VW) visited Iraq in late May 1997, as part of a delegation in support of a campaign to end the US-supported UN economic sanctions against Iraq. For the sixth time since January 1991 the delegation had travelled to Iraq, this time nearly six months after the UN 'Oil for Food' Resolution 986. The delegation visited hospitals in Baghdad and the southern port city of Basra. Members met with UN and relief officials, doctors, government workers, religious leaders and Iraqis from all walks of life. Instead of improvements in the availability of food and medicine the delegation 'found, instead, a deterioration of all conditions necessary for the sustenance of life. Travelling to Iraq for the third time in nine months, I encountered a resigned hopelessness amongst the people, a population historically known for its resilience.' A decade of 'the most comprehensive sanctions in modern history have reduced Iraq and its people to utter destitution,' observed McDowell. 'The United Nations Security Council's economic sanctions, invoked only ten times since the inception of the United Nations, and applied eight times since the end of the cold war, constitute an extension of the devastating Allied bombing campaign of 1991.'[255]

By 1999, UN figures projected that more than 1.7 million Iraqi civilians had died as a result of the sanctions, between 500,000 and 600,000 of whom were children.[256] Other experts have independently come to similar conclusions. Richard Garfield, for example, a renowned epidemiologist at Colombia University in New York, concluded that 'most' excess child deaths between August 1990 and March 1998 were 'primarily associated with sanctions'.[257] Garfield further observed that the death rate of Iraqi children in Iraq, tripling since 1990, was unique since 'there is almost no documented case of rising mortality for children under five years in the modern world'.[258] British and American government officials publicly to this day deny that sanctions have contributed to the suffering in Iraq. Yet since their implementation in 1991, the state of Iraq has steadily degraded under the UN sanctions regime, as documented in successive UN reports. In 1995 UNICEF reported:

> Sanctions are inhibiting the importation of spare parts, chemicals, reagents, and the means of transportation required to provide water and sanitation services to the civilian population of Iraq ... What has become increasingly clear is that no significant movement towards food security can be achieved so long as the embargo remains in place. All vital contributors to food availability, agricultural production, importation of foodstuffs, economic stability and income generation are dependent on Iraq's ability to purchase and import those items vital to the survival of the civilian population.[259]

The UN Food and Agricultural Organization (FAO) reported in September 1995 that:

> Famine threatens four million people in sanctions-hit Iraq – one fifth of the population – following a poor grain harvest ... The human situation is deteriorating. Living conditions are precarious and are at pre-famine level for at least four million people ... The deterioration in nutritional status of children is reflected in the significant increase of child mortality, which has risen nearly fivefold since 1990.[260]

The World Health Organization (WHO) observed in March 1996 that: 'Since the onset of sanctions, there has been a sixfold increase in the mortality rate for children under five and the majority of the country's population has been on a semi-starvation diet.'[261] The United Nations Children's Fund (UNICEF) reported in the same year that: '4500 children under the age of five are dying each month from hunger and disease ... The situation is disastrous for children. Many are living on the margin of survival.'[262] A year later in April 1997, UNICEF, in association with the UN's World Food Program (WFP), reported that: 'One out of every four Iraqi infants is malnourished ... Chronic malnutrition among children under five has reached 27.5 per cent. After a child reaches two or three years of age, chronic malnutrition is difficult to reverse and damage on the child's development is likely to be permanent.'[263] Six months on, UNICEF noted that: '32 per cent of children under five, some 960,000 children, are chronically malnourished − a rise of 72 per cent since 1991. Almost one quarter ... are underweight − twice as high as the levels found in neighboring Jordan and Turkey.'[264] By April 1998 the situation had deteriorated further:

> The increase in mortality reported in public hospitals for children under five years of age (an excess of some 40,000 deaths yearly compared with 1989) is mainly due to diarrhoea, pneumonia and malnutrition. In those over five years of age, the increase (an excess of some 50,000 deaths yearly compared with 1989) is associated with heart disease, hypertension, diabetes, cancer, liver or kidney diseases.

Approximately 250 people die every day in Iraq due to the effect of the sanctions, the UNICEF report added.[265]

The UN's Department of Humanitarian Affairs reported that Iraq's public health services were nearing a total breakdown from a lack of basic medicines, lifesaving drugs and essential medical supplies. The lack of clean water (50 per cent of all rural people have no access to potable water) and a collapse of water treatment facilities in most urban areas contributed to the rapidly deteriorating state of public health. The prohibition of critical items under the sanctions meant that Iraq lacked the spare parts and minerals essential to the task of repairing and maintaining its water and sewage treatment facilities. Because of this, the condition of many Iraqis barely improved at all, even by the food they received. The untreated water contributed immensely to disease and death.

> Since 1991, hospitals and health centres have remained without repair and maintenance. The functional capacity of the health care system has degraded further by shortages of water and power supply, lack of transportation and the collapse of the tele-communications system. Communicable diseases, such as waterborne diseases and malaria, which had been under control, came back as an epidemic in 1993 and have now become part of the endemic pattern of the precarious health situation, according to WHO.[266]

As airborne and waterborne diseases proliferated, deaths related to diarrhoea diseases tripled in an increasingly un-healthy environment. There was a dramatic increase in child-hood cancers, including leukaemia, Hodgkin's disease, lymph-omas, congenital diseases and deformities in foetuses, along with limb reductional abnormalities and increases in genetic abnormalities throughout Iraq, which may also be linked to the use of depleted uranium during the Persian Gulf War by the Western allies. The children born since the 1991 Gulf War have suffered in silence, often without access to painkillers, drugs, antibiotics or hope. Some childhood cancers realized an 80 per cent cure rate prior to sanctions. Following the imposition of sanctions, without cancer-fighting drugs, the survival rate for children with these same cancers was 0 per cent.[267] All this is directly related to the comprehensive collapse of Iraq's infrastructure as a consequence of the sanctions regime:

> In addition to the scarcity of resources, malnutrition problems also seem to stem from the massive deterioration in basic infrastructure, in particular in the water supply and waste disposal systems. The most vulnerable groups have been the hardest hit, especially children under five years of age who are being exposed to unhygienic conditions, particularly in urban centres. The WFP estimates that access to potable water is currently 50% of the 1990 level in urban areas and only 33% in rural areas.[268]

Due to the absence of hard currency the economy of Iraq, estimated to have the second largest oil reserves in the world, collapsed. Average public sector wages for the few in employment have fallen to less than $5 per month, while hyper-inflation resulted in astronomical rises in the price of goods. Prior to sanctions, the Iraqi dinar was worth $3. By May 1997 this was reduced to $.000625. While skilled workers, including doctors and engineers, deserted their jobs to become taxi drivers or cigarette salesmen, Iraqi professionals have left the country in increasing numbers. With an estimated 80 per cent of Iraqis affected by sanctions, families were forced to take recourse to selling household and personal possessions just to buy food and medicine. This was accompanied by the disintegration of the social fabric, as evidenced by the widespread rise in begging, street children, crime and prostitution. The UN's Humanitarian Panel reported to the Security Council in 1999:

> ... the cumulative effects of sustained deprivation on the psychosocial cohesion of the Iraqi population ... the following aspects were frequently mentioned: increase in juvenile delinquency, begging and prostitution, anxiety about the future and lack of motivation, a rising sense of isolation bred by absence of contact

with the outside world, the development of a parallel economy replete with profiteering and criminality, cultural and scientific impoverishment, disruption of family life ... UNICEF spoke of a whole generation of Iraqis who are growing up disconnected from the rest of the world.[269]

Rick McDowell cites several examples of the dire situation faced by Iraqi civilians under the sanctions regime. One young doctor at a Baghdad hospital summed up Iraqi feelings in a sentence: 'Our life is over.' Another doctor asked the delegation, 'What does your country gain from our suffering?' He makes 3000 dinar a month – equivalent to $2 – although he has practised for eight years. Yet, a single bottle of milk for his children costs 3500 dinars. An Iraqi reporter is quoted as despairingly stating, 'the world is upside down, nothing makes sense any more, it's all gone mad.' McDowell refers to 'the pain in the eyes of the mothers who wait in hospitals, with their children – for far too many mothers it is a death watch.'[270]

As a consequence of sanctions then, Iraq 'has experienced a shift from relative affluence to massive poverty' according to the United Nations.

> The data provided to the panel point to a continuing degradation of the Iraqi economy with an acute deterioration in the living conditions of the Iraqi population and severe strains on its social fabric ... In marked contrast to the prevailing situation prior to the events of 1990–91, the infant mortality rates in Iraq today are among the highest in the world, low infant birth weight affects at least 23% of all births, chronic malnutrition affects every fourth child under five years of age, only 41% of the population have regular access to clean water, 83% of all schools need substantial repairs. The ICRC states that the Iraqi health-care system is today in a decrepit state. UNDP calculates that it would take 7 billion US dollars to rehabilitate the power sector country-wide to its 1990 capacity.[271]

The UN Humanitarian Panel further noted that the alleviation of these conditions could only be achieved by a complete revival of the Iraqi economy, entailing the lifting of the sanctions regime:

> Regardless of the improvements that might be brought about — in terms of approval procedures, better performance by the Iraqi Government, or funding levels — the magnitude of the humanitarian needs is such that they cannot be met within the context of [the Oil for Food program]. Nor was the program intended to meet all the needs of the Iraqi people ... Given the present state of the infrastructure, the revenue required for its rehabilitation is far above the level available under the program. The humanitarian situation in Iraq will continue to be a dire one in the absence of a sustained revival of the Iraqi economy, which in turn cannot be achieved solely through remedial humanitarian efforts.[272]

Indeed, the UN admitted that it is principally because of the sanctions that the Iraqi people have suffered: '[T]he Iraqi people would not be undergoing such deprivations in the absence of the prolonged measures imposed by the Security Council and the effects of the war.'[273]

In terms of providing an objective assessment of the sanctions regime in Iraq, it is entirely reasonable to conclude that the policy since 1991 constituted an act of genocide, perpetrated by the United Nations at the primary insistence of Anglo-American power. As Sean Gondalves reports: 'Dennis Halliday, former UN humanitarian coordinator in Iraq, and his successor Hans von Sponeck both resigned in protest of the sanctions, calling them genocidal. Add to that list Scott Ritter, chief UNSCOM inspector in Iraq, the Pope and 53 US Catholic bishops.'[274] Head of the Middle East program at the New York based Center for Economic and Social Rights (CESR), Abdullah Mutawi, elaborates that:

Genocide has been unambiguously defined in international law as one of a number of acts, including killing or causing serious bodily or mental harm with intent to destroy – in whole or in part – a national, ethnic, racial or religious group. It is no longer too controversial to suggest that the sanctions policy against Iraq has targeted a 'national group' which has led to hundreds of thousands of deaths – not to mention the countless number who have suffered serious bodily and/or mental harm. All humanitarian agencies, UNICEF included, now freely admit to this. This leaves us with intent. It is inconceivable that the effects of combining a large scale military devastation of civil infrastructure with a sanctions policy unprecedented in its comprehensiveness, could not have been foreseen. Even if it can be argued that there was no intent at the outset, once the manifestations became obvious, intent can be said to have formed … The Harvard Study Team and the Center for Economic and Social Rights demonstrated in 1991 and 1996, respectively, the connection between malnutrition, the loss of civil infrastructure (most notably water and sanitation facilities) and excess child deaths. Given all this information, how can it be said that there was no intent?[275]

Oil for Food or Oil for Blood?

UN Security Council Resolution 986, issued on 14 April 1995, called on the international community to implement the 'Oil for Food' program in Iraq. The exact nature of the program was established in an agreement between the UN Secretariat and the Iraqi Government from May 1996. The resolution, which came into effect in December 1996, stipulated that Iraq can export oil and use a portion of the money raised to purchase basic goods from other countries. However, the 'Oil for Food' program was never meant to be an adequate substitute for the independent functioning of the Iraqi economy. Security Council Resolution 986 refers to the program as a 'temporary measure'. As noted in the March 1999 report of the UN Humanitarian Panel to the Security Council, 'in order for Iraq to aspire to social and economic indicators comparable to the ones reached at the beginning of the decade humanitarian efforts of the kind envisaged under the 'Oil for Food' system alone would not suffice and massive investment would be required in a number of key sectors, including oil, energy, agriculture and sanitation'.

> 'Oil for Food' can admittedly only meet but a small fraction of the priority needs of the Iraqi people ... [T]he magnitude of the humanitarian needs is such that they cannot be met within the context of the parameters set forth in Resolution 986 (1995) and succeeding resolutions, in particular Resolution 1153 (1998). Nor was the program intended to meet all the needs of the Iraqi people ... [The sanctions regime] does not contribute to stimulate the economy and has an indirect negative impact on agriculture, while increasing state control over a population whose private initiative is already under severe constraints of an internal and external nature.[276]

As a consequence, 'Oil for Food' could never have prevented the humanitarian crisis in Iraq. The 1999 report of the UN Humanitarian Panel to the Security Council observes that:

> The gravity of the humanitarian situation of the Iraqi people is indisputable and cannot be overstated. Irrespective of alleged attempts by the Iraqi authorities to exaggerate the significance of certain facts for political propaganda purposes, the data from different sources as well as qualitative assessments of bona fide observers and sheer common-sense analysis of economic variables converge and corroborate this evaluation.

The report finds that even if 'Oil for Food' worked perfectly the humanitarian situation in Iraq would continue to be dire as long as the sanctions regime subsisted.[277] Indeed, by the end of May 1997, Iraq had exported 120 million barrels of oil but had received only 692,000 metric tons of food — 29 per cent of what had been expected under the deal according to the WFP. Of the 574 contracts submitted to the Sanctions Committee for exports of humanitarian supplies to Iraq, 311 were approved, 191 placed on hold, 14 blocked, and 38 were awaiting clarification. Of the $2 billion in Iraqi oil revenue authorized for a six-month period, 30 per cent was designated for war reparations, 5 to 10 per cent for UN operations, 5 to 10 per cent covered maintenance and repair of the oil pipeline, and 15 per cent was earmarked for humanitarian supplies for the Kurdish population in northern Iraq. Only the minimal amount of $800,000 was available for central southern Iraq, which is equivalent to approximately 25 cents per person per day for food and medicine.[278]

Since the UN policy stipulated that all 15 members of the Sanctions Committee must approve contract applications made by the Iraqi Government, the arbitrary obstruction of entirely legitimate contracts became a routine aspect of 'Oil for Food'. The UN Secretary-General's report of 29 November 2000 warns that such holds are:

> ... certainly one of the major factors that are impeding program delivery in the centre and south. Current holds on such sectors as electricity, water and sanitation and agriculture impact adversely on the poor state of nutrition in Iraq. Similarly, holds on trucks badly needed for transportation of food supplies may soon affect distribution of food rations, which is also compounded by collapsing telecommunications facilities.[279]

It is noteworthy that such obstructions from the international community continued to increase in number, and in proportion to the total value of contracts. Indeed, 20 per cent of holds by value were established entirely without any reason given by the holding missions.

In light of these horrifying facts, the 'Oil for Food' resolution that was so often cited by the American and British governments as the sign of their commitment to the Iraqi people and the international instrument through which the needs of Iraqis could be adequately met since 1991 has been completely insufficient. Even assuming that food distribution was adequate, the devastation of the Iraqi economy meant that the population continued to starve. When Tun Myat, the UN Humanitarian Coordinator in Iraq, returned to New York in October 2000 after spending six months in Iraq, he noted that escalating poverty nullified the ongoing distribution of food:

> The food distribution system ... now ensures that under the new Distribution Plan over 2470 kcal of energy of food is being made available to every man, woman and child in the country ... but the fact is, of course, people have become so poor, in some cases, that they can't even afford to eat the food that they've been given free because for many of them the food ration represents the major part of their income ... they have to sell it in order to buy clothes and shoes or hats or whatever other things that they would require. So the sort of upturn in nutrition that we would all want to be seeing is not happening.[280]

In his June 2000 report, the UN Secretary-General noted that 'clean water and reliable electrical supply are of paramount importance to the welfare of Iraqi people'.[281] Such basic needs could not be provided through the imports allowed to Iraq under 'Oil for Food'. The resolution did not provide for critically needed parts to repair Iraqi water sanitation and medical infrastructure, both of which were devastated during the 1991 Gulf War. Indeed, the importation of such basic items as chlorine, fertilizers and pencils is prohibited.

Thus, at the beginning of 1997, the World Health Organization reported on the escalation of the humanitarian crisis despite 'Oil for Food':

Iraq's health system is close to collapse because medicines and other life-saving supplies scheduled for importation under the 'oil-for-food' deal have not arrived … Government drug warehouses and pharmacies have few stocks of medicines and medical supplies. The consequences of this situation are causing a near-breakdown of the health-care system, which is reeling under the pressure of being deprived of medicine, other basic supplies and spare parts.[282]

By November of the same year, 'Oil for Food' continued to remain ineffective in addressing the humanitarian crisis. UNICEF observed: 'There is no sign of any improvement since Security Council Resolution 986/1111 ['Oil for Food'] came into force.'[283] By April 1998, UNICEF again noted the sheer impotence of the 'Oil for Food' program: 'The Oil-for-Food plan has not yet resulted in adequate protection of Iraq's children from malnutrition and disease. Those children spared from death continue to remain deprived of essential rights addressed in the Convention of Rights of the Child.'[284] By March 1999, a UN report concluded that Iraq had fallen into a state of 'massive poverty' due to the sanctions, and that the country should be allowed to receive foreign investments in oil and other exports. Moreover, the report declared that 'Oil for Food' had failed to meet the needs of the Iraqi people.[285]

The United States and United Kingdom have actively continued to espouse the myth that the 'Oil for Food' program provided adequately for the needs of the Iraqi people. The blame for ongoing mass starvation, disease and so on, is laid squarely on Iraqi corruption in the distribution of goods due to Saddam Hussein. The disparity in development between the north and southern/central Iraq was one of the factors that the US has claimed proves its case. Data indicates that Iraqis inhabiting the northern region that is autonomous from Saddam's regime were better off than those elsewhere in the country who are subject to the regime's rationing system. Among the conclusions of an August 1999 UNICEF report on this matter were that in the autonomous northern region, under-five mortality rose from 80 deaths per 1000 live births in the period 1984–89, to 90 deaths per 1000 live births during the years 1989–94, but then *fell* to 72 deaths per 1000 live births between 1994 and 1999. Infant mortality rates followed a similar pattern. This discrepancy between child mortality in the north, where the UN controlled distribution under the 'Oil for Food' program, and in the rest of the country, where the Iraqi Government controlled distribution, has been highlighted by the Western powers to conclude that the humanitarian crisis was wholly a result of Saddam Hussein's corrupt distribution policies and wilful starvation of the Iraqi people.

This conclusion, however, flies in the face of rather stark realities. The March 1999 report of the UN Security Council's Humanitarian Panel highlighted the lack of evidence against Iraq in relation to the government's alleged lack of cooperation with the 'Oil for Food' program:

> While there is agreement that the Government could do more to make the 'Oil for Food' program work in a better and more timely fashion, it was not clear to what extent the problems encountered could be attributed to deliberate action or inaction on the part of the Iraqi Government. It is generally recognized that certain sectors such as electricity work smoothly while drug supplies suffer from delays in distribution. But mismanagement, funding shortages (absence of the so-called 'cash component') and a general lack of motivation might also explain such delays. While food and medicine had been explicitly exempted by Security Council Resolution 661, controls imposed by Resolution 986 had, at times, created obstacles to their timely supply.

This UN report clearly illustrates that whether there was any deliberate obstruction or otherwise by the Iraqi Government is at the very least unclear. It further clarifies a number of other factors inhibiting the potential benefits of 'Oil for Food', particularly funding shortages and arbitrary holds by members of the UN Security Council. Furthermore, with respect to funding shortages, absence of the 'cash component' under the 'Oil for Food' deal is particularly critical. In government-controlled areas of Iraq, the government is not given cash in return for oil sales under the 'Oil for Food' program, but only receives delivery of goods. The consequence of this is that the government is extremely inhibited in its ability to provide for the needs of the Iraqi people – for example, to hire a lorry to make a delivery if it does not have one available at the time.

Indeed, the Iraqi Government's own initiative has helped to alleviate the crisis for the population in spite of these problems. An authoritative FAO study points out that:

> The government of Iraq introduced a public food rationing system with effect from within a month of the imposition of the embargo. It provides basic foods at 1990 prices, which means they are now virtually free. This has a life-saving nutritional benefit ... and has prevented catastrophe for the Iraqi people.[286]

But this has simply not been enough. On a political level, the role which the Saddam administration has played increasingly consolidated its control over the civilian population. On a socio-economic level, as reported by former United Nations Assistant Secretary-General Dennis Halliday, head of the UN's 'Oil for Food' program until his resignation in September 1998, 5–6000 Iraqi civilians have died every month under the sanctions regime, irrespective of 'Oil for Food', and despite an 'efficient' and 'equitable' Iraqi rationing system.[287] Refuting statements by then British Foreign Office minister Peter Hain to the effect that

'Oil for Food' could have worked if not for Saddam's obstruction, Halliday countered that:

> There's no basis for that [kind of] assertion at all. The Secretary-General [Kofi Annan] has reported repeatedly that there is no evidence that food is being diverted by the government in Baghdad. We have 150 observers on the ground in Iraq. Say the wheat ship comes in from God knows where, in Basra, they follow the grain to some of the mills, they follow the flour to the 49,000 agents that the Iraqi Government employs for this program, then they follow the flour to the recipients and even interview some of the recipients – there is no evidence of diversion of foodstuffs whatsoever in the last two years.[288]

UN official Michael Stone similarly observed that:

> Ministers and senior members of the Opposition frequently state that the Iraqi leadership have diverted supplies under this program. This is a serious error. Some 150 international observers, travelling throughout Iraq, reported to the United Nations Multidisciplinary Observer Unit, of which I was the head. At no time was any diversion recorded. I made this clear in our reports to the UN Secretary-General, and he reported in writing to the Security Council accordingly. In the case of private donations outside the Oil for Food program, those which arrived by air were observed by us, and no diversion was recorded. Humanitarian supplies arriving by road were not within our remit, although my contact with the Iraq Red Crescent, which has a co-ordination role, would suggest no diversion. With regard to private medical donations, again nothing directly to do with the Oil for Food program, there has sometimes been confusion. All supplies, in accordance with international practice, should have been vetted before distribution by the testing authority, Kimadia. (Some suppliers, in ignorance, tried to avoid this.) I know of more than one occasion when outdated medicines arrived, and Kimadia was naturally reluctant for them to be distributed.[289]

By February 2000, the most senior UN aid official in Iraq, German diplomat Hans von Sponeck, who has served in the UN for 36 years, resigned his post after 17 months in opposition to the effects of the sanctions on the civilian population. Like Stone and Halliday he 'also rejected American allegations that the Iraqi regime was hindering the distribution of supplies'. Ironically, Von Sponeck's resignation followed the actions of his Irish predecessor who had similarly quit in opposition to the sanctions.[290] Notably, two days after Von Sponeck's resignation, head of the World Food Program in Iraq, Jutta Burghadt, also resigned, asserting that the situation imposed on Iraq by the sanctions regime was intolerable and unjustified.[291]

UN spokesperson in Iraq, Adnan Jarra, informed the *Wall Street Journal*: 'The [Oil for Food] distribution network is second to none. They [the Iraqis] are very efficient. We have not found anything that went anywhere it was not supposed to.'[292] Administrator of the UN 'Oil for Food' program Tun Myat told the *New York Times*: 'I think the Iraqi food-distribution system is probably second to none that you'll find anywhere in the world. It gets to everybody whom it's supposed to get to in the country.' Dennis Halliday elaborates:

> As most Iraqis have no other source of income, food has become a medium of exchange; it gets sold for other necessities, further lowering the calorie intake. You also have to get clothes and shoes for your kids to go to school. You've then got malnourished mothers who cannot breastfeed, and they pick up bad water. What is needed is investment in water treatment and distribution, electric power production for food processing, storage and refrigeration, education and agriculture.[293]

The real reasons for the discrepancy between northern and southern Iraq thus has little to do with the Iraqi regime, and is more a direct product of the protocols of the UN sanctions regime. The north receives 22 per cent more per capita from the 'Oil for Food' program than does the centre/south; the autonomous north receives a cash component for distribution of goods, while the centre/south receives only goods; there are 34 non-governmental organizations working in the north, while there are only 11 in the rest of the country; there was a massive influx of aid to the north immediately after the Gulf War, whereas the rest of the country did not receive any aid during that time; goods have been approved by the UN for distribution in the north far faster than in the centre/south; the north enjoys porous borders with Turkey, Syria and Iran, so more goods are able to penetrate through to the north by smuggling than in the rest of the country; finally, 85 per cent of the Iraqi population live in southern/central Iraq.[294]

The real cause of the devastation of Iraq thus lies in the nature of the sanctions regime. For instance, UN Secretary-General Kofi Annan criticized the US Government for 'using its muscle to put indefinite "holds" on more than $500 million in humanitarian goods that Iraq would like to buy'.[295] The British Government implements similar policies by, for instance, preventing the shipment of vaccines to Iraq for children in 1999, which was justified on the pretext that Saddam may use them to create weapons of mass destruction. Former UN Assistant Secretary-General Dennis Halliday has also harshly criticized such policies, noting that they appear to be intended to sabotage the possibility that 'Oil for Food' genuinely helps the Iraqi people:

> [T]he Sanctions Committee weighed in and they would look at a package of contracts, maybe ten items, and they would deliberately approve nine but block the tenth, knowing full well that without the tenth item the other nine were of no use. Those nine then go ahead – they're ordered, they arrive – and are stored in warehouses; so naturally the warehouses have stores that cannot

in fact be used because they're waiting for other components that are blocked by the Sanctions Committee . . . Washington, and to a lesser extent London, have deliberately played games through the Sanctions Committee with this program for years – it's a deliberate ploy. For the British Government to say that the quantities involved for vaccinating kids are going to produce weapons of mass destruction, this is just nonsense. That's why I've been using the word 'genocide', because this is a deliberate policy to destroy the people of Iraq. I'm afraid I have no other view at this late stage.[296]

Another example is the claim by then British Foreign Office Minister Peter Hain that 'about $16bn of humanitarian relief was available to the Iraqi people last year'. Citing official UN documents, Hans von Sponeck refuted Hain's statement, pointing out that the figure was for *four* years, and further noting that the vast proportion of the 'relief' is spent on reparations to Kuwait and oil companies, leaving Iraq with a paltry $100 a year to keep a single person alive.[297]

Both the United States and the United Kingdom have deliberately obstructed Iraq's purchase of necessary humanitarian supplies on fallacious grounds, claiming one or more of the following: that they might be turned into weapons (although the delivery and distribution of those goods is rigorously monitored by the UN); that they are not essential humanitarian supplies despite clear evidence that they are; that they will be inputted into Iraqi industry, although industry is also an essential aspect of civilian life. Karol Sikora, Chief of the Cancer Program of the World Health Organization (WHO) and Professor of International Cancer Medicine at Imperial College, London, reports that: 'Requested radiotherapy equipment, chemotherapy drugs and analgesics are consistently blocked by United States and British advisers. There seems to be a rather ludicrous notion that such agents could be converted into chemical or other weapons.' Iraq expert Dr Eric Herring of the Department of Politics at the University of Bristol describes this Western intransigence in detail. He notes that during Phase V of the oil sales program (i.e., between 26 November 1998 and 25 May 1999), the UN Sanctions Committee had by 16 August 1999 'considered 999 applications for humanitarian contracts'.

> Those which had been blocked included sugar from Vietnam; veterinary medicine from Spain; vegetable ghee from Egypt and Tunisia; generator, boiler and measuring system equipment from Italy; laboratory equipment from Germany; soya bean meal from India; cheese, chillers, water treatment chemicals, pumps and compressors from France; and distribution network equipment from Turkey.[298]

The British Foreign Office claimed in 1999 that only 4 per cent of items requested by Iraq were vetoed or 'blocked' by the Sanctions Committee. But Herring points out that in Britain any application 'to supply Iraq with goods' must 'first be approved by the Sanctions Unit within the Export Control Organization of the British Department of Trade and Industry' before the application 'can even be seen by the Sanctions Committee'. The figure of 4 per cent excluded 'all items which were blocked at national level before being allowed to go forward for approval to the Sanctions Committee'. Furthermore, although an item might not be blocked, there remained 'tremendous potential for disruptive stalling through the use of "holds"' which could last indefinitely. A member of the Sanctions Committee 'can delay approval of an application, and only that same Sanctions Committee member can release that hold'. Thus by 16 August 1999, Herring reports that the Sanctions Committee had placed holds 'on 141 of the 999 Phase V humanitarian contracts from many countries'.

None of the holds were for food, but 18 were for medicines and medical equipment, including one for X-ray equipment from Austria. The holds were principally aimed at supplies for the electricity industry, but also water treatment, cranes, excavators, educational equipment and materials, trucks and vehicle spare parts, dental equipment, toilet soap, computers, pesticides, veterinary supplies and, strangely enough, wheelbarrows.

By the same date in August, 524 proposed contracts for oil industry spare parts had been presented to the committee. Out of these, '164 – one third with about one third of the total dollar value of the contracts, mostly from China, Russia, France and the United Arab Emirates – had been placed on hold and six blocked'. The situation was worsened by the fact that the Sanctions Committee routinely took '66 days to approve a food contract, whereas delivery takes only 59 days and distribution seven days'. Although UN documentation does not identify which holds were imposed by which committee members throughout the sanctions period – nor the reasons for the holds or their duration – 'it is generally believed that the United States has imposed most of the holds, with most of the rest being imposed by Britain'.

The impact of this combination of blocks and holds by the US and UK governments was described by Benon Sevan, Executive Director of the UN Office of the Iraq Program (OIP), in his report to the Security Council in July 1999 as follows: '[T]he improvement of the nutritional and health status of the Iraqi people through [a] multi-sectoral approach ... is being seriously affected as a result of [the] excessive number of holds placed on supplies and equipment for water, sanitation and electricity.' As Herring observes, Sevan cited specific examples proving 'that the absence of even one small item can be enough to stall an entire project'.[299]

Accusations that Saddam deliberately withheld medical supplies from the Iraqi people in order to prevent them from accessing medicines are similarly flawed, Herring points out, citing authoritative UN reports. Analysing these documents, Herring shows that much of the problems of the Iraqi distribution system were a direct or indirect consequence of the sanctions regime – either directly because of Security Council policies in the form of obstructions, holds, and so on, or indirectly because of the perennially poor conditions of Iraqi infrastructure which could not be developed due to the blocking of essential items under the sanctions regime.

For instance, the British Government has argued that Iraq's 'stockpiling of medical supplies' is 'conclusive proof of Saddam Hussein's diabolical nature and the irrelevance of sanctions to the suffering of ordinary Iraqis'. This bizarre interpretation is contradicted by UN reports reviewed in detail by Eric Herring. Indeed, as Herring records, in the period before such allegations surfaced, 'not only did the UN favour stockpiling, but the WHO argued for more of it'. In November 1997, for instance, Kofi Annan reported approvingly that Iraq maintained a buffer stock for emergencies. The regime 'releases supplies from the buffer stock as newly arrived stock becomes available as replacement'. Again in June 1998, Annan observed that: 'The current stock, consisting of a 5 to 10 per cent reserve has been designed to cope with emergencies and has assisted in ensuring the availability of needed items ... WHO has indicated that a more substantial reserve is the only practical solution to the procurement cycle with a delay of some four to five months before the start of arrivals [of replacements for depleted items].' As Herring records, he did express concerns about distribution problems, which were caused not by a deliberate conspiracy on the part of the regime but by 'poor logistics, the absence of proper warehousing, inadequate management tools and a lack of staff support and training'. These problems, according to Annan, were worsened by 'a surge in arrivals of commodities from April 1998 onwards', with further problems caused by 'lack of transport, bulky equipment, and failure of some suppliers to indicate how to test supplies', in Herring's words.

In February 1999, Annan acknowledged that stockpiles were 'alarmingly high', but only due to 'slow contracting by Kimadia, the Iraqi state company for drug imports' as a result of technical and logistical problems with Kimadia's efforts to computerize the ordering process with inexperienced staff. Another 'more serious' factor noted by Annan was 'the slow pace of distribution from Kimadia central warehouses to the governorate warehouses, and further to health centres' as a consequence of 'lack of modern managerial tools . . . poor working conditions within the warehouses . . . lack of transport for moving the supplies . . . the rigid hierarchy in the Ministry of Health administration which makes it difficult for functionaries to approve deliveries without approval of superiors . . . [and the possibility that] superiors may have deliberately withheld supplies in anticipation of emergency needs'. The last point, Herring reports, 'refers to bombing by the US and British air forces'. Finally, Annan confirmed that another reason for stockpiling was 'over-prescribing by physicians and the Iraqi Ministry of Health's desire to prevent waste of medicines by controlling supplies more tightly'.

By May 1999, Annan reported that Iraq's distribution problems had 'multiple and complex' causes, including 'the decline in professional competence and motivation' which as Herring observes was probably a result of 'eight years of poverty and ill health' under sanctions. Other critical contributory factors identified by Annan included ' "erratic arrivals", confusion caused by the fact that various brand-names refer to the same generic product, space problems caused by the recent delivery of bulky equipment, increased total volume of deliveries, and delays in the arrival of complementary parts and technical staff...'

In July 1999, Sevan indicated that 'lengthy delays' caused by the UN Sanctions Committee approval process meant that previously reliable suppliers had withdrawn, and so Iraq had been 'obliged to procure through less reliable brokers'. Sevan indicated that he wanted 'to demystify' the issue of warehoused humanitarian supplies through a comprehensive inventory. Initial results from the inventory showed the situation to be improving. By 31 July 1999, of drugs delivered to Iraq, 68.8 per cent had been distributed with 26.7 per cent set aside as buffer and working stock. Of medical supplies delivered to Iraq, 65 per cent had been distributed, and 15 per cent was being quality tested, had failed quality testing or was awaiting complementary accessories.[300]

As thus noted by the Washington DC-based anti-war group founded by former US Attorney-General Ramsey Clark – the International Action Center (IAC) – 'Oil for Food' is designed less to help the people of Iraq than to lend the sanctions regime a humanitarian gloss for public relations purposes:

The oil-for-food deal cannot solve the health problems in Iraq and it's not meant to. The oil-for-food deal is and always will be used by the US to divert attention from the genocidal effects of the sanctions. It is only a complete lifting of the sanctions and a withdrawal of the US from the region that can end the crisis in Iraq.[301]

The Objective of the Sanctions: Paying the Price

In May 1996 then US Ambassador to the UN – later Secretary of State – Madeleine Albright, appeared on the American documentary TV show, *60 Minutes*. Host Lesley Stahl asked: 'We have heard that a half a million children have died. I mean, that's more children than died in Hiroshima. Is the price worth it?' Albright replied: 'I think this is a very hard choice, but the price – we think the price is worth it.'[302] The question we are led to ask in light of this horrifying declaration is: the price is worth what exactly?

Rather than damaging Saddam Hussein and his brutal dictatorship, the sanctions have in fact had the entirely opposite effect. According to a House Select Committee report on sanctions to the British Parliament in 2000:

> Those who should be targeted, the political leaders and elites who have flouted international law, continue to enrich themselves. Much discussion has taken place of targeted sanctions, in particular financial sanctions, as a 'smarter' and more just approach. We conclude, however, that neither the United Kingdom nor the international community have made real efforts to introduce such sanctions. There has been much talk but little action. There is a clear consensus that the humanitarian and developmental situation in Iraq has deteriorated seriously since the imposition of comprehensive economic sanctions whilst, at the same time, sanctions have clearly failed to hurt those responsible for past violations of international law as Saddam Hussein and his ruling elite continue to enjoy a privileged existence ... However carefully exemptions are planned, the fact is that comprehensive economic sanctions only further concentrate power in the hands of the ruling elite. The UN will lose credibility if it advocates the rights of the poor whilst at the same time causing, if only indirectly, their further impoverishment.[303]

The fundamental basis of legitimacy for the establishment of the sanctions regime was, at least officially, the objective of blocking Saddam Hussein's access to materials that could be used in programs to develop weapons of mass destruction. Yet an examination of some of the materials banned from reaching Iraq under the sanctions discloses that many of them are irrelevant to this objective. Indeed, a vast number of materials and technologies banned under the sanctions have absolutely no connection with any possibility of being used in Saddam's weapons programs. The banned materials are supposed to be 'dual-use' technologies, i.e., they have both civilian and military applications. Yet many of the goods banned by the sanctions regime appear to be, in fact, only single use items with solely civilian applications. Voices in the Wilderness has compiled a partial list of some of these items that only by a convoluted twist of the imagination could be used to contribute to nuclear, chemical and biological weapons development programs:

> Accumulators; Adhesive paper; Aluminium foil; AM-FM receivers; Ambulances; Amplifiers; Answering machines; Armoured cable; Ashtrays; Auto polish; Axes; Bags; Baking soda; Balls (for children, for sport); Baskets; Bath brushes; Batteries; Battery chargers; Beads; Bearings; Bed lamps; Belts; Benches; Bicycles; Books (all categories included); Bottles; Bowls; Boxes; Broil Busses; Calculators; Cameras; Candles; Candlesticks; Canvas; Carpets; Cars; Carts; Carving knives; Cellophane; Chalk; Chess boards; Chiffon; Children's wear; Chisels; Clocks; Clutches; Coats; Coaxial cable; Cogs; Coils; Colors for painting; Combs; Compressors (for cooling); Computers and computer supplies; Copper; Cupboards; Cups; Desks; Desk lamps; Detergents; Dictaphones; Dish ware; Dishwashers; Dolls; Doorknobs; Doormats; Drawing knives; Dresses; Drills; Dryers; Dust cloths; Dyes; Dynamos; Easels; Electric cookers; Electric cords; Envelopes; Eyeglasses; Fabrics; Fans; Fax machines; Fibres; Files; Filing cabinets; Filing cards; Films; Filters; Flashlights; Flowerpots; Forks; Fountain pens; Furniture polish; Fuses; Gas burners; Gauges; Generators; Girdles; Glass; Glue; Gowns; Grills; Grindstone; Hairpins; Hammers; Handkerchiefs; Hats; Headlights; Headphones; Hearing aids; Hedge-trimmers; Helmets; Hoes; Hooks; Hookup wires; Hoses; Hydraulic jacks; Ink (the prohibition on writing); Ink cartridges; Insulator strips; Interrupters;

Jackets; Jacks; Joints; Jumpers; Kettles; Knives; Lampshades; Lathes; Lawn mowers; Leather; Levers; Light bulbs; Light meters; Lime; Magazines (including journals); Magnesium; Magnets; Masonite; Mastic; Matches; Measuring equipment; Mica; Microfiche; Microphones; Microscopes; Mirrors; Mops; Motorbikes; Motors; Mufflers; Mugs; Music cassettes; Music CDs; Musical instruments; Nail brushes; Nailfiles; Napkins; Notebooks; Oil cans; Oil gauges; Oil lamps; Oscillators; Packaging materials; Pails; Painters brushes; Paints; Pans; Paperclips; Paper for printing; Paper for wrapping; Paper for writing; Pens; Percolators; Pesticides; Photocopiers; Photometers; Pincers; Pincettes; Pins; Plastics; Plates; Plexiglas; Pliers; Plugs; Plywood; Porcelain; Pots; Potties; Press drills; Pressure cookers; Printing equipment; Pulleys; Putty; Radiators for cars; Razor blades; Razors; Reels; Relays; Riveters; Roasters; Rubber; Rugs; Rulers; Sandals; Sandpaper; Saucers; Saws; Scales; Scoreboards; Screws; Seals; Seats; Shampoo; Sheers; Shelves; Shirts; Shock absorbers; Shoe polish; Shoes; Shopping carts; Shovels; Silicon; Silver polish; Skirts; Soap; Soap pads; Sockets; Socks; Solder; Soldering irons; Spark plugs; Spatulas; Sponges; Spoons; Stamps; Staplers; Starters; Stoves; Straps; Suits; Sun hats; Swimming suits; Switches; Tables; Tacks; Tags; Telephone cables; Telephones; Tents; Thermometers; Threads; Timber; Timers; Tin; Tire pumps; Tissue paper; Toasters; Toilet paper; Tongs; Toothbrushes; Toothpicks; Towels; Toys; Tractors; Transformers; Trash cans; Tripods; Troughs; Typewriters; Vacuum cleaners; Valves; Vans; Vaseline; Vases; Venetian blinds; Ventilators; Videotapes; Voltage regulators; Waffle irons; Wagons; Wallets; Wallpapers; Washing machines; Wastepaper baskets; Watches; Water pumps; Wax; Welders; Wheelbarrows; Window shades; Wood; Wool; Wrenches; Zoom lenses.[304]

Given that the many items banned under the sanctions regime clearly have a primarily civilian application with only a negligible/arbitrary military use (e.g. the banning of pencils because their graphite can theoretically be used in the process of creating nuclear weapons), the idea that the sole objective of the sanctions was the obstruction of Saddam Hussein's weapons programs is disingenuous. For if that were the case, then there would be no need to ban items with a fundamentally civilian use. The specifically civilian application of such a vast number of items banned by the sanctions illustrates that the aim of the sanctions regime is far broader, and designed deliberately to target the civilian population. Former Chief UN Relief Coordinator for Iraq, Dennis Halliday, who resigned his post in protest against the sanctions regime, stated in November 1998 that:

> [S]anctions continue to kill children and sustain high levels of malnutrition. Sanctions are undermining cultural and educational recovery. Sanctions will not change governance to democracy. Sanctions encourage isolation, alienation, and possibly fanaticism. Sanctions may create a danger to peace in the region and in the world. Sanctions destroy Islamic and Iraqi family values. Sanctions have undermined the advancement of women and have encouraged a massive brain drain. Sanctions destroy the lives of children, their expectations and those of young adults. Sanctions breach the Charter of the United Nations, the Conventions of Human Rights, and the Rights of the Child. Sanctions are counterproductive, and have no positive impact on the leadership, and sanctions lead to unacceptable human suffering, often the young and the innocent ... I can find no legitimate justification for sustaining economic sanctions under these circumstances.[305]

Halliday asserted that he resigned his post 'because the policy of economic sanctions is totally bankrupt. We are in the process of destroying an entire society. It is as simple and terrifying as that.'

Five thousand children are dying every month ... I don't want to administer a program that results in figures like these ... I had been instructed to implement a policy that satisfies the definition of genocide: a deliberate policy that has effectively killed well over a million individuals, children and adults. We all know that the regime, Saddam Hussein, is not paying the price for economic sanctions; on the contrary, he has been strengthened by them. It is the little people who are losing their children or their parents for lack of treated water. What is clear is that the Security Council is now out of control, for its actions here undermine its own Charter, and the Declaration of Human Rights and the Geneva Convention.[306]

His disgust is mirrored even by those who formerly appeared to be supporters of US policy. Scott Ritter, an ex-US Marine and former head of the United Nations weapons inspection team in Iraq, certainly does not agree that the sanctions could ever be justified: 'We're killing 5000 kids under the age of five every month. Now people say Saddam's killing them, but ultimately, sanctions are killing them, and we shouldn't be supportive of something that causes innocent people to suffer to such a degree.'[307]

The anti-humanitarian cynicism that lies behind the sanctions policy was illustrated when then President Bill Clinton attempted to justify the policy when he argued that 'without the sanctions', there would be 'less food for [Iraq's] people ... so long as Iraq remains out of compliance [with UN inspections], we will work with the international community to maintain and enforce the economic sanctions.'[308] Clinton's audacious claim that the sanctions meant more food for the Iraqi people directly contradicts successive US and UN reports, which consistently prove that the sanctions have been the principal cause of starvation, disease and death in Iraq. His willingness to attempt to deceive the public so flagrantly indicates the rather deceptive nature of the entire sanctions policy. Indeed, US officials have repeatedly indicated that the sanctions were imposed independently of the UN weapons inspection process, and were in fact instituted for other political and strategic reasons. The real objective of the sanctions was admitted by US Deputy National Security Adviser Robert M. Gates in May 1991:

> Saddam is discredited and cannot be redeemed. His leadership will never be accepted by the world community. Therefore, Iraqis will pay the price while he remains in power. All possible sanctions will be maintained until he is gone ... Any easing of sanctions will be considered only when there is a new government.[309]

In other words, Gates asserted, sanctions are to continue irrespective of Iraqi compliance with the requirements of UN weapons inspections. This reveals that the elimination of weapons of mass destruction has never been the reason for the sanctions. On the contrary, the sanctions were designed to punish the Iraqi people until a new pro-Western government is installed. They aimed to prostrate the entire country, smash it until it would surrender to Western demands. In Gates's words, 'Iraqis will pay the price.' The real US position was articulated again in March 1997 by US Secretary of State Madeleine Albright: 'We do not agree with the nations who argue that if Iraq complies with its obligations concerning weapons of mass destruction, sanctions should be lifted.'[310] The cavalier US approach is further confirmed by the observation of an anonymous US official 'with responsibility for Iraq': 'We bought seven years and that's not bad ... The longer we can fool around in the council and keep things static the better.'[311]

It is noteworthy that the US policy regarding sanctions violates international law, standing in contravention of UN Resolution 687 which asserts that 'sanctions shall have no further force or effect' when Iraq complies with inspections. US policy always stipulated that sanctions are to remain in effect as long as Saddam Hussein remains in power. It is no surprise considering the nature of this policy that the Iraqi regime never saw any substantial point in attempting to comply with any sort of UN weapons inspection process, given that the US had always intended to impose sanctions indefinitely regardless of such compliance. The US concern regarding the initiation of sanctions on Iraq was therefore not related to the removal of Saddam's alleged weapons. Accusations of Iraqi weapons programs instead have consistently played the propagandist role of providing a justification for an illegal, anti-humanitarian sanctions policy, and were thus issued solely for the purpose of public relations. As French Foreign Minister Hubert Vedrine observed: '[The] United States is insensitive to the human catastrophe under way in Iraq ... Iraq is not just made up of Saddam Hussein himself ... There are men, women, and children, a whole society which is being destroyed.'[312]

An Illegal Policy

According to an authoritative report on Iraq prepared for the UN Secretary-General by Professor of International Law Marc Bossuyt, a renowned authority in his field, the 'sanctions regime against Iraq is unequivocally illegal under existing human rights law' and 'could raise questions under the Genocide Convention'. Professor Bossuyt is not alone in his conclusions. Specialist in International Politics at the University of Bristol, Dr Eric Herring – formerly Visiting Scholar at George Washington University (Washington DC) and Social Science Research Council MacArthur Fellow in International Peace and Security at Columbia University (New York) – observes that an expanding body of authoritative legal opinion agrees that the proposed International Criminal Court has a responsibility to investigate 'the UN bombing and sanctions which have violated the human rights of Iraqi civilians on a vast scale by denying them many of the means necessary for survival. It should also investigate those who assisted [Saddam Hussein's] programs of now prohibited weapons, including Western governments and companies.'[313]

To comprehend the entirely illegal nature of the UN sanctions regime imposed under US pressure, it suffices to review several related stipulations of international law. The World Declaration on Nutrition states that: 'We recognize that access to nutritionally adequate and safe food is a right of each individual. We affirm ... that food must not be used as a tool for political pressure.'[314] This statement is rooted in the basic principles of international law. The Constitution of the United Nations World Health Organization affirms that: 'The enjoyment of the highest standard of health is one of the fundamental rights of every human being without distinction of race, religion, political belief, economic or social condition.'[315] Indeed, the Universal Declaration of Human Rights (1948) stipulates that:

> Everyone has the right to a standard of living adequate for the health and well-being of himself and of his family, including food, clothing, housing and medical care and necessary social services, and the right to security in the event of unemployment, sickness, disability, widowhood, old age or other lack of livelihood in circumstances beyond his control.

As such, any action pursued to jeopardize the rights enshrined as above is prohibited under international law. According to the Geneva Conventions:

> 1. Starvation of civilians as a method of warfare is prohibited.
> 2. It is prohibited to attack, destroy, remove, or render useless objects indispensable to the agricultural areas for the production

of foodstuffs, crops, livestock, drinking water installations and supplies, and irrigation works, for the specific purpose of denying them for their sustenance value to the civilian population or to the adverse Party, whatever the motive, whether in order to starve out civilians, to cause them to move away, or for any other motive.[316]

A United Nations Resolution issued on December 1989 elaborates as follows:

> Economic measures as a means of political and economic coercion against developing countries: Calls upon the developed countries to refrain from exercising political coercion through the application of economic instruments with the purpose of inducing changes in the economic or social systems, as well as in the domestic or foreign policies, of other countries; Reaffirms that developed countries should refrain from threatening or applying trade and financial restrictions, blockades, embargoes, and other economic sanctions, incompatible with the provisions of the Charter of the United Nations and in violation of undertakings contracted multilaterally and bilaterally, against developing countries as a form of political and economic coercion that affects their political, economic, and social development.[317]

As Abdullah Mutawi, head of the Middle East Program at the New York-based Center for Economic and Social Rights (CESR), thus points out: '[T]he sanctions policy against Iraq has proven to be the single largest violation of the International Covenant on Economic and Social Rights, a violation committed by the Security Council itself ... Collective punishment is prohibited by the Fourth Geneva Convention of 1949.'[318]

The Iraq sanctions policy — and those bodies and governments that have supported and promoted the policy throughout its existence — have therefore done so illegally. The sanctions regime has been entirely illegitimate from the perspective of international law, human rights and moral norms. This fact is perhaps best articulated in the charge sheet against the Western powers drawn up by the president of the International Commission of Inquiry on Economic Sanctions, legal expert Ramsey Clark — former US Attorney-General under the Kennedy and Johnson administrations. The charges were issued at the International Court On Crimes Against Humanity Committed by the UN Security Council on Iraq, held in Madrid in November 1996. Clark charges American, British and UN officials with 'causing the deaths of more than 1,500,000 people including 750,000 children under five, and injury to the entire population of Iraq by genocidal sanctions'.

> The criminal acts charged include the deliberate and intentional imposition, maintenance and enforcement of an economic blockade and sanctions against the people of Iraq from August 6, 1990 to this date with full knowledge constantly communicated that the blockade and sanctions were depriving the people of Iraq of essentials to support and protect human life. These essentials include medicines and medical supplies, safe drinking water, adequate food, insecticides, fertilizers, equipment and parts required for agriculture, food processing, storage and distribution, hospital and medical clinic procedures; a multitude of common items such as light bulbs and fluorescent tubes; equipment and parts for the generation and distribution of electricity, telephone and other communications, public transportation and other essential human services. Also denied the people of Iraq is knowledge of the existence of, and procedures and equipment to provide protection from, depleted uranium and dangerous chemical pollution released in the environment of Iraq by defendants. The United States has further subjected Iraq to random missile assaults which have killed civilians.

The formal criminal charges are extremely significant, since they have been issued not merely by a renowned US legal expert, but by one who was formerly an official legal expert for the US Government under the presidencies of Kennedy and Johnson. Furthermore, the panel of judges of the International War Crimes Tribunal presided over by Ramsey Clark — which ruled US, British and UN officials to be guilty of these charges among many others in relation to the Gulf War — consisted of many legal and human rights experts from around the world, including: leading British QC and member of the House of Lords, Lord Tony Gifford; US Attorney, former President of the National Lawyers Guild and Director of the Center for Constitutional Rights, Michael Ratner; US lawyer and first Vice-President of the American Association of Jurists, Deborah Jackson; Organizing Secretary for the American Association of Jurists in Canada, John Philpot; former Japanese Judge and Attorney, Susumu Ozaki; former member of the German Bundestag and Lieutenant-Colonel in the German Bundeswehr, Dr Alfred Mechtersheimer; Resident Magistrate of the High Court in Arusha, Tanzania, Aisha Nyerere; member of Tunisian Bar Association and former President of Association of Young Lawyers, Abderrazak Kilani; former Chief Justice of the Gujarat High Court and elected President of the All-India Lawyers Union (1989) P. S. Pot; among others. The charges are reproduced below in their entirety:

> 1. The United States and its officials aided and abetted by others engaged in a continuing pattern of conduct from August 6, 1990 until this date to impose, maintain and enforce extreme economic sanctions and a strict military blockade on the people of Iraq for the purpose of injuring the entire population, killing its weakest members, infants, children, the elderly and the chronically ill, by depriving them of medicines, drinking water, food, and other essentials in order to maintain a large US military presence in the region, and dominion and control over its people and resources including oil.

2. The United States, its President Bill Clinton and other officials, the United Kingdom and its [former] Prime Minister John Major and other officials have committed a crime against humanity as defined in the Nuremberg Charter against the population of Iraq and engaged in a continuing and massive attack on the entire civilian population in violation of Articles 48, 51, 52, 54 and 55 of Protocol I Additional to the Geneva Convention 1977.

3. The United States, its President Bill Clinton and other officials, the United Kingdom and its Prime Minister John Major and other officials have committed genocide as defined in the Convention against Genocide against the population of Iraq including genocide by starvation and sickness through use of sanctions as a weapon of mass destruction and violation of Article 54, Protection of Objects Indispensable to the Civilian Population, of Protocol I Additional to the Geneva Convention 1977.

4. The United States, its President Bill Clinton and other officials, the United Kingdom and its Prime Minister John Major and other officials have committed and engaged in a continuing course of conduct to prevent any interference with the long-term criminal imposition of sanctions against the people of Iraq in order to support continuing US presence and domination of the region.

5. The United States, its President Bill Clinton and other officials, the United Kingdom and its Prime Minister John Major and other officials with US Ambassador Madeleine Albright as a principal agent have obstructed justice and corrupted United Nations functions, most prominently the Security Council, by political, economic and other coercions using systematic threats, manipulations and misinformation to silence protest and prevent votes or other acts to end sanctions against Iraq despite reports over a period of five years by every major UN agency concerned including UNICEF, UN World Food Program, UN Food and Agriculture Organization, which describe the deaths, injuries and suffering directly caused by the sanctions.

6. The United States, its President Bill Clinton and other officials have engaged in a continuing concealment and cover-up of the criminal assaults during January through March 1991 on nuclear reactors, chemical, fertiliser, insecticide plants, oil refineries, oil storage tanks, ammunition depots and bunkers in violation of humanitarian law including Article 56, Protecting Works and Installations Containing Dangerous Forces, exposing the civilian population of Iraq, and military personnel of Iraq, the United States and other countries to radiation and dangerous chemical pollution which continues for the population of Iraq causing deaths, sickness and permanent injuries including chemical and radiation poisoning, cancer, leukaemia, tumours and diseased body organs.

7. The United States and its officers have concealed and failed to help protect the population of Iraq from the cover-up of the use by US forces of illegal weapons of a wide variety including rockets and missiles containing depleted uranium which have saturated soil, ground water and other elements in Iraq and are a constant presence affecting large areas still undefined with deadly radiation causing death, illness and injury which will continue to harm the population with unforeseeable effects for thousands of years.

8. The United States and its officials have endeavoured to extort money tribute from Iraq and institutionalize forced payments of money on a permanent basis by demanding more than one half the value of all oil sales taken from Iraq be paid as it directs as the price for reducing the sanctions to permit limited oil sales insufficient to feed the people and care for the sick. This is the functional and moral equivalent of holding a gun to the head of the children of Iraq and demanding of Iraq, pay half your income or we will shoot your children.

9. The United States has violated and condoned violations of human rights, civil liberties and the US Bill of Rights in the United States, in Kuwait, Saudi Arabia and elsewhere to achieve its purpose of complete domination of the region.

10. President Clinton, Ambassador Albright, Nicholas Burns and Rolf Ekeus have systematically manipulated, controlled, directed, misinformed, concealed from and restricted press and media coverage about conditions in Iraq, compliance with UN require-ments, and the suffering of the people of Iraq to maintain over-whelming and consistent media support for genocide. This has been done in the face of their proclaiming that the deaths of more than half a million children is 'worth it' to control the region, that Saddam Hussein is responsible for all injury and could prevent this genocide by not putting 'his yacht on the Euphrates this winter', or by shutting down his 'palace for the winter and using that money to buy food and medicine' and by insisting that the sanctions will be maintained until a government acceptable to the US is installed in Iraq.[319]

That this wholesale policy of genocide in Iraq was initiated and legitimized through the United Nations is an instructive indi-cation of the extent to which the UN has become a tool of Western, and particularly Anglo-American power, in the inter-national system, in violation of the very international law that the UN is obliged to protect. In this respect, former adviser to the UN Secretary-General, Erskine Childers, describes in detail how the UN has become an instrument of Western policy. He notes that the Western policy of using 'economic bribery and intimi-dation' to determine affairs at the World Bank and IMF 'has now been extended to the United Nations ...'

Whenever the [Western] powers are determined to get a given vote through either the Security Council (i.e., the Gulf crisis and sanctions against Libya) or the General Assembly (i.e., rescind-ment of the Zionism is Racism resolution), governments are warned. If they do not 'behave' they will not get debt relief, World Bank capital projects, easier IMF 'adjustment conditionalities' or urgently needed hard currency IMF credit to pay oil bills. Reduction or cut-off in bilaterial aid is an additional threat ... [I]n effect, the [Western] powers have taken to employing a form of state terrorism at the UN – the threat being more death, malnutrition, disease or no education among millions of already poor people ... [T]he Council is now regarded as a captive [by most of the UN membership], where the North secures decisions by economic intimidation, abuses the peaceful-redress procedures inscribed in the charter and authorizes a kind of vigilantism against countries of the North's own choosing.[320]

In other words, the functioning of the United Nations, as illustrated here with reference to the sanctions on Iraq, has become disfigured by Western power, to the extent the institution has in many respects effectively become an instrument of Anglo-American foreign policy which embellishes that policy with a rubber-stamp of contrived international legitimacy. In this manner, the United Nations might be likened to a rehabilitated version of its predecessor the League of Nations, providing a means by which Western power can police, maintain and manipulate the international system in its own interests.

7

False Pretexts

Weapons of Mass Destruction: Permissible for Our Clients

Saddam's previous programs for the development of weapons of mass destruction and his use of such weapons, are publicly cited by Western officials as the key reason that the sanctions against Iraq were initiated. Our examination of the facts has shown that in reality the Western powers have been motivated by other interests.

But the absurdity of the West's justification for the sanctions policy is also evident in relation to the inconsistency of its policies. Not only does Western acquiescence and complicity in other humanitarian catastrophes throughout the world and throughout history belie this justification, but the reality of Western policy towards Iraq itself exposes the irrelevance of human rights in relation to the fundamental principles of Western foreign policy. Indeed, the Western powers had previously provided Saddam Hussein with the technology, materials and know-how to develop weapons of mass destruction while he played a role that suited Western economic and strategic interests in the Middle East, despite the tyrannical and genocidal nature of his regime.[321] These weapons programs were not a problem when they were directed at tens of thousands of Iraqi civilians. They were not a problem when they were used to attack Iran. Yet they became a problem when Saddam Hussein began openly demonstrating his growing propensity towards independence and opposition towards US domination of Middle East oil.

It is, in fact, rather unlikely that the Western powers have a principled stand against the development and use of weapons of mass destruction for anti-humanitarian purposes. This is illustrated by a wide variety of cases. For instance, even before Indonesia invaded the island of East Timor, it had deployed the chemical weapon napalm against villagers in Irian Jaya. The *Observer* Foreign News Service reported that in July 1977: '1279 villagers were killed by napalm and antipersonnel cluster bombs'.[322] And during its invasion of East Timor – which was notoriously supported by the US, Britain and Australia, among other Western powers – Indonesia again used weapons of mass destruction, employing napalm to bomb and strafe East Timorese villages. Yet these appalling acts of terrorism were met not with Western outrage, but with jubilant Western investment in Indonesia, along with exultant Western exploitation of East Timorese oil – not to mention vast inputs of arms and military training.[323]

Turkey, a member of NATO and a subservient US/Western client-regime, has similarly made ample use of its weapons of mass destruction – with Western support – in its war on the Kurds in the south. Turkish forces have massacred whole villages, indiscriminately targeting civilians along with combatants. One particular example is relevant here. The *Coastal Post* reports that Turkey used chemical and biological weapons during an airborne offensive against Kurds around Mt Djoudi in 1989, employing napalm and defoliants, along with toxic and nerve gas. Meanwhile the international community remained silent, and Western military and financial support of the Turkish regime continues unabated.[324] Notably, this attack occurred not long before the 1991 Gulf War.

The principal US client-regime in the Middle East, Israel, also manufactures weapons of mass destruction and uses them to consolidate its over 30 year long illegal occupation of Palestine, which has continued with repeated – indeed routine – condemnation by the UN Security Council and General Assembly in what has now become hundreds of resolutions. During its illegal occupation of portions of the West Bank, Gaza, Lebanon and Syria, Israel has brutalized the Palestinians, massacred refugees in Lebanon, and deliberately bombed the UN refugee camp at Qana. As the London *Times* reports:

> Israel has repeatedly accused Arab and Islamic countries hostile to it of manufacturing [weapons of mass destruction] on a large scale but has never admitted possessing biological or chemical weapons, just as it has never owned up to a nuclear capability, although it is an open secret that the country has at least 200 nuclear warheads.

The Times refers to the existence in Israel of a 'shadowy biological institute situated in the growing suburban community of Nes Ziona ... believed by many foreign diplomats to be one of the most advanced germ warfare institutions in the Middle East'.[325] Israel's notorious nuclear, chemical and biological weapons programs are well known, but little discussed – and the US has not raised concerns about the issue.[326] Credible reports of the use by Israel of a toxic poisonous gas against Palestinian children have been ignored. British journalist Johnathan Cook, who writes for The *Guardian* and *Observer* newspapers, reported from the West Bank in April 2001:

> The school playground in the village of Al-Khader, near Bethlehem, has been a children's battleground for the past six months: pupils finish classes at midday and congregate to throw stones at the Israeli soldiers stationed in the hills around their homes. The confrontation was relatively trouble-free until last month when soldiers fired tear gas into the playground. One canister landed

only a few feet from 13-year-old Sliman Salah, enveloping him in a cloud of gas described by witnesses as an unfamiliar, yellow color. Within a minute he was unconscious.

By the time Salah arrived at the private Yamamah hospital, his body was racked by violent spasms and convulsions, his breathing was sporadic and his pupils tightly constricted. The French doctor who admitted him was baffled. Annie Dudin, a paediatrician who has worked in the West Bank for 15 years, has treated dozens of victims of gas inhalation, including many between 1987 and 1993, during the first Intifada, but had never seen symptoms like Salah's before.

As Cook points out, tear gas does not have such effects, with victims usually recovering after only a few minutes. More severe effects such as coughing fits or streaming eyes can normally be eliminated using oxygen and an injection of glucose. But neither treatment worked with Salah. Instead, his 'seizures continued until he was given large doses of anti-convulsants and only slowly did he regain consciousness'. French paediatrician Annie Dudin who treated Salah stated: 'I have seen nothing like this before. I would have expected these sorts of symptoms in a case of severe poisoning. But to treat him properly, I needed to know what chemicals he had been exposed to.'

Dudin's concerns were corroborated when Salah was later transferred to Hussein Hospital Beit Jala, to be treated by neurologist Nabir Musleh. According to hospital tests there was no reasonable doubt that Salah had been poisoned, but by what was unclear. His doctors could only advise him to shower regularly in the hope that chemical traces remaining on his skin would be washed away. But within 24 hours of being released 'Salah was having convulsions and had to be readmitted to the Hussein'. It took five days since his exposure to the Israeli gas for his symptoms to be brought under control. Nevertheless, according the boy's father, he continues to suffer from 'stomach pains, vomiting, dizziness and breathing problems'. Salah's case, however, is just 'one of a spate of such cases in the Bethlehem area in the past month', reports Cook.

> Another tear gas victim recently arrived unconscious at the Yamamah having convulsive fits and Hussein Hospital has reported a rapid increase in untreatable patients since the first such case was admitted in late February ... The new cases in Bethlehem follow a pattern first seen in the Gaza Strip in mid-February, when a large crowd was tear-gassed near Khan Younis refugee camp. Ten men were admitted to Nasser Hospital suffering from seizures that doctors could not treat. Many other patients vomited for days afterwards.

The Israeli Defence Force has denied accusations that the gases used were anything but standard CS gas and, more rarely, smokescreen gases, arguing that the symptoms experienced by Palestinian victims are only due to 'anxiety'. But Israeli denials have been dismissed by doctors, including a Western medic, Helen Brisco of the international humanitarian medical group Doctors Without Borders (Médecins Sans Frontières), who testified that patients she treated as a result of Israeli gassings were clinically ill, and in the more serious cases had severe muscle paralysis — symptoms quite unrelated to normal CS or smokescreen gases. French paediatrician Dudin was similarly sceptical of Israeli claims:

> Sliman's condition was certainly not one of anxiety. It is very difficult for me to say what he was exposed to. Without knowing the chemicals involved, I cannot run the necessary tests, but his symptoms were compatible with exposure to a strong poison. This suggests to me that the gas being used by Israel is no longer safe.

These observations have been corroborated in tests of air samples at the site of one of the gassings, along with blood samples of patients, by the Palestinian Ministry of Health. The preliminary findings indicated that Israel had been using a cocktail of different gases in unprecedentedly higher concentrations, forming a new chemical weapon designed specifically to poison Palestinian civilians.[327]

The concern that Saddam Hussein has employed weapons of mass destruction is therefore disingenuous. On the contrary, regimes backed by the United States have used weapons of mass destruction against their own people and others with US support. As noted by Howard Zinn, Professor Emeritus of History at Boston University, with respect to then President Clinton's televised assertions just before the Anglo-American bombing campaign of Iraq in December 1998:

> President Clinton has just told another lie, this time not about the relatively trivial matter of his sexual activities, but about matters of life and death. In explaining his decision to bomb Baghdad, he said that other nations besides Iraq have weapons of mass destruction, but Iraq alone has used them. He could only say this to a population deprived of history. The United States has supplied Turkey, Israel and Indonesia with such weapons and they have used them against civilian populations.[328]

Weapons of Mass Destruction: Reserving the Right

While selectively condemning the development of weapons of mass destruction by its 'enemies', the US actively supports such programs when undertaken by its own clients, and when it thus serves to consolidate US hegemony. Such hypocrisy is further evident in light of the fact that the US itself has reserved the right to use such weapons, having amply deployed chemical and biological weapons in past military ventures. For instance, US forces used chemical weapons – including napalm, agent-orange and nerve gas – against Vietnamese civilians and combatants from 1970 onwards. Bill Mesler reported in *The Nation* on a Time/CNN exposé of the subject based on an 'exhaustive eight-month investigation': 'The excellent investigative story that aired on the Time/CNN television magazine *NewsStand* on June 7 [1998] revealed the unthinkable: US Special Forces units on more than 20 occasions used the nerve gas sarin on civilians and combatants during the Vietnam War.' The story featured a prominent incident about 'an attack in 1970 on a camp' in which 'US gas killed hundreds of civilians as well as enemy soldiers'. Nerve gas was 'used on more than 20 missions'. Mesler adds that:

> [This was] confirmed by retired Adm. Thomas Moorer, Chairman of the Joints Chief in 1970, who added that the use of sarin would have required permission from the National Security Council, then headed by Henry Kissinger, who had no comment ... Asia has three times been the site of our colonial wars (the Philippines, Korea and Vietnam) and twice the target of our weapons of mass destruction (Japan and, we now know, Vietnam) ... [W]e would have more credibility if we shipped Henry Kissinger off to the Hague for a long-overdue war crimes trial.[329]

The US also tested chemical weapons on its own troops in Panama in the early 1970s.[330] But the West's fatal infatuation with weapons of mass destruction is not merely a fact of history. It is an ongoing reality that reared its ugly head during the 1991 Gulf War when the Allies were able to test their new nuclear DU (Depleted Uranium) weapons in combat conditions. Between themselves, they managed to fire 5–6000 DU tank rounds, and 940,000 bullets from aircraft such as A10 Warthog.[331] A secret report of the British Atomic Energy Authority (BAEA) estimated that Western forces had left at least 40 tonnes of DU in Iraq and Kuwait, enough to cause '50,000 potential deaths'. The Western military refuses to officially classify DU as a 'radiological weapon', and publicly denies that it has had any adverse effects on the people of Iraq or its own soldiers.[332] Yet contrary to the public denials of Western officials insisting that Depleted Uranium is not a nuclear weapon, is free of radioactive side-effects, and is neither devastating the Iraqi people nor Gulf War veterans through radiation, the BAEA report admitted that this huge amount of DU 'indicates a significant problem'.[333]

Depleted Uranium is a low-level radioactive metal that is almost three times as heavy as steel. The pyrophoric explosions associated with the use of DU weapons create microscopic air-borne particles that spread across distances as far as kilometers. Their solubility allows them to contaminate soil, ground water and surface water. These microscopic, radioactive heavy metal particles of DU can enter the body through ingestion and inhalation. Ingestion results in the permanent accumulation of DU in the bones and kidneys, and thus results in the growth of tumours as well as irreversible damage to the kidneys. During pregnancy, DU crosses the placenta with particularly dangerous results, since children are especially vulnerable to its toxic effects because their cells divide rapidly as they grow. The inhalation of DU results in some DU particles being perma-nently trapped in the lungs, increasing the risk of cancer. Other particles will settle in the bones and the bloodstream – again with horrifying results.

In May 1991, the US Defense Department finally confessed that the use of DU weapons effectuates 'the potential to cause adverse impacts on human health, primarily through the water pathway'.[334] Yet while officials have refused to go any further, independent scientific studies have confirmed the devastating consequences of the use of DU due to nuclear radiation. For instance, two leading scientific authorities on the effects of DU stated that DU weapons should be banned because their use constitutes a crime against humanity, contaminating the environment, and causing suffering to civilians. Professor Sharma (Professor Emeritus of Chemistry, University of Waterloo, Ontario) told the BBC: 'Based on the samples I have examined, I think between 5% and 12% of those who were exposed to DU may expect to die of cancer.'[335] US scientist Asaf Durakovic, Professor of Nuclear Medicine at Georgetown University in Washington DC, came to similar conclusions. He told a conference of nuclear scientists in Paris (European Association of Nuclear Medicine) that 'tens of thousands' of British and American soldiers were dying from radiation from DU shells fired during the Gulf War. Referring to tests on Gulf War veterans showing DU in the urine and bones of 70 per cent, Professor Durakovic stated:

> I doubt whether the MoD or Pentagon will have the audacity to challenge these results. I can't say this is the solitary cause of Gulf War Syndrome, but we now have clear evidence that it is a leading factor in the majority of victims. I hope the US and UK governments finally realize that, by continuing to use this ammunition, they are effectively poisoning their own soldiers.[336]

Reports from aid workers and doctors working in Iraq have similarly documented the massive escalation in new illnesses and deformities amongst children in Iraq, subsequent to the Gulf War. UN personnel and aid workers have seen children playing with empty shells and destroyed tanks in the former battlefields – weapons that have been linked to the rise in childhood cancers in these areas.[337]

Indeed, as US Senator Russel Feingold pointed out in September 1998: '[The Pentagon's] assertion that no Gulf War veterans could be ill from exposure to DU .... contradicts numerous pre- and post-war reports, some from the US Army itself.'[338] A restricted UK Ministry of Defence document dated 25 February 1991 states that full protective clothing and respirators should be worn when close to DU shells, and that human remains exposed to DU should be hosed down before disposal. The document – coded 25/22/40/2 – also warns that inhalation or ingestion of particles from DU shells is a health risk and that exposure should be treated as 'exposure to lead oxide'. It adds that DU dust on food would result in radioactive contamination. A 1992 document from the US Defence Nuclear Agency describes DU particles as a 'serious health threat'.[339] According to the Army Environmental Policy Institute (AEPI):

> DU is inherently toxic. This toxicity can be managed, but it cannot be changed ... If DU enters the body, it has the potential to generate significant medical consequences. The risks associated with DU in the body are both chemical and radiological ... Personnel inside or near vehicles struck by DU penetrators could receive significant internal exposures.[340]

The US General Accounting Office similarly observes: 'Inhaled insoluble oxides stay in the lungs longer and pose a potential cancer risk due to radiation. Ingested DU dust can also pose both a radioactive and a toxicity risk.'[341] A Science Applications International Corporation (SAIC) report included in the Appendix of an AMMCOM study concluded that: 'Short-term effects of high doses can result in death, while long-term effects of low doses have been implicated in cancer. Aerosol DU exposures to soldiers on the battlefield could be significant with potential radiological and toxicological effects.[342]

Other US Army documents categorically confirm the potentially fatal radioactive effects of DU in ample detail:

> Aerosol DU (Depleted Uranium) exposures to soldiers on the battlefield could be significant with potential radiological and toxicological effects ... Under combat conditions, the most exposed individuals are probably ground troops that re-enter a battlefield following the exchange of armour-piercing munitions

... We are simply highlighting the potential for levels of DU exposure to military personnel during combat that would be unacceptable during peacetime operations ... DU is ... a low level alpha radiation emitter which is linked to cancer when exposures are internal, [and] chemical toxicity causing kidney damage ... Short-term effects of high doses can result in death, while long-term effects of low doses have been linked to cancer ... Our conclusion regarding the health and environmental acceptability of DU penetrators assume both controlled use and the presence of excellent health physics management practices. Combat conditions will lead to the uncontrolled release of DU ... The conditions of the battlefield, and the long-term health risks to natives and combat veterans may become issues in the acceptability of the continued use of DU kinetic penetrators for military applications.[343]

Another startling document clearly illustrates US knowledge of the long-term dangers of DU contamination, yet attempts to play down the serious implications and advises future reports on the issue to do the same to avoid the banning of DU:

There has been and continues to be a concern regarding the impact of DU on the environment. Therefore, if no one makes a case for the effectiveness of DU on the battlefield, DU rounds may become politically unacceptable and thus be deleted from the arsenal. I believe we should keep this sensitive issue in mind when action reports are written.[344]

In fact, the linkage between disease and DU is well documented.[345] It has also been authoritatively confirmed by former Pentagon scientist Doug Rokke, Professor of Nuclear Physics and Environmental Engineering at Jacksonville State University in Alabama. Professor Rokke's combat operations and medical military experience span over 30 years from the Vietnam War to Operation Desert Storm. He was assigned to the Theatre Depleted Uranium Assessment Team as the team health physicist and medic, with responsibility for identifying, planning and implementing the clean-up of all US Depleted Uranium equipment, providing initial medical care recommendations and emergency medical care for contaminated casualties. He was then recalled to active duty in the US Army as Director of the Pentagon's Depleted Uranium Project, during which he conducted research to develop radioactive materials management procedures and to write education and training curricula. Tasked by the US Department of Defense with organizing the DU clean-up of Saudi Arabia and Kuwait after the Gulf War, Professor Rokke – also a former US Army Colonel – had briefed the UK Commons Defence Select Committee on the risks of DU in 1999. 'Since 1991, numerous US Department of Defense reports have stated that the consequences of DU were unknown,' he testified. 'That is a lie. They were told. They were warned.' Rokke, who as a former Pentagon scientist specializing in DU gave military personnel briefings on the hazards of DU shells, 'warned the allied powers as far back as 1991 that the explosives could cause cancer, mental illness and birth defects...'

> I can confirm that medical and tactical commanders knew all the hazards. DU is the stuff of nightmares. It is toxic, radioactive and pollutes for 4500 million years. It causes lymphoma, neuro-psychotic disorders and short-term memory damage. In semen, it causes birth defects and trashes the immune system. The United States and British military personnel, as part of Nato, wilfully disregarded health and safety and the environment by their use of DU, resulting in severe health effects, including death. I and my colleagues warned the US and British officials that this would occur. They disregarded our warnings because to admit any correlation between exposure and health effects would make them liable for their actions wherever these weapons have been used.[346]

At an international conference hosted by Cambridge University's Campaign Against Sanctions on Iraq (CASI) that included the participation of prominent historians, diplomats, public health specialists, anthropologists, journalists, activists and Iraqi citizens, Professor Rokke explained that the effects of DU were known as early as 1943:

> The possible hazards were known before the use of depleted uranium munitions during the Gulf War. In 1943, a letter from the Manhattan Project to Brigadier General Groves who was in charge of the project discusses the use of DU as a terrain contaminant, a gas warfare instrument for inhalation and ingestion, and a contaminator of the environment. In 1943 they knew explicitly that the deliberate release of uranium dust would cause respiratory problems within days of anybody exposed and permanent lung damage within a few months to a few years.

Citing a US Defense Nuclear Agency memorandum written by Lt.-Col. Greg Lyle that was sent to his DU team in Saudi Arabia, Rokke observed that it is 'indisputable that United States Department of Defense officials were and still are aware of the unique and unacceptable hazards associated with using DU munitions'.[347] The former US Army scientist further noted that:

> There can be no reasonable doubt about this. As a result of the heavy metal and radiological poison of DU, people in southern Iraq are experiencing respiratory problems, breathing problems, kidney problems, cancers. Members of my own team have died or are dying from cancer.

Indeed, out of his primary DU clean-up team, 21 members are dead — a fifth of the staff. Rokke himself is now ill, with 5000 times the permissible level of radiation in his body. 'At various meetings and conferences, the Iraqis have asked for the normal medical treatment protocols. The US Department of Defense and the British Ministry of Defence have refused them.'[348]

DU weapons have also been used in Kosovo despite prior warnings from DU experts including Rokke himself. 'In April of this year [1999], myself and a few other individuals were called up to Washington DC to discuss the use of this in Kosovo,' he stated. 'We sat with members of the Cabinet, the President of the United States and others from the Department of State and warned them. We got to the end of the meeting and the head guys in charge promised "don't worry about it, we won't use it".'[349] NATO nevertheless proceeded to use its nuclear arsenal in Kosovo to devastating effect. The UN Environment Program has already found traces of radiation at eight sites in Kosovo hit by NATO DU shells.[350] As British journalist John Pilger thus concludes in the *New Statesman*:

> The truth about the effects of depleted uranium in shells fired in the 1991 Gulf War and Nato's 1999 attack on Yugoslavia is that the Americans and British waged a form of nuclear warfare on civilian populations, disregarding the health and safety of their own troops.[351]

The impact of Western DU weapons on Iraqi civilians has been horrific. UN statistics published in the *British Medical Journal* illustrate a sevenfold increase in cancer in southern Iraq between 1989 and 1994. Before the 1991 Gulf War, cancer wards did not exist. After the war, they became abundant – and overflowing. Cancer specialist Dr Jawad Al-Ali, a member of the Royal College of Physicians in Britain, reported that Iraqi medical studies:

> ... indicate that more than 40 per cent of the population in this area will get cancer in five years' time to begin with, then long afterwards. Most of my own family now have cancer, and we have no history of the disease. It has spread to the medical staff of this hospital. We are living through another Hiroshima ... We suspect depleted uranium. There simply can be no other explanation.

Professor Karol Sikora, head of the cancer program of the World Health Organization (WHO) further noted in the *British Medical Journal* that: 'Requested radiotherapy equipment, chemotherapy drugs and analgesics are consistently blocked by United States and British advisers [to the Sanctions Committee]. There seems to be a rather ludicrous notion that such agents could be converted into chemical or other weapons.' Over 1000 life-saving items remain 'on hold' in New York despite calls from UN chief Kofi Annan for the items to be released 'without delay'. Professor Sikora commented:

> The saddest thing I saw in Iraq was children dying because there was no chemotherapy and no pain control. It seemed crazy they couldn't have morphine, because for everybody with cancer pain it is the best drug. When I was there, they had a little bottle of aspirin pills to go round 200 patients in pain.[352]

All this clarifies that it is redundant for the West to attempt to provide humanitarian justification for the bombing and sanctioning of Iraq by citing Saddam's development and use of weapons of mass destruction. Saddam employed and developed his weapons under Western aid and tutelage; other governments, some of which have been mentioned here, have developed and used weapons of mass destruction to commit massive atrocities, often with Western weapons and training or to Western indifference; the United States has itself used chemical and biological weapons against civilians; the Western allies under US leadership have used nuclear weapons – depleted uranium – in the first Gulf War with tragic results for both allied soldiers and Iraqi civilians.

The United Nations Weapons Inspections

According to American and British government officials, the Iraqi government of Saddam Hussein systematically obstructed and undermined the weapons inspections program conducted by the United Nations Special Commission (UNSCOM). Iraq's alleged failure and refusal to comply with the weapons inspections and their requirements allegedly justified the renewed bombing campaign that ensued in December 1998, which was purportedly aimed at eliminating Saddam's weapons of mass destruction. The sanctions regime in particular, as already noted, was justified on the pretext of preventing Saddam's access to materials and technology that could be used to develop weapons of mass destruction. But the facts are far more complex than conventional opinion would have us know.

The United States pointed to a 1998 report to the UN Security Council by the Executive Chairman of UNSCOM Richard Butler as proof of Iraqi intransigence in relation to the weapons inspection process. An analysis of the factual record, however, illustrates that the ever-looming threat of Saddam's weapons of mass destruction was deliberately exaggerated, and in that respect somewhat fabricated, by the US to justify both a new bombing campaign and the continuation of the UN sanctions regime.

According to former UNSCOM Executive Chairman from 1991 to 1997 Rolf Ekeus:

> UNSCOM was highly successful in identifying and eliminating Iraq's prohibited weapons — but not to the degree that everything was destroyed. The loopholes in the presentation by Iraq and the contradictions in Iraq's declarations mean there is reason to be careful. Iraq did not make a coherent presentation in the biological field or in the chemical field. There was a slightly better one in the missile field, and there was a coherent presentation with regard to the nuclear program ... In my view, there are no large quantities of weapons. I don't think that Iraq is especially eager in the biological and chemical area to produce such weapons for storage. Iraq views those weapons as tactical assets instead

of strategic assets, which would require long-term storage of those elements, which is difficult.[353]

Scott Ritter, who was chief UN weapons inspector for five years, stated that UNSCOM had successfully destroyed over 90 per cent of Iraq's weapons and weapon-making facilities.[354] Rolf Ekeus corroborates Ritter's testimony, similarly confirming that more than 90 per cent of Iraq's weapons of mass destruction programs were dismantled in this six-year period. This assessment was corroborated by another member of UNSCOM, Raymond Zalinskas, who observed in February 1998 that '95 per cent of work proceeds unhindered'.[355]

The relatively small amount of material or weapons that remained unaccounted for after the UNSCOM process is of no military significance, and does not pose a threat. Robert Gallucci, former Deputy Directory of UNSCOM commented that: 'Possession of the weapons themselves doesn't, in my view, offer a proximate threat to the United States or to our friends in the region, and I'm including Israel in that.'[356] Moreover, there is good reason to believe that despite unaccounted for materials UNSCOM managed to effectively eliminate Iraq's weapons of mass destruction capability. In March 1999 Ritter elaborated that: 'Today, Iraq no longer possesses arms of mass destruction.' He added that Iraq's nuclear program and long-range missiles had already been 'destroyed and dismantled'.[357] In a detailed explanation in the journal *Arms Control Today*, Ritter further noted that:

> Iraq had been disarmed, [it] no longer possessed any meaningful quantities of chemical or biological agent, if it possessed any at all, and the industrial means to produce these agents had either been eliminated or were subject to stringent monitoring [since as early as 1997]. The same was true of Iraq's nuclear and ballistic missile capabilities ... [F]rom 1994 to 1998, Iraq was subjected to a

strenuous program of ongoing monitoring of industrial and research facilities ... [which] provided weapons inspectors with detailed insight into the capabilities, both present and future, of Iraq's industrial infrastructure. It allowed UNSCOM to ascertain, with a high level of confidence, that Iraq was not rebuilding its prohibited weapons programs.[358]

In an interview with the award-winning British journalist John Pilger, Scott Ritter testified that:

By 1998, the chemical weapons infrastructure had been completely dismantled or destroyed by UNSCOM (the UN inspections body) or by Iraq in compliance with our mandate. The biological weapons program was gone, all the major facilities eliminated. The nuclear weapons program was completely eliminated. The long-range ballistic missile program was completely eliminated. If I had to quantify Iraq's threat, I would say zero.[359]

Ritter's account has been confirmed by his colleague, former UN weapons inspector Raymond Zalinskas, Associate Professor at the Biotechnology Institute, University of Maryland, who noted in 1998 that:

UNSCOM has destroyed all the chemical facilities, the chemical weapons facilities, and also all known chemical weapons ... In the biological area, UNSCOM has destroyed the dedicated biological weapons facility at al-Hakam, plus other ones at other institutes. And as far as we know, they have no biological weapons stored up ... [T]here are no weapon sites that I know of ... Because if UNSCOM knew about it, they would have been destroyed already ... 95 per cent of UNSCOM and the agency's work continues unhindered, and this is what they call 'the ongoing monitor and verification program'. And all these 80 facilities are visited, sometimes on a weekly basis, sometimes on a monthly basis.

He affirmed that inspectors had wiped out any possible Iraqi chemical and biological weapons sites as early as 1995. In June of that year, the Executive Chairman of UNSCOM, Richard Butler, submitted a report to the Security Council confirming fulfilment of the inspection's essential requirements in the missile and chemical fields, as well as confirming the destruction of the launchers and missile engines.[360]

Others involved in the inspection process have testified similarly. For example, Hans Blix, then Director of the International Atomic Energy Agency (IAEA), which for six years has overseen the inspections of Iraq's nuclear capability, publicly stated that the IAEA is 'sure Iraq has no remaining infrastructure for nuclear weapons production'.[361] Rosemary Hollis, head of the Middle East program at the Royal Institute of International Affairs, concludes that: 'Iraq does not have the capacity to build nuclear weapons': She suggests that 'the emphasis now on Saddam's nuclear ambitions is dictated by Washington's plans for a pre-emptive strike on Iraq.'[362] Middle East specialist Professor Stephen Zunes of the University of San Francisco has also observed that: 'The International Atomic Energy Agency and other United Nations inspectors have since overseen the total dismantling of Iraq's nuclear apparatus.'[363]

In other words, it is clear that UNSCOM had succeeded in not only eliminating Saddam's weapons of mass destruction, but in dismantling the military and technological infrastructure essential to provide the capability to manufacture such weapons. Executive Chairman of the new weapons inspection system, the United Nations Monitoring, Verification and Inspections Commission (UNMOVIC), Hans Blix, has explicitly confirmed the same. In an interview with *Arms Control Today* in July 2000, Blix was asked: 'Is there any indication that Iraq is trying to rearm?' He replied: 'No, I don't think you can say that. Sometimes there are reports in the media from intelligence organizations that they are watching the procurement efforts here and there, but we have nothing to substantiate that.'[364] Citing Blix's more recent statements in February 2003, Director of the Middle East Project and Fellow at the Institute for Policy Studies in Washington DC Phyllis Bennis reported that:

> US Secretary of State Colin Powell's presentation to the UN Security Council on February 5 wasn't likely to win over anyone not already on his side. He ignored the crucial fact that in the past several days (in Sunday's *New York Times* and in his February 4 briefing of UN journalists) Hans Blix denied key components of Powell's claims. Blix, who directs the UN inspection team in Iraq, said the UNMOVIC inspectors have seen 'no evidence' of mobile biological weapons labs, has 'no persuasive indications' of Iraq-Al Qaeda links, and no evidence of Iraq hiding and moving material used for Weapons of Mass Destruction (WMD) either outside or inside Iraq. Dr Blix also said there was no evidence of Iraq sending scientists out of the country, of Iraqi intelligence agents posing as scientists, of UNMOVIC conversations being monitored, or of UNMOVIC being penetrated.[365]

These authoritative testimonials on the general annulment of Iraq's weapons programs find explicit confirmation in the actual texts of official UNSCOM documents. As noted by current affairs commentator Professor Edward Said of the University of Columbia: '[It] is clear from the UNSCOM reports that he [i.e., Saddam Hussein] neither has the missile capacity nor the chemical arms, nor the nuclear arsenal, nor in fact the anthrax bombs that he is alleged to be brandishing.'[366] A brief review of these documents is thus in order. The last UNSCOM report dated 15 December 1998, which was issued before the withdrawal of UN inspectors, records that 'the majority of the inspections of facilities and sites under the ongoing monitoring system were carried out with Iraq's cooperation'.[367] According to an October 1997 UNSCOM report, 'the majority of these inspections were conducted in Iraq without let or hindrance'.[368]

Further UN reports clearly demonstrate the successful disarmament of Iraqi weapons of mass destruction and related technological infrastructure by UNSCOM.

A UN Panel established by the Security Council reported in March 1999 that 'the [IAEA] is able to state that there is no indication that Iraq possesses nuclear weapons or any meaningful amounts of weapon-usable nuclear material or that Iraq has retained any practical capability (facilities or hardware) for the production of such material'.[369] Indeed, the IAEA had reported in December 1998 that Iraq had allowed inspections, interviews with personnel and site visits to ascertain that Saddam's nuclear weapons program had been eliminated. Iraq had cooperated sufficiently to ensure that the IAEA's work was completed 'efficiently and effectively'.[370] Even a year before then, in November 1997, UNSCOM recorded its conclusions that 'there are no indications that any weapon-usable nuclear material remains in Iraq and that the ongoing monitoring and verification activities of IAEA have not revealed indicators of the evidence in Iraq of prohibited materials, equipment or activities'.[371]

With regards to Iraq's chemical weapons programs, UNSCOM reported that in November 1997: 'The members of the Commission recognize the significant progress of UNSCOM in this area. Considerable quantities of chemical weapons, their components and chemical weapons-related equipment have been destroyed by Iraq and UNSCOM, in cooperation.'[372] Similarly, Iraq's main biological weapons production facility was destroyed by UNSCOM, as noted by the Security Council Panel on Disarmament in March 1999:

> UNSCOM ordered and supervised the destruction of Iraq's main declared BW production and development facility, Al Hakam. Some 60 pieces of equipment from three other facilities involved

in proscribed BW activities as well as some 22 tonnes of growth media for BW production collected from four other facilities were also destroyed. As a result, the declared facilities of Iraq's BW program have been destroyed and rendered harmless.[373]

Iraq's prohibited missile capabilities were also effectively dismantled. UNSCOM admitted in November 1997 that 817 out of 819 proscribed missiles had been accounted for, i.e., destroyed.[374] UNSCOM had clarified a month earlier that:

> Significant progress has been achieved in the missile area. The Commission is now in a position to be able to account for practically all, except two, imported combat missiles that were once the core of Iraq's proscribed missile force. The Commission has also accounted for all declared operational missile launchers, both imported and indigenously produced.[375]

The Security Council Panel on Disarmament also noted in March 1999 that: 'UNSCOM has also concluded that Iraq does not possess a capability to indigenously produce either BADR-2000 missiles or assets known as the "Supergun".'[376]

There is, in fact, no evidence that in recent years Iraq had any meaningful capabilities with regards to weapons of mass destruction, nor that Iraq presented a military threat due to such capabilities. Indeed, in May 2001 the Congressional Research Service — the official body that provides information to the US Congress — admitted that 'there is no hard evidence that Iraq is reconstituting banned WMD programs'.[377]

It is worth further exploring the observations of former weapons inspector and chief of the Concealment Unit for the United Nations Special Commission on Iraq (UNSCOM), Scott Ritter. In a sober and extensive overview of the subject published by the authoritative journal of the Washington DC-based Arms Control Association, Ritter states that: '... from 1994 to 1998 Iraq was subjected to a strenuous program of ongoing monitoring of industrial and research facilities that could be used to reconstitute proscribed activities.' This program provided a detailed insight into the present and future capabilities of Iraq's industrial infrastructure, allowing 'UNSCOM to ascertain, with a high level of confidence, that Iraq was not rebuilding its prohibited weapons programs and that it lacked the means to do so without an infusion of advanced technology and a significant investment of time and money'. Ritter goes on to discuss the 'disarmament obligation set forth in Resolution 687', whose 'absolute nature' meant that only '100 per cent disarmament' would be defined as 'compliance' — while anything less would be evidence of Saddam's defiance.

> There was no latitude for qualitative judgements. As such, the world found itself in a situation where the considerable accomplishments of the UNSCOM weapons inspectors—the elimination of entire categories of WMD and their means of production—were ignored in light of UNSCOM's inability to verify that every aspect of these programs was fully accounted for. Quantitative disarmament (the accounting of every last weapon, component or bit of related material) took precedence over qualitative disarmament (the elimination of a meaningful, viable capability to produce or employ weapons of mass destruction).

UNSCOM's attempts to verify Iraq's complete disarmament was complicated due to the fact that Iraq 'undertook a systematic program of "unilateral destruction", disposing of munitions, components, and production equipment related to all categories of WMD' in the summer of 1991. In the process, Iraq had disregarded 'its obligation to submit a complete declaration of its WMD programs'. When this was admitted to UNSCOM, Iraq denied possessing sufficient documentation to prove its comprehensive destruction of its weapons programs.

Thus, observes Ritter, 'UNSCOM was able to verify that Iraq

had in fact destroyed significant quantities of WMD-related material,' but the lack of documentation or other hard evidence meant 'it was impossible to confirm Iraq's assertions that it had disposed of all its weapons'. Consequently, the quantitative mandate established in Resolution 687 'had become a trap'. Nevertheless, extensive investigations allowed UNSCOM 'to ensure that the vast majority of Iraq's WMD arsenal, along with the means to produce such weaponry, was eliminated. Through monitoring, UNSCOM was able to guarantee that Iraq was not reconstituting that capability in any meaningful way.'

Since December 1998, the absence of weapons inspectors in Iraq led to a 'vacuum of available data on which to base an assessment of Iraq's current activities'. That vacuum was swiftly filled with 'a series of speculative reports', largely supported by the US and UK governments, 'that have attributed certain capabilities to Iraq that are incompatible with what UNSCOM learned from eight years of experience with Iraq's WMD programs'. In reality, without weapons inspections 'no one knows for sure what has transpired in Iraq since the last inspectors were withdrawn'. But disregarding speculation and conjecture, 'there is absolutely no reason to believe that Iraq could have meaningfully reconstituted any element of its WMD capabilities in the past 18 months'. In Ritter's words, with respect to weapons of mass destruction, 'Iraq today is not the Iraq of 1991.' The weapons Iraq had constituted by 1991 over a 'period of decades' by spending 'billions of dollars', could not 'under any rational analysis, have been reconstituted since December 1998'. Due to the work of UNSCOM, 'Iraq was qualitatively disarmed at the time inspectors were withdrawn ...'

> While no one can say for certain what has transpired inside Iraq since then, the resumption of monitoring-based inspections would easily determine if Iraq had made any effort to reconstitute

its WMD programs ... Resolution 687 demanded far more than the dismantling of viable weapons and weapons-production capabilities. Most of UNSCOM's findings of Iraqi non-compliance concerned either the inability to verify an Iraqi declaration or peripheral matters, such as components and documentation, which by and of themselves do not constitute a weapon or program. By the end of 1998, Iraq had, in fact, been disarmed to a level unprecedented in modern history, but UNSCOM and the Security Council were unable – and in some instances unwilling – to acknowledge this accomplishment.

Concerning nuclear capabilities, Ritter specifies that while Iraq had established a 'massive infrastructure' to support its nuclear weapons programs, this 'had been eliminated by 1995' by the IAEA. Even assuming that some components remained, these 'would be of no use to Iraq given the extent to which Iraq's nuclear program was dismantled by the IAEA'.

This is not to say that problems were ruled out. Ritter notes the potential danger posed by VX nerve agent and mustard gas loaded onto 155 mm artillery shells, but points out that VX mass-production equipment turned over to UNSCOM in 1996 had never actually been used. He further reports that 'numerous inspections' of possible VX storage and production sites had found nothing – this 'minimizes the likelihood that Iraq maintains any significant stockpile of VX weapons'. While there remained 750 mustard gas artillery shells unaccounted for, Ritter observes that: 'A meaningful CW attack using artillery requires thousands of rounds ... a few hundred 155 mm mustard shells have little military value for use on the modern battlefield ... [and] cannot be viewed as a serious threat.'[378]

It has often been argued by supporters of military action against Iraq that chemical weapon production equipment could have easily been distributed throughout Iraq's commercial chemical-related facilities. A similar myth concerning biological weapons has been widely promoted, with pro-war ideologues suggesting that Iraq could have been producing such weapons in secret facilities anywhere in the country. The novel idea of 'mobile biological labs' is a particularly absurd example. Ritter responds to these notions by highlighting the crucial fact that the manufacture of chemical weapons 'would require the assembling of production equipment into a single integrated facility, creating an infrastructure readily detectable by the strategic intelligence capabilities of the United States'. Meanwhile, 'the CIA has clearly stated on several occasions since the termination of inspections in December 1998 that no such activity has been detected'. Indeed, unaccounted for stocks of chemical and biological weapons 'would no longer be viable'. Ritter emphasizes that: 'Weapons built before the Gulf War that slipped through the UNSCOM net would by now have passed their sell-by date.'[379] 'The Iraqis do have enough equipment to carry out laboratory-scale production of BW agent,' Ritter elaborates on the particular threat of biological weapons.

> However, without an infusion of money and technology, expanding such a capability into a viable weapons program is a virtual impossibility. Contrary to popular belief, BW cannot simply be cooked up in the basement; it requires a large and sophisticated infrastructure, especially if the agent is to be filled into munitions. As with CW, the CIA has not detected any such activity concerning BW since UNSCOM inspectors left Iraq.[380]

In an interview with the *Cape Cod Times*, Ritter summarizes the essential aspects of the subject of Iraqi programs for the development of weapons of mass destruction in very clear and unequivocal terms: 'In 1991, did Iraq have a viable weapons of mass destruction capability? You're darn right they did. They had a massive chemical weapons program. They had a giant biological weapons program. They had long-range ballistic

missiles and they had a nuclear weapons program that was
about six months away from having a viable weapon ...'

> ... after seven years of work by UNSCOM inspectors, there was no
> more (mass destruction) weapons program. It had been elimi-
> nated ... When I say eliminated I'm talking about facilities
> destroyed ... The weapons stock had been, by and large,
> accounted for — removed, destroyed or rendered harmless. Means
> of production had been eliminated, in terms of the factories that
> can produce this ... There were some areas that we didn't have
> full accounting for. And this is what plagued UNSCOM. Security
> Council 687 is an absolute resolution ... Iraq will not be found in
> compliance until it has been disarmed to a 100 percent level ...
>
> And this was the Achilles tendon, so to speak, of UNSCOM.
> Because by the time 1997 came around, Iraq had been quali-
> tatively disarmed. On any meaningful benchmark — in terms of
> defining Iraq's weapons of mass destruction capability; in terms
> of assessing whether or not Iraq posed a threat, not only to its
> immediate neighbors, but the region and the world as a whole —
> Iraq had been eliminated as such a threat ...

Primarily, Ritter notes, Iraq has hidden documentation: 'documents that would enable them to reconstitute — at a future date —
weapons of mass destruction capability'. However, such documentation remains 'useless unless Iraq has access to the tens, if
not hundreds, of millions of dollars required to rebuild the
industrial infrastructure [necessary] to build these weapons',
funds which were not available to Iraq in 1998, nor thereafter.
'This paranoia about what Iraq is doing now that there aren't
weapons inspectors reflects a lack of understanding of the reality
in Iraq,' namely, the impact of the economic sanctions which
'have devastated this nation'. Combined with the effects of the
first Gulf War, the sanctions 'have assured that Iraq operates as a
Third World nation in terms of industrial output and capacity',
to the extent that 'enormous resources' were invested 'in trying

to build a 150-kilometer range ballistic missile called the Al Samoud'.

> In 1998 they ran some flight tests of prototypes that they had built of this missile. They fizzled. One didn't get off the stand. The other flipped over on the stand and blew up. The other one got up in the air and then went out of control and blew up. They don't have the ability to produce a short-range ballistic missile let alone a long-range ballistic missile...
>
> The other thing to realize is: they are allowed to build this missile. It's not against the law. The law says anything under 150 kilometers they can build and yet people are treating this missile as if it's a threat to regional security ... It's a tactical battlefield missile, that's it. Yet, (Congressman Tom) Lantos and others treat this as though it's some sort of latent capability and requires a ballistic missile defence system to guard against it. It's ridiculous. Iraq has no meaningful weapons of mass destruction program today.
>
> Now, having said that, I firmly believe we have to get weapons inspection back in for the purpose of monitoring ... especially if we lift economic sanctions. And I believe that there should be immediate lifting of economic sanctions in return for the resumption of meaningful arms inspections ... a) Iraq represents a threat to no one, and b) Iraq will not represent a threat to anyone if we can get weapons inspectors back in. Iraq will accept these inspectors if we agree to the immediate lifting of economic sanctions.[381]

Of crucial significance to this subject is the authoritative testimony of Saddam's son-in-law, General Hussein Kamel, the former Iraqi Minister of Military Industry and head of Iraq's weapons programs, who defected to Jordan on the night of 7 August 1995, along with his brother Colonel Saddam Kamel. General Hussein Kamel is best known for exposing Iraq's deceptions about the extent of its pre-1991 Gulf War weapons programs, having provided crates of documents revealing past weapons programs to UNSCOM. General Kamel's defection was repeatedly characterized by the American and British governments as evidence of Iraq's weapons programs and of how defectors such as Kamel are the most reliable source of evidence in this regard.[382]

The American and British governments frequently referred to large quantities of biological and chemical weapons material produced by Iraq before the 1991 Gulf War, as well as weapons that were produced but remain unaccounted for. All such claims, however, have referred to weapons produced before 1991. But as revealed by *Newsweek* in February 2003, General Kamel had also told UN inspectors in 1995 that Iraq had destroyed its entire stockpile of nuclear, chemical and biological weapons and banned missiles in 1991, exactly as the Iraqi regime always claimed.[383]

General Kamel was interviewed on 22 August 1995 in Amman by the following UN inspection officials: Rolf Ekeus, then Executive Chairman of UNSCOM; Professor Maurizio Zifferero, Deputy Director of the IAEA and then head of the inspections team in Iraq; Nikita Smidovich, then head of UNSCOM's ballistic missile team and Deputy Director for Operations of UNSCOM. In his interview – a complete copy of which was obtained by British academic Glen Rangawala of Cambridge University – General Kamel confirmed categorically that: 'I ordered destruction of all chemical weapons. All weapons – biological, chemical, missile, nuclear were destroyed' (p. 13). When General Kamel was asked about anthrax ('Were weapons and agents destroyed?'), he responded: 'Nothing remained.' The destruction occurred 'after visits of inspection teams. You have an important role in Iraq with this. You should not underestimate yourself. You are very effective in Iraq.' Concerning prohibited missiles, General Kamel explained that there was 'not a single missile left but they had blueprints and moulds for production. All missiles were destroyed' (pp. 7–8). Regarding VX production, he clarified that Saddam's regime 'put it in bombs during the last days of the Iran-Iraq War. They were not used and the program was terminated' (p. 12). When asked whether the regime chose to 'restart VX production after the Iran-Iraq War?' he noted: 'We changed the factory into pesticide production. Part of the establishment started to produce medicine ... We gave instructions not to produce chemical weapons' (p. 13). This testimony is all the more extraordinary because of General Kamel's credibility – endorsed by the American and British governments – as well as his open opposition to Saddam's regime: 'They are only interested in themselves and not worried about economics or the political state of the country. I can state publicly I will work against the regime' (p. 14).[384]

Summarizing the implications of the interview, *Newsweek's* John Barry reported that:

> Hussein Kamel, the highest-ranking Iraqi official ever to defect from Saddam Hussein's inner circle, told CIA and British intelligence officers and UN inspectors in the summer of 1995 that after the Gulf War Iraq destroyed all its chemical and biological weapons stocks and the missiles to deliver them ... Kamel told his Western interrogators that he hoped his revelations would trigger Saddam's overthrow. But after six months in exile in Jordan, Kamel realized the United States would not support his dream of becoming Iraq's ruler after Saddam's demise. He chose to return to Iraq—where he was promptly killed ... Kamel's revelations about the destruction of Iraq's WMD stocks were hushed up by the UN inspectors, sources say ... NEWSWEEK has obtained the notes of Kamel's UN debrief, and verified that the document is authentic.[385]

The idea that by 2003 Saddam's Iraq constituted an unprecedented threat to regional and international security, used to legitimize the sanctions and drive for war, is therefore not merely inaccurate, but quite baseless. In the words of former US Secretary of Defense William Cohen to the incoming President Bush on 10 January 2001: 'Iraq no longer poses a military threat to its neighbors.'[386]

Indeed, while the US has consistently argued that Saddam's Iraq posed an extreme danger to regional peace, Iraq's actual neighbors – the supposed potential victims of Iraqi aggression – did not seem to think so. The *New York Times* reported in December 1998 that the reactions to the Anglo-American military intervention in that month 'from countries like Egypt, Qatar and Syria have ranged … from regret to concern to outright condemnation. Even Kuwait, which was liberated from Iraqi occupation by the Persian Gulf War, has stopped short of endorsing the military action.'[387] Even Iran, which was previously attacked by Iraq, failed to see any necessity in the Anglo-American attack, describing it as unacceptable.

The notion of Iraq as a regional military threat, thus justifying a humanitarian intervention to destroy Iraq's military capabilities coupled with ongoing sanctions designed to contain these capabilities, was aptly refuted by Paul Routledge, chief political commentator of the London *Daily Mirror*:

> The justification for these casual murders is that – in the Prime Minister's words – Iraq's military capability has to be diminished 'for the safety of the world' … This is preposterous nonsense. The Iraqi dictator may be among the nastiest of his type. He has certainly treated his own people with the utmost cruelty. But he is in no position to threaten the rest of the world. He is not even in much of a position to threaten the folks next door. His neighbor Israel, on whom he unleashed his arsenal of Scud missiles seven years ago to no very great effect, has more weapons of mass destruction than he could ever dream of acquiring – including nuclear bombs. His other neighbor Saudi Arabia is armed to the

teeth with the latest American and British military hardware, including Patriot missiles. The Saudis could annihilate him in an afternoon. Never mind that Israel has repeatedly invaded her neighbors and has totally ignored United Nations resolutions of the kind that Blair and Clinton cling to as a pretext for the legitimacy of their missile raids on Iraq. The difference is that we sell billions of pounds worth of arms to the Saudis and the Americans are locked into a military-political alliance with Israel that US politicians 'degrade' at their peril ... OK, Saddam Hussein is a tyrant. But the world is full of tyrants. Most of them, including ex-dictator Pinochet of Chile and ex-president Suharto of Indonesia, were customers of Britain. We took their money and turned a blind eye to their human-rights record. In fact, we did the same with Mad Sad.[388]

Former chief UN weapons inspector Ritter went even further by completely debunking the notion of Iraq as a military threat:

The Iraqi army is in total disarray, capable of little more than manning security pickets along the Iran-Iraq border, in northern Iraq (Kurdistan), and in southern Iraq. I have visited numerous Iraqi military barracks and have seen soldiers in tattered uniforms and bare feet. Military training is without substance, barely sufficient to convert recruits into simple soldiers, let alone provide skills in the intricacies of modern combined arms combat – the integration of infantry, armour, artillery, and air power in a single military action ... I have seen the Republican Guard, too ... enough to put down internal unrest, but not enough to match the armed forces of any of its neighbors ... Even at its best, the Republican Guard was decimated in a matter of hours once it engaged the US Army in 1991. Any international threat from today's Republican Guard is imaginary ... Saddam's air force in action could be shot out of the sky by any of the modern air forces of its neighbors ... Iraq simply lacks the stocks of chemical and biological agent needed to have any militarily significant effect.[389]

Saddam's regime therefore no longer posed a threat to its neighbors, although of course it remained a highly repressive regime with respect to domestic matters. In this regard, it bears similarity to many other repressive regimes supported by the United States in the Middle East. The idea that Iraq could ever pose a threat to the entire world, as suggested by the American and British governments in justification of sanctions and other policies, is thus completely preposterous. Middle East expert Stephen Zunes notes that:

> Iraq has never had the industrial capacity, the self-sustaining economy, the domestic arms industry, the population base, the coherent ideology or political mobilization, the powerful allies, or any of the necessary components for large-scale military conquest that the German, Italian, and Japanese Fascists of the 1930s and 1940s had. Though better off than most of the non-Western world, Iraq was still a Third World country and was quite incapable of seizing or holding large amounts of territory.[390]

Manufacturing a Pretext for War

Iraq's relative military impotence was only compounded by the destruction of the materials and infrastructure for its weapons programs. Yet on 15 December 1998, UNSCOM Executive Chairman Richard Butler reported to the Security Council that Iraq had failed to grant UNSCOM full and unconditional access to at least four sites in Iraq. It has been widely claimed by the Western media that Saddam Hussein unilaterally expelled the UN weapons inspectors in response to Butler's unfavourable report. In fact, it is the United States that unilaterally withdrew the inspectors. Butler, anticipating US-UK air strikes against Iraq in response to this alleged intransigence, ordered weapons inspectors to be withdrawn the next day, 16 December. According to the *New York Times*:

While the 133 [UN humanitarian] workers had been left behind, more than 185 others, most of them arms inspectors, had been evacuated yesterday by air to neighboring Bahrain and by car to Jordan ... Butler abruptly pulled all of his inspectors out of Iraq shortly after handing Annan a report yesterday afternoon on Baghdad's continued failure to cooperate with UNSCOM.[391]

Butler had, however, acted without a mandate from the Security Council, which had as yet not even assessed his report. Instead, he had acted under unilateral US insistence. Butler admits the same in his book *Saddam Defiant*:

I received a telephone call from US Ambassador Peter Burleigh inviting me for a private conversation at the US mission ... Burleigh informed me that on instructions from Washington it would be 'prudent to take measures to ensure the safety and security of UNSCOM staff presently in Iraq'. I told him that I would act on his advice and remove my staff from Iraq.[392]

Since UNSCOM had successfully destroyed Saddam's weapons and infrastructure to create them, at least by a quantitative standard, the question remains as to how UNSCOM Executive Chairman Richard Butler was able to report contrary to the facts, many of which he himself had documented, in his unfavourable 1998 report to the Security Council. In fact, an analysis of the factual details of Butler's report shows that, overall, Iraq had cooperated with the inspections process. Indeed, the specific instances of alleged Iraqi defiance referred to by Butler are trivial in the extreme. The *Economist* succinctly pointed out that Butler's 'report cites a bare handful of violations out of more than 300 inspections...'

One was a delay of 40 minutes in giving access, another was a demand for the presence of a UN Secretary-General's representative as a witness to the handing over of documents. A further violation was a refusal to allow college students to be interviewed and two more related to inspections on Friday.[393]

Ramsey Clark's anti-war group, the International Action Center, has elaborated on these acute observations, noting that out of 427 inspections – 128 of them at new sites – Butler was able to cite only five alleged 'obstructions' that were supposed to have completely sabotaged the whole weapons inspection process:

> One was a 45-minute delay before allowing access. Another was a rebuff to an outrageous demand by a US arms inspector, Dianne Seamons, that inspectors be allowed to interview all of the undergraduate students in Baghdad University's Science Department. Another, on December 9, was the inspection of a small headquarters of the Ba'athist political party. Inspectors left those premises after they were asked what is the relation between the small headquarters of a party and the disarmament mission. The last two cases of so-called Iraqi noncompliance were this: UNSCOM asked to inspect two establishments on Fridays – the Muslim holy day. The Iraqis told UNSCOM that since these establishments were not open on Friday, the inspectors could visit the establishments, but they would need to be accompanied by Iraqi officials. This is in accordance with the agreement between Iraq and UNSCOM about Friday inspections.[394]

However, the documentary record suggests that the unfavourable aspects of Butler's UNSCOM report were inserted or influenced by members of the US Government. Minor incidents were apparently manipulated to manufacture a justification for a renewed attack on Iraq. According to the *Washington Post*:

> Among the circumstances [supporting the conclusions that] Butler [was] coordinating with Washington on a rationale for war, three stand out. One is that Butler made four visits to the US mission to the United Nations on Monday, the day before finishing his report. A second is that administration officials

acknowledge they had advance knowledge of the language he would use and sought to influence it, as one official said 'at the margins'. The third is that Butler ordered his inspectors to evacuate Baghdad, in anticipation of a military attack, on Tuesday night – at a time when most members of the Security Council had yet to receive his report.

Other UN diplomats reported that: 'Butler gave far more equivocal progress reports to them, in the days leading up to his written report, than his final conclusion that he is "not able to conduct the substantial disarmament work" because of the "absence of full cooperation by Iraq".' One New York-based diplomat highlighted the discrepancy between Butler's last report and the optimistic tenor of all his previous reports: 'What we were told by Butler for weeks was yes, we've hit some roadblocks but the inspections were going on.'[395]

The IAC provides some important background to the drafting of the report:

> The US [claims to have] based its attack on the report by Richard Butler, chairman of UNSCOM, but UNSCOM is answerable only to the UN Security Council and the Security Council did not authorize a US bombing of Iraq. In fact, both Russia and China – two of the five members of the Security Council – have demanded that Butler be fired for having withdrawn UN weapons inspectors without first receiving the support of the Security Council. The unilateral decision to withdraw the weapons inspectors was clearly a US, not a UN, operation. The Washington Post, on December 16 [1999], suggested that the administration had carefully orchestrated the timing and content of Richard Butler's unfavourable report about Iraq. The New York Times, on December 18, says that the US air strikes have been planned since December 1 and that Butler's report was simply a 'formality'.[396]

That the report was a mere 'formality' to justify long-established military plans is further supported by the fact that the US

President had been anticipating an unfavourable report from Butler which would warrant action. The Associated Press reported that Clinton discussed preparation for an attack on Iraq earlier on in the week with Israeli Prime Minister Netanyahu. Netanyahu stated: 'He [Clinton] told me that he was about to get a very difficult report by Richard Butler on Iraq's failure to fulfil its commitments, and that it would apparently obligate him to act.'[397]

The Washington Times similarly reported that an attack on Iraq had been planned and consented to before Butler's report:

> The White House notified the Joint Chiefs of Staff on Sunday (December 13) that President Clinton would order air strikes this week, 48 hours before he saw a United Nations report declaring Iraq in noncompliance with weapons inspectors, it was learned from authoritative sources last night.[398]

The Washington Post, citing sources, thus reported that:

> Butler's conclusions were most welcome in Washington, which helped orchestrate the terms of the Australian diplomat's report. Sources in New York and Washington said Clinton administration officials had played a direct role in shaping Butler's text during multiple conversations with him at secure facilities in the US mission to the UN. Spokesmen for Butler and the Clinton administration declined to comment on those conversations.[399]

The US administration thus appears to have had a direct role in manipulating Butler's report to manufacture justification for an attack on Iraq. Former chief inspector of UNSCOM Scott Ritter harshly condemned the US manoeuvre: 'What Richard Butler did last week with the inspections was a set-up. This was designed to generate a conflict that would justify a bombing.' Ritter stated that he was informed by US government sources when the inspections resumed that 'the two considerations on the horizon were Ramadan and impeachment'. He continued: 'If you dig around, you'll find out why Richard Butler yesterday ran to the phone four times. He was talking to his National Security adviser. They were telling him to sharpen the language in his report to justify the bombing.'[400]

Inspections or Intelligence Gathering?

Having manipulated and falsified Butler's report, the US utilized the new document to legitimize an intervention and renew claims that the sanctions regime against Iraq is justified. But the falsification of Butler's report was only the latest in a series of escalating ploys against Iraq related to the weapons inspection programs. Summarizing the nature of the inspection process, James Petras, Professor of Sociology at the State University of New York, reported that by the end of 1998, despite ongoing 'United Nations inspections and inspectors, including CIA operatives, nothing has been discovered ... First, the US surveillance airplanes covered Iraqi airspace taking detailed aerial photographs. Nothing turned up. But Washington then claimed the secret weapons were hidden,' insisting that UN inspectors on the ground have 'unlimited rights to inspect every crevice and cage, building and laboratory. Every building, basement, toilet, and outhouse was inspected for secret weapons for seven years. Nothing was turned up.' The US then urged the inspection of the presidential palace, 'including the shelter where Hussein fled to avoid US bombing attempts'. Understandably, Iraq initially responded with considerable resistance to the idea of revealing the areas of presidential security; but the government eventually consented: 'Nothing was found: no deadly weapons, no germs, no poison gases.' It appears that the US was becoming desperate for evidence. 'Washington then lined up some pseudo-scientists to testify that traces of anthrax were found. Objective studies in Switzerland disproved Washington's claim.' Despite the fact that no evidence was found of Saddam's alleged programs to develop weapons of mass destruction, the US would not relent. Instead, the US publicly declared its conclusion that the absolute lack of evidence was, indeed, clear proof that Saddam was cleverly hiding the weapons: 'Absence of evidence is not evidence of absence,' to paraphrase one Bush administration official explaining why the US could escalate the war on Iraq in 2002 without justification.

The UN inspections, combined with the genocidal sanction regime, thus continued at ever-increasing intensities. 'The charges were no longer that hidden weapons were discovered,' notes Petras. 'Instead the new charges were the capability to produce weapons.' As a result every single Iraqi scientist became suspect, 'every laboratory a "potential" centre of germ warfare — even if there was no evidence that any deadly weapons were produced in the past or the present'. The unfortunate logical import of the US position was that 'any pharmaceutical firm producing antibiotics could be a "potential" source of dangerous weaponry and the "inspections" could continue.' To support this position the US 'invented the concept of "dual capability" — civilian scientists or laboratories which were engaged in research were a "potential source of germ warfare". So as evidence failed to materialize, the net was thrown wider, the inspections became more intensive and never ending.' Scott Ritter even began launching 'surprise visits' without forewarning, 'forcing his way into strategic defence areas. Nothing was found.' Petras therefore concludes that according to this twisted logic, 'any educated Iraqi, any scientific laboratory and military installation is suspect, and reason to continue the search for the missing secret deadly weapons'.[401]

The UN inspections were in fact motivated by more fundamental objectives. Not long after the Anglo-American bombing
campaign of December, evidence began surfacing that the
inspections were designed to provide inside information on Iraq
that could not have been otherwise obtained. The inspections
were, in other words, penetrated by a covert US intelligence
operation designed to develop knowledge of the inner workings
of Saddam's regime in order to aid the formulation of military
plans. UNSCOM was in this respect an American-Israeli operation to gather strategic information on Iraq, with the view to aid
the policy of attempting to sponsor an overthrow of Saddam
Hussein. The *Washington Post* reported that:

> According to three officials with direct knowledge of the re-
> lationship, Israel had become by July 1995 the most important
> single contributor among the dozens of UN member states that
> have supplied information to UNSCOM since its creation in April
> 1991 ... Israel and UNSCOM have protected the operation among
> their most sensitive secrets.[402]

According to the BBC, British Member of Parliament George
Galloway of the Labour Party affirmed that: '[F]our members of
the United Nations inspection team in Iraq are Israeli spies.'
Galloway, who has campaigned against air strikes on Iraq,
'named four people he alleged were agents of Mossad, the Israeli
secret service, working under false names and papers with the
UNSCOM team'.[403] Peter J. Boyer noted in the *New Yorker* that
UNSCOM inspector Scott Ritter began exchanging information
with Israeli intelligence in 1994, providing, for example, U-2 spy
plane photos which could be used to target Iraq.[404] Ritter has
admitted the Israeli role, but denied knowledge that the latter
was part of an Israeli intelligence operation to gain information
for military targeting. Brian Jenkins of CNBC reported that
according to NBC confirmation through its own sources, various

UNSCOM inspectors were providing intelligence information, including that related to the establishment of targets in a military assault, to the US Government.[405] The *Washington Post* additionally found that UN Secretary-General Kofi Annan had obtained convincing evidence that UN weapons inspectors were inadvertently helping the US to collect intelligence to be employed in efforts to undermine Saddam's regime. The *Post* quoted one Annan confidant as follows: 'The Secretary-General has become aware of the fact that UNSCOM directly facilitated the creation of an intelligence collection system for the United States in violation of its mandate.' The source added that 'what's wrong with the UNSCOM operation' is that according to the UN Charter the 'United Nations cannot be party to an operation to overthrow one of its member states'.[406]

Scott Ritter also confirmed the US plot: 'The US has perverted the UN weapons process by using it as a tool to justify military actions, falsely so ... The US was using the inspection process as a trigger for war.'[407] Other statements by US officials clarify that the context of this policy was the objective of removing Saddam Hussein. Not long after sanctions were first imposed against Iraq, then US Secretary of State James Baker stated: 'We are not interested in seeing a relaxation of sanctions as long as Saddam Hussein is in power.'[408] More recently, Ritter similarly referred to the 'current US policy of trying to overthrow Saddam'.[409]

In actuality therefore Western policies have succeeded in destroying Iraq's military capabilities, economy and capacity to feed its people. The West's insistence on the reality of an Iraqi threat despite the utter vacuum of evidence was nothing but an attempt to justify, in the words of Professor Petras, 'its massive military presence in the Gulf and the need to be the undisputed owner and boss of the Gulf's energy resources'.

The 1998 Intervention

The ensuing Anglo-American bombing campaign against Iraq which continued until the 2002 war drive has received little publicity. British Prime Minister Tony Blair claimed that the US-UK planes were 'performing vital humanitarian tasks' over Iraq, specifically the monitoring and protection of Iraqi civilians from Saddam's regime through the 'no-fly zones'.[410] Immediately after the 1991 Gulf War, the US and Britain established the 'no-fly zones' in the north and south of Iraq on the pretext of protecting the Kurds and Shi'ite Muslims living in those areas. Yet those civilians were the very ones suffering from the air patrols. Indeed, the Pentagon had predicted that the missile attack planned for December 1998 could result in the killing of up to 10,000 Iraqi civilians.[411] 'During 1999, US and British warplanes bombed Iraq on 138 separate days, attacking more than 450 targets and dropping more than 1800 bombs,' reported Cable News Network (CNN).[412]

Agence France Press (AFP) reported the humanitarian results: 'The air strikes from December 1998 to December 1999 have left 156 dead and wounded another 371, according to an AFP casualty toll compiled from Iraqi military statements.'[413] This estimate is comparable to the 168 people killed in the 1995 Oklahoma City bombing. Indeed, the US and British air raids which signalled the beginning of the December bombing campaign commenced their 'humanitarian task' by flattening an agricultural school, damaging at least a dozen other schools and hospitals, and knocking out water supplies for 300,000 people in Baghdad – facts documented by the United Nations. A large storehouse in Tikrit, filled with 2600 tonnes of rice, was destroyed. A maternity hospital, a teaching hospital and an outpatients' clinic were also damaged, as well as parts of the Health Ministry. The severing of water supplies to 300,000 civilians was accomplished when a cruise missile destroyed one of the main water systems in Karrada, a Baghdad suburb. Ten schools suffered damage in Basra, while a secondary school in Kirkuk in the Kurdish north sustained a direct hit.[414]

By February 1999, British and American aircraft had staged well over 70 air strikes over Iraq in only five weeks, accompanied by the systematic massacre of Iraqi civilians. On 25 January, for example, an American missile exploded in a Basra housing complex, killing 17 civilians and injuring more than 100. Most of the victims were children.[415] On 27 February, American F-14, F-15 and F-18 planes implemented 28 sorties against civilian and military targets, injuring 23 people. The next day witnessed US air raids on farming villages in the northern 'no-fly zone' in the Ninevah province, killing three Iraqis, including a child. Several others were injured. US strikes also hit a power station and communications centre for a major oil pipeline, cutting off the flow of Iraqi oil to Turkey – 56 per cent of Iraq's oil exports flowed through the pipeline, and the export was used to pay for food and medicine for civilians under the UN 'Oil for Food' deal.

These repeated attacks on civilians and civilian structures continued systematically on a daily basis. In early March 1999, Anglo-American forces bombed northern Iraq, killing one Iraqi and injuring nine. Two additional raids were undertaken against a residential complex. After about a month's lull due to the concentration of forces on the military intervention in Kosovo, US-UK fighters returned to destroy two homes in southern Iraq, wounding two people. The next day, the alliance attacked yet another Iraqi oil installation, hitting Iraq's main crude oil pumping stations with the view to cripple oil sales already extremely limited under sanctions. Another house was destroyed the next day in US-UK raids on military and civilian sites, and an oil pipeline control station was destroyed the day after. On 29 April, with such attacks continuing daily, US air-craft attacked a residential quarter in the northern city of Mosul, wounding 20 people, and destroying four houses. On 9 May, US-UK warplanes bombarded a private house in southern Iraq, killing three people and wounding three more. The allies carried out a similar raid on a separate civilian site, killing another Iraqi, and wounding two. The purposeful nature of these systematic attacks on Iraqi infrastructure was particularly exemplified on 12 May, when American and British warplanes raided northern Iraq, killing 12 civilians and destroying livestock — 200 sheep were killed. Notably, the planes attacked the shepherds twice, the second time striking farmers who were trying to help the injured. On 25 May US warplanes bombed a communications site and destroyed several civilian installations in the 'no-fly zone' over northern Iraq. By the end of May 1999, the total number of air strikes since January was more than 200.[416]

This ruthless bombing campaign continued without cess-ation. Sarah Sloan, an analyst with Ramsey Clark's IAC reported a year after the commencement of the bombing campaign:

> On November 28 [1999], the US carried out 18 bombing sorties over three northern provinces of Iraq. These are on top of the 10,000-plus combat and non-combat sorties tallied over the 10 months since the US and Britain carried out a massive bombing campaign from December 16 to 19, 1998. This time, US bombs hit a school in Mosul, injuring eight people, including children, as well as damaging the school building and cars parked in the surrounding area. This came less than a week after ten civilians were wounded in another series of sorties. The bombing continued again the next week.[417]

As John Pilger observed: 'Britain and the United States are still bombing Iraq almost every day; it is the longest Anglo-American bombing campaign since the Second World War.'[418] Indeed, the

Pentagon admitted in 2000 to having flown over 280,000 sorties since imposing the 'no-fly zones' in 1991. British Ministry of Defence figures in 2000 indicated that since mid-December 1998 RAF bombers alone dropped 78 tons of bombs on Iraqi military targets, compared with 2.5 tons between April 1991 and December 1998. The average monthly release of bombs rose from 0.025 tons to 5 tons. According to Iraqi government figures, between December 1998 and the beginning of 2001, 323 civilians were killed and 960 injured by the Anglo-American attacks in the 'no-fly zones'. These figures have been contested, but there is little doubt that they are not far off the mark.[419]

With the passing of time, the campaign's anti-humanitarian nature only became clearer. Thus, for example, on 15 August 2000, Anglo-American air strikes killed dozens of civilians and destroyed a train station, several homes, and a food rations storage and distribution facility that stored food allowed into Iraq under the United Nations 'Oil for Food' program.[420] As recorded in an internal UN Security Sector report for a single five-month period of bombing via the 'no-fly zones':

> 41 per cent of victims of the bombing were civilians in civilian targets: villages, fishing jetties, farmland and vast, treeless valleys where sheep graze. A shepherd, his father, his four children and his sheep were killed by a British or American aircraft, which made two passes at them.

Pilger points out that a single year of this bombing campaign against the Iraqi people 'cost the British taxpayer £60 million'.[421] By the end of 2002 the total cost amounted to a billion.[422] This secret war, legitimized by the supposedly humanitarian 'no-fly zones' and buttressed by a variety of propaganda ploys, continued without public knowledge and understanding. The stark reality of the Anglo-American air war has been aptly clarified by Hussein Ibish, Communications

Director of the Arab-American Anti-Discrimination Committee (ADC), who notes how US government officials 'argue that the attacks were in self-defence, prompted by Iraqi "aggression" against American warplanes "defending the no-fly zones" in northern and southern Iraq'. In reality, the zones 'have no basis in a United Nations resolution or any other element of international law, and were not part of the Gulf War cease-fire agreements'. As 'a unilateral dictate by the United States', Ibish concludes, they amount to 'a direct and clear violation of Iraq's sovereignty and territorial integrity, which is guaranteed by international law, the UN Charter and numerous Security Council resolutions, including the Gulf War cease-fire agreements...'

> If Iraqi civilians die as a result of illegitimate and illegal US attacks on military targets in Iraq, this is the moral equivalent of targeting them directly – a form of international 'felony murder'. The enforcement of the 'no-fly zones' is supposed to be for the protection of the civilian population of northern and southern Iraq. [The] killings clearly demonstrate that Iraqi civilians are its victims.[423]

Indeed, as British journalist Pilger reported at the end of 2002 in the London *Mirror*, in the aftermath of the 11 September 2001 terrorist attacks, the Bush administration in tandem with the Blair government escalated the secret air war to unprecedented proportions. 'The American and British attack on Iraq has already begun. While the Blair government continues to claim in Parliament that "no final decision has been taken", Royal Air Force and US fighter bombers have secretly changed tactics and escalated their "patrols" over Iraq to an all-out assault on both military and civilian targets ...'

> American and British bombing of Iraq has increased by 300 per cent. Between March and November, according to Ministry of

Defence replies to MPs, the RAF dropped more than 124 tonnes of bombs.

From August to December, there were 62 attacks by American F-16 aircraft and RAF Tornadoes – an average of one bombing raid every two days. These are said to have been aimed at Iraqi 'air defences', but many have fallen on mostly populated areas, where civilian deaths are unavoidable.

... The bombing is a 'secret war' that has seldom been news ... The US and British governments justify it by claiming they have a UN mandate to police so-called 'no-fly zones' which they declared following the Gulf War. They say these 'zones', which give them control of most of Iraq's airspace, are legal and supported by UN Security Council Resolution 688.

This is false. There are no references to no-fly zones in any Security Council resolution. To be sure about this, I asked Dr Boutros Boutros-Ghali, who was Secretary-General of the United Nations in 1992 when Resolution 688 was passed. 'The issue of no-fly zones was not raised and therefore not debated: not a word,' he said. 'They offer no legitimacy to countries sending their aircraft to attack Iraq.'[424]

Thus, despite the fact that the 'no-fly zones' were purportedly designed to protect Iraqis, in fact they have done nothing of the sort. Not only have they allowed American and British planes to kill Iraqi civilians, they failed to prevent massive human rights abuses from occurring in Iraq. For example, just outside the northern zone is the city of Kirkuk, where 'Kurds are at most direct risk from the Iraqi regime, which has pursued a policy of Arabization of the city and the surrounding region...

Kurds have been forced to resettle elsewhere in Iraq or move to the Kurdish-controlled areas, stripped of their ration cards and all their possessions. According to Kurdish sources quoted by Amnesty International, over 94,000 Kurdish and Turkmen inhabitants have been expelled from Kirkuk since 1991.[425]

The integrity of the zones is further in question in light of the fact that although Iraqi planes were prohibited from entering the northern zone, Turkish craft were not. Sarah Graham-Brown reports that:

> ... the Turks, pursuing their war with the PKK, continue to use both air and ground troops on a regular basis inside Iraqi Kurdistan, often causing civilian deaths, injuries and destruction of property. The US has never challenged Turkey's incursions — the latest when 10,000 Turkish troops crossed the border in December 2000.

As for the southern zone, 'it has never actually contributed anything to the safety of the civilian population...'

> In fact, the role assigned to the mission was to 'observe' violations, not to stop them. As early as 1994, the US State Department's annual report on the human rights situation in Iraq acknowledged that, although the no-fly zone prevented aerial attacks on the southern marshes, it did not prevent artillery attacks or other army actions. By the end of 1996, the same source noted that civilians were not protected from ground attack in either zone.[426]

Indeed, American and British forces were heavily complicit in facilitating the Turkish attacks on Kurds in the Iraqi 'no-fly zones' which they were supposed to be protecting. 'In 1999, Tony Blair claimed the no-fly zones allowed the US and Britain to perform 'a vital humanitarian task' in protecting the Kurds in the north of Iraq and the ethnic Marsh Arabs in the south. In fact, British and American aircraft have actually provided cover for neighboring Turkey's repeated invasions of northern, Kurdish Iraq ...

> Hundreds of thousands of Turkish Kurds have been displaced and an estimated 30,000 killed. Turkey, unlike Iraq, is 'our friend'. In 1995 and 1997, as many as 50,000 Turkish troops,

backed by tanks and fighter aircraft, occupied what the West called 'Kurdish safe havens'. They terrorized Kurdish villages and murdered civilians. In December 2000, they were back, committing the atrocities that the Turkish military commits with impunity against its own Kurdish population ... So great is the collusion of the Blair government that, virtually unknown to Parliament and the British public, the RAF and the Americans have, from time to time, deliberately suspended their 'humanitarian' patrols to allow the Turks to get on with killing Kurds in Iraq.[427]

9/11, Anthrax and War Plan Iraq

These anti-humanitarian policies were granted a new lease of legitimacy in the aftermath of the 11 September 2001 terrorist attacks and the climate of fear that thereupon resulted. The Bush administration with Prime Minister Blair on side was eager to grab the opportunity to implement wide-ranging military plans on the pretext of fighting the new 'War on Terror'. Targeting Iraq was among the most prominent objectives of those plans.

On the same day as the attacks, five hours after the attack on the Pentagon, US Defense Secretary Donald Rumsfeld was taking notes based on incoming intelligence reports. As CBS News reported, in an official memo that day Rumsfeld demanded 'best info fast. Judge whether good enough [to] hit S.H. [Saddam Hussein] at the same time. Not only UBL [i.e., Osama bin Laden]. Go massive. Sweep it all up. Things related and not.'[428]

That demand to 'hit Saddam' was the product of years of planning for a comprehensive military assault on Iraq. From 1997 onwards, Rumsfeld, his top deputy Paul Wolfowitz, Vice-President Dick Cheney, his top aide I. Lewis Libby, Deputy Secretary of State Richard Armitage, US Trade Commissioner Robert Zoellick, US special envoy to Afghanistan Zalmay

Khalilzad, and Bush's brother Jeb, had begun making the case for a US invasion of Iraq. Their case was made through their sponsoring of a neo-conservative think-tank, The Project for the New American Century, which in January 1998 had written to then President Clinton as follows: 'We urge you to ... enunciate a new strategy that would secure the interests of the US and our friends and allies around the world. That strategy should aim, above all, at the removal of Saddam Hussein's regime from power.'[429]

It is not surprising then that immediately after the 11 September terrorist attacks the Bush administration exploited the resulting climate of fear and hostility to pave the way for the long-planned war on Iraq. As noted by Middle East expert Ian Lustick, Professor of Political Science at the University of Pennsylvania: 'What happened was 9/11, which had nothing to do with Iraq but produced an enormous amount of political capital which allowed the government to do anything it wanted as long as they could relate it to national security and the Middle East.'[430]

Thus by the beginning of October 2001 at the height of the sudden anthrax outbreak in the United States, desperate attempts were made by US officials to somehow link that out-break to the clandestine activities of Saddam's regime *vis-à-vis* his alleged programs to manufacture weapons of mass destruction. The London *Observer* noted in mid-October 2001 in a report headlined 'Iraq "behind US anthrax outbreaks" – Pentagon hardliners press for strikes on Saddam' that: 'American investigators probing anthrax outbreaks in Florida and New York believe they have all the hallmarks of a terrorist attack – and have named Iraq as prime suspect as the source of the deadly spores.'

Their inquiries are adding to what US hawks say is a growing mass of evidence that Saddam Hussein was involved, possibly indirectly, with the 11 September hijackers. If investigators' fears are confirmed – and sceptics fear American hawks could be publicizing the claim to press their case for strikes against Iraq – the pressure now building among senior Pentagon and White House officials in Washington for an attack may become irresistible.[431]

In fact, it soon became clear that there was absolutely no evidence of an Iraqi connection to the anthrax attacks. On the contrary, somewhat ironically, US investigators following the anthrax trail were led inexorably back to US governmental agencies, bearing dire implications for the US role in the increasingly contentious issue of weapons of mass destruction.

On 11 September 2001, prior to the anthrax attacks, White House staff were put on the anti-anthrax drug Cipro. The Associated Press reported on 24 October 2001 that:

> At least some White House personnel were given Cipro six weeks ago. White House officials won't discuss that, or who might be receiving the anthrax-treating antibiotic now ... On the night of the September 11 attacks, the White House Medical Office dispensed Cipro to staff accompanying Vice-President Dick Cheney as he was secreted off to the safety of Camp David, and told them it was a precaution, according to one person directly involved.[432]

Citing this AP report, Washington DC's public interest law firm Judicial Watch concludes 'that the White House knew of the anthrax attacks much sooner than admitted ... When asked yesterday if he had been tested for anthrax, President George W. Bush refused to answer on two occasions ... This buttresses the conclusion that the White House has known of the full extent of the problem for some time, but will not discuss it with the American people.' Judicial Watch Chairman and General Counsel Larry Klayman commented: 'It is a scandal in the making that the White House and Congress, which have full information, have adequately protected themselves with testing and antibiotics, while the rest of the populace is kept in the dark and not treated like the political elite.'[433] Thus, the US Government seemed to have anticipated an imminent anthrax crisis and taken measures to protect a political elite, as opposed to the general public. There can be little doubt therefore that the White House had some sort of advanced warning of the anthrax attacks.

Five days after 9/11, the Bush administration proposed the totalitarian USA Patriot Act.[434] On 18 September the first anthrax letters were mailed out. By 4 October, the anthrax crisis was in full swing with the first outbreak of the sickness being confirmed.[435] Meanwhile, the Patriot Act was received with little enthusiasm in Congress, so much so that Attorney-General John Ashcroft accused Senate Majority leader Tom Daschle and the Democrat-controlled Senate of deliberately obstructing the passage of the bill – Daschle had stated that he was unlikely to take up the bill within the one-week timetable required by the administration. Senate Judiciary Committee Chairman Patrick J. Leahy had also accused the administration of reneging on an agreement with respect to the proposed anti-terrorism legislation.[436]

On 9 October, lethal doses of anthrax were mailed to the offices of both Daschle and Leahy.[436] Within the next two days, the original batch of the Ames strain of anthrax was destroyed with the prior approval of the FBI. This, of course, made it far more difficult to trace the type of anthrax used in the letters. On 9 November, the *New York Times* reported that:

> Last month, after consulting with the FBI, Iowa State University in Ames destroyed anthrax spores collected over more than seven decades and kept in more than 100 vials. A variant of the so-called Ames strain had been implicated in the death of a Florida man

from inhalation anthrax, and the university was nervous about security. Now, a dispute has arisen, with scientists in and out of government saying the rush to destroy the spores may have eliminated crucial evidence about the anthrax in the letters sent to Congress and the news media.

Nonetheless, a week later Daschle's office opened its anthrax letter and 28 Congressional staffers tested positive for anthrax – investigators confirmed that the anthrax used in the letters was indeed the Ames strain.[438] By 26 October the Senate had passed the final version of the Patriot Act, with the full support of Senators Daschle and Leahy.[439]

The subsequent FBI investigation was systematically replete with stalling and stonewalling. It took the FBI five months to finally begin subpoenaing laboratories working with the Ames strain used in the attacks. When the labs complied by sending their samples, they were told to wait yet another month to allow the FBI to build a new room to store them. Scientists and outside investigators thus believe that: 'The FBI's delay in requesting the samples – and the government's lack of readiness to receive them – is part of a pattern that ... may have permanently damaged any chance of resolving the bioterrorism attack that killed five people, including 94-year-old Ottilie Lundgren of Oxford.' Other elements of the pattern of FBI stalling include taking six months to begin testing mailboxes surrounding Trenton, New Jersey, where the anthrax letters were post-marked, or nearly a year to return to the American Media building in Boca Raton, Florida, to search for the source of anthrax that killed the first victim.[440]

Why was the FBI stalling in this manner? According to Reuters, the environmental pressure group Greenpeace Germany reported that the anthrax attacks were 'the work of a member of a US biological warfare program ... It seems the attacker ...

wanted to force through an increase in the budget for US research on biological weapons.' Citing 'information from a US delegation source at the United Nations biological weapons conference in Geneva' that occurred in mid-November 2001, a reporter for the group's magazine Kirsten Brodde told Reuters: 'The US delegation believe it is an inside job ... Their members also have more information than has been made public.'[441]

As the FBI investigation proceeded, the Ames strain of anthrax used in the attacks was eventually traced back to a single high-level source in the US Army. According to the *Washington Post*: 'Genetic fingerprinting studies indicate that the anthrax spores mailed to Capitol Hill are identical to stocks of the deadly bacteria maintained by the US Army since 1980, according to scientists familiar with the most recent tests ...'

> Although many laboratories possess the Ames strain of anthrax involved in this fall's bioterrorist attacks, only five laboratories so far have been found to have spores with perfect genetic matches to those in the Senate letters, the scientists said. And all those labs can trace back their samples to a single US military source: the US Army Medical Research Institute of Infectious Disease (USAM-RIID) at Fort Detrick, MD.

Following the trail further, the FBI was led inevitably to the CIA:

> The FBI's investigation into the anthrax attacks is increasingly focusing on whether US government bio-weapons research programs, including one conducted by the CIA, may have been the source of deadly anthrax powder sent through the mail, according to sources with knowledge of the probe. The results of the genetic tests strengthen that possibility. The FBI is focusing on a contractor that worked with the CIA, one source said.

Law enforcement sources insist that the CIA connection is 'the best lead they have at this point'.[442] Moreover, there is credible evidence that US intelligence knows the identity of the perpetrator of the attacks, but has been prevented from arresting the individual under high-level government pressure.

This information comes from a leading US expert on biological warfare, Barbara Hatch Rosenberg, Director of the Chemical and Biological Weapons Program for the Federation of American Scientists, and a Research Professor of Environmental Science at the State University of New York. Rosenberg, according to BBC correspondent Susan Watts, has high-level government connections and states that the FBI had already identified the perpetrator of the winter 2001 anthrax attacks, but was not pressing charges for fear that secret government activities would be exposed. The *Trenton Times* reported that according to Rosenberg, 'the Federal Bureau of Investigation has a strong hunch about who mailed the deadly letters. But the FBI might be "dragging its feet" in pressing charges because the suspect is a former government scientist familiar with "secret activities that the government would not like to see disclosed".'[443]

The charge was made in an 18 February address at the Woodrow Wilson School of Public and International Affairs at Princeton University. Rosenberg cited informed sources she described as 'government insiders' with whom she has been in contact. She testified that the FBI had known since last October the identity of the person who mailed lethal quantities of anthrax in letters to Senate Majority Leader Tom Daschle, Senator Patrick Leahy, and several media outlets. Her sources further informed her that although the individual in question had been interrogated several times, he had not been arrested. 'We know that the FBI is looking at this person, and it's likely that he participated in the past in secret activities that the government would not like to see disclosed,' Rosenberg said. And she went on to raise the question of whether the FBI was deliberately stalling its investigation because it 'may not be so anxious to bring to public light the person who did this'.

> I know that there are insiders, working for the government, who know this person and who are worried that it could happen that some kind of quiet deal is made so that he just disappears from view. I hope that doesn't happen, and that is my motivation to continue to follow this and to try to encourage press coverage and pressure on the FBI to follow up and publicly prosecute the perpetrator.[444]

Other experts concur. Professor Steven Block of Stanford University, for example – another expert on biological warfare – told the *Dallas Morning News* that: 'It's possible, as has been suggested, that they may be standing back because the person that's involved with it may have secret information that the United States Government would not like to have divulged.'[445] Soviet defector Ken Alibek – the former First Deputy Director of Biopreparat from 1988 to 1992, anthrax expert, and a US government consultant – also confirmed that the person behind the anthrax attacks 'may, in fact, have been advising the US Government. After having passed a lie detector test, Alibek was cleared of any suspicion.'[446]

US investigative journalist Wayne Madsen – who has some 20 years experience in national security and intelligence matters having worked as an intelligence officer for the US National Security Agency, the Naval Telecommunications Command, and the State Department – has written a particularly comprehensive analysis of the available data on the anthrax attacks. Madsen's conclusions are worth noting:

> ... the FBI has never been keen to identify the perpetrator because that perpetrator may, in fact, be the US Government itself. Evidence is mounting that the source of the anthrax was a top secret US Army laboratory in Maryland and that the perpetrators involve

high-level officials in the US military and intelligence infrastructure ... Forget unfounded conspiracy theories. The evidence is overwhelming that the FBI has consistently shied away from pursuing the anthrax investigation [under government pressure].[447]

Perhaps the most glaring evidence of the US Government's connection to the anthrax attacks is the fact that it has refused to release information about the attacks and government foreknowledge of them to the public under the Freedom of Information Act. Washington DC's public interest law firm Judicial Watch, which investigates and prosecutes government corruption and abuse, reported in June 2002 that it had filed lawsuits against the Federal Bureau of Investigation ('FBI'), the Department of Health and Human Services ('HHS'), the Center for Disease Control ('CDC'), the US Army Medical Research Institute of Infectious Diseases ('USAMRIID') and the US Postal Service ('USPS') for those agencies' failures to produce documents concerning the terrorist anthrax attacks of October 2001, under the provisions of the Freedom of Information Act ('FOIA'):

> Judicial Watch has additional anthrax-related FOIA requests pending with the White House and other government agencies that will see legal action ... Judicial Watch represents hundreds of postal workers from the Brentwood Postal Facility in Washington, DC. Until the Brentwood facility was finally condemned by the CDC, Brentwood postal workers handled all of the mail for Washington, DC, including the 'official mail' that contained the anthrax-laden envelopes addressed to Senators Daschle and Leahy. While Capitol Hill workers received prompt medical care, Brentwood postal workers were ordered by USPS officials to continue working in the contaminated facility. Two Brentwood workers died from inhalation anthrax, and dozens more are suffering from a variety of ailments related to the anthrax attacks. A

variety of legal actions are being planned for the disparate treatment and reckless endangerment the Brentwood postal workers
faced.

In October 2001, press reports revealed that White House staff
had been on a regimen of the powerful antibiotic Cipro since the
September 11 terrorist attacks. Judicial Watch is aggressively
pursuing the disclosure of the facts and the decision for White
House staff, and President Bush as well, to begin taking Cipro
nearly a month before anthrax was detected on Capitol Hill. 'The
American people deserve a full accounting from the Bush
administration, the FBI, and other agencies concerning the
anthrax attacks. The FBI's investigation seems to have dead-
ended…,' stated Judicial Watch Chairman and General Counsel
Larry Klayman. 'One doesn't simply start taking a powerful antibiotic for no good reason. The American people are entitled to
know what the White House staffers knew nine months ago,' he
added.[448]

The anthrax outbreak thus bears ominous implications for the
dubious US role in the proliferation and use of weapons of mass
destruction, demonstrating clearly that the Bush administration
has no credibility on this issue. Exploited by the administration
to generate a pretext for a military intervention against Saddam's
regime in Iraq, the anthrax attacks – apparently issuing from
elements of the US military-intelligence infrastructure – were
soon forgotten as the evidence leaned further towards governmental responsibility therein. Thus, the administration began
searching for new ways of legitimizing its plans for Iraq. In an
editorial column for the right-wing journal *National Review*,
which has close connections to the Bush White House, Richard
Lowry vociferously called for a military intervention in Iraq just
one month after 9/11: 'At the very least, Iraq should be allowed
to be dismembered by its perpetually warring factions, or, ide-
ally, invaded and occupied by the American military and made

into a protectorate.' The goal 'would be a pro-Western and reasonably successful regime, somewhere between the Shah of Iran
and the current government of Turkey ... It would guarantee the
West's access to oil, and perhaps break up OPEC ... And it
would be a nice economic benefit to the United States.'[449]

Manufacturing a New War: 'Regime Change'?

Lacking entirely any substantial justification for a sudden new
invasion of Iraq by US forces – but committed to the same based
on longstanding strategies and interests – the Bush administration began attempting to revive the stale issue of weapons of
mass destruction in order to build international momentum in
support of the new US regional war drive. The political capital
for the war drive against Iraq in 2002/2003 deriving from the
9/11 terrorist attacks was insufficient. As the London *Times*
reported in February 2002:

> Initially, Washington included Iraq on its list of countries with
> links to al-Qaeda, but when European governments insisted that
> there was no intelligence evidence connecting Baghdad to Osama
> bin Laden's organization, the US changed tack. 'Now the
> emphasis is on Iraq's weapons of mass destruction program and
> the danger that Saddam might send out his own agents armed
> with chemical or biological devices,' one [British] official said.[450]

The day after the anniversary of the World Trade Center terrorist attacks in 2002, President Bush addressed the United
Nations General Assembly demanding the elimination of 'all
weapons of mass destruction, long-range missiles, and all related material ... if the Iraqi regime wishes peace'. The international community responded by insisting on the need to
establish a new UN weapons inspection system in the country to
ascertain the annulled status of Iraqi weapons programs that

had been almost completely achieved by the previous inspection system UNSCOM.

The US Government, however, was more concerned with generating a pretext for war, and immediately began undermining the concept and reality of UN weapons inspections. The goal in Iraq was not disarming a threat to regional and global security, but simply the removal of a regime considered hostile to US regional interests. In May 2002, for example, US Secretary of State Colin Powell described the aims of the Bush administration's war plans: 'US policy is that, regardless of what the inspectors do, the people of Iraq and the people of the region would be better off with a different regime in Baghdad. The United States reserves its option to do whatever it believes might be appropriate to see if there can be a regime change.' UN inspections are a 'separate and distinct and different' issue from the overarching objective of regime change.[451]

Regime change entails not the democratization of Iraq, but on the contrary merely the replacement of the country's pro-Saddam leadership – including of course Saddam himself – by a suitably pro-Western administration. The policy of maintaining the stability of the general political infrastructure of the Ba'athist regime in the immediate aftermath of a military intervention has always been a crucial element of the US concept of 'regime change' in Iraq – notwithstanding restructuring that might occur subsequently under US control. During the first Gulf War, Richard Haass – former Special Assistant to President Bush Snr, then Senior Director of Near East Affairs at the US National Security Council, and later Director of Policy Planning in the State Department under the administration of President Bush Jnr – confirmed in March 1991 that: 'Our policy is to get rid of Saddam, not his regime.'[452]

Credible reports corroborate this. For example, Daniel Neep – head of the Middle East and North Africa Program at the Royal

United Services Institute for Defence Studies in London – reports that when the US war is launched: 'The ideal scenario is someone within Iraq, preferably within the army, killing Saddam and taking control. That would mean that entering Baghdad would not be necessary and would also solve the problem of who will govern once he has gone.'[453] In other words, the ideal solution was to provoke a military coup from within the current regime to establish a new military dictatorship without Saddam Hussein.

The Bush administration had already seriously considered at least two dubious Iraqi generals to replace Saddam. One of them, the exiled General Nizar al-Khazraji who possesses the most 'credibility' with the Iraqi army, is currently under investigation in Denmark for the war crime of gassing 5000 Kurds in 1988. Brigadier-General Najib al-Salhi was also favoured by the US purportedly for his public support of the idea of a 'multiparty democracy' in Iraq. General al-Salhi, however, inadvertently revealed his real hopes for a future Iraqi military junta. He highlighted, according to the Sunday Telegraph, 'the need to encourage Iraqi military leaders to switch sides by promising that no more than 20 of Saddam's closest henchmen would be treated as criminals by an incoming Iraqi government'.[454]

In March 2002, Newsweek confirmed that Lieutenant-General Mahdi Al-Deleimi and General Fawzi Al-Shmari were among other possible candidates to lead a military coup against Saddam and replace him. Like General al-Salhi, they may also have played substantive roles in attacks on the Kurds during the 1998 Anfal campaign.[455] Clearly, the US has always aimed to ensure the stability of the Ba'athist military dictatorship while replacing its leadership – Saddam Hussein and his immediate entourage – with a new group of Iraqi generals subservient to US regional designs. As the New York Times elaborated in late February 2003, 'outraged Iraqi exiles report that there won't be any equivalent of post-war de-Nazification, in which accomplices of the defeated regime were purged from public life...'

> Instead the Bush administration intends to preserve most of the current regime: Saddam Hussein and a few top officials will be replaced with Americans, but the rest will stay. You don't have to be an Iraq expert to realize that many very nasty people will therefore remain in power ... and that the US will in effect take responsibility for maintaining the rule of the Sunni minority over the Shi'ite majority.[456]

British academic Patrick Cockburn, Visiting Fellow at Washington DC's Center for Strategic and International Studies (CSIS), further commented that: 'The US is abandoning plans to introduce democracy in Iraq after a war to overthrow Saddam Hussein' – as if such plans had ever existed in the first place – 'according to Kurdish leaders who recently met American officials...'

> The Kurdish leaders are enraged by an American plan to occupy Iraq but largely retain the government in Baghdad. The only changes would be the replacement of President Saddam and his lieutenants with senior US military officers. It undercuts the argument by George Bush and Tony Blair that war is justified by the evil nature of the regime in Baghdad ... The US appears to be returning to the policy it pursued at the end of the Gulf War in 1991. It did seek to get rid of President Saddam but wanted to avoid a radical change in Iraq. The US did not support the uprisings of Shia Muslims and Kurds because it feared a transformation in Iraqi politics that might have destabilized its allies in the Middle East or benefited Iran ... The change in American policy means marginalizing the Iraqi opposition which has been seeking to unite.[457]

Furthermore, superimposed over the entrenched Ba'athist military-political regime structure, the US had been drawing up extensive plans to establish a colonial-style administration of direct control. Citing documents summarizing the conclusions of 17 State Department working groups, the London *Independent* noted in February 2003 how 'Britain and America have been working for months on detailed proposals on how to rebuild Iraq after President Saddam ... In the initial aftermath of any war, Iraq would be governed by a senior US military officer, probably General Tommy Franks, with a civilian administrator.' General Franks would be expected to 'initially impose martial law', while Iraqis would be relegated to the sidelines as 'advisers' to the US administration.[458] The *Washington Post* elaborated that the 'blueprints for Iraq's future ... outline a broad and protracted American role in managing the reconstruction of the country'. In particular, US forces are expected to control Iraq's oil reserves.

> The [Bush] administration's plans, which are nearing completion, envision installing a civilian administration within months of a change of government, US officials said. But the officials said that even under the best of circumstances, US forces likely would remain at full strength in Iraq for months after a war ended, with a continued role for thousands of US troops there for years to come ... Among key roles for US forces would be the preservation of Iraq's borders against any sudden claims by neighbors and the defence of the country's oilfields. Oil revenue is considered the primary source of funds for Iraq's reconstruction, and the proceeds of the oil trade are seen as the glue most likely to hold the country's communities together.[459]

Indeed, White House plans outlined in late February 2003 revealed that the US intended to take 'complete control of post-Saddam Iraq "for an indefinite period".'[460] Meanwhile, the administration announced plans to install an 'American of stature' entasked to 'direct the reconstruction of the country' and to orchestrate the creation of a new Iraqi government.[461] By March, US officials finally revealed that they intended to carve up Iraq into at least three sectors of control, with Baghdad under the rule of former US Ambassador to Yemen Barbara Bodine, and the northern and southern sectors administrated by two retired US generals.[462] The details of the plan were reported by the Jerusalem-based investigative news service DEBKAfile which noted that the White House intended to 'effectively partition Iraq into three or possibly four military zones after the war is over', granting the United Kingdom control of one key sector.

> The American zone will stretch from the northern oilfields, taking in the cities of Kirkuk and Mosul as well as Baghdad and Tikrit in the central sector and the southern city of Nassririyah – up to the Kuwaiti border.
>
> Bush's decision to carve out a British military zone in south-eastern Iraq is by far the most spectacular strategic and political news for post-war Iraq ... The British army will, furthermore, have military jurisdiction over a triangular sector in southeastern Iraq, a sector that extends from Basra in the east, Sug Al Shuyukh in the west and Khozistan in the north. This wedge of land includes such strategic assets as the oilfields of the Basra and the Khozistan regions, Al Qurnah in the east and the Hawr Al Hammar southern marshlands up to the Iranian border, which British and American units will jointly patrol.
>
> The oilfields in the south, like those in the north, will be under American administration. The British have been given to understand that a portion of oil revenue will be allotted to defray their military expenses and the costs of maintaining an army in Iraq.[463]

In the context of this strategic objective of 'regime change', the Bush administration resolutely and consistently attempted to manufacture a pretext for full-fledged military invasion and occupation of Iraq. Thus in November 2002, a senior Pentagon official commented that: 'The inspections cannot work. Period.

Military power works. Period. All this is a side-show which, the longer it drags on, the greater the need to break the cycle becomes and the need to get involved militarily.'[464] These remarks revealed the sentiments behind what one top US Senate foreign policy aide referred to in May that year: 'The White House's biggest fear is that UN weapons inspectors will be allowed to go in.'[465] In other words, official US policy was that UN inspections – finding scant or no evidence of weapons of mass destruction – might prevent the US from building the momentum necessary for war. Thus, they were irrelevant to the need to wage war to topple Saddam and install a more obedient tyrant. As Seymour Hersh reported in the *New Yorker* in December 2001, 'Inside the Administration, there is general consensus on one issue, officials told me: there will be no further effort to revive the UN inspection regime withdrawn in late 1998.'[466]

Manufacturing a New War: UN Inspections

As British human rights activist and Iraq expert Milan Rai proves without doubt, the only possible function of weapons inspections as far as White House policy was concerned was to generate the desired justification for military intervention.[467] The London *Times* reported in February 2002 that: 'Key figures in the White House believe that demands on Saddam to readmit United Nations weapons inspectors should be set so high that he would fail to meet them unless he provided officials with total freedom.'[468] In other words, the sole objective of any UN inspections system would be to engineer a war crisis. To that end, for instance, the US demanded that UN inspectors fly Iraqi weapons scientists and their families out of the country to be questioned and offered asylum in the US. Iraq predictably protested at this idea, a stance that for the Bush administration was supposed to provide at least one example of Iraqi intransigence, thus building justification for war. Hans Blix, chief of the new inspections system UNMOVIC, opposed the US proposal: 'We are not going to abduct anyone. The UN is not a defection agency.'[469]

Perhaps the only single slightly substantial piece of 'evidence' that surfaced was the discovery at the beginning of 2003 of eleven empty 'chemical warheads' and 'one warhead that requires further evaluation' at the Ukhaider ammunition dump 75 miles south of Baghdad. A UN spokesperson commented: 'They were in excellent condition and were similar to ones imported by Iraq during the late 1980s.' The London *Telegraph* observed that: 'In the White House there was a sense of near-jubilation as aides realized immediately that the empty warheads, plus another one that the inspectors said required "further evaluation", represented the political equivalent of manna from heaven ... it suddenly seemed that the crucial evidence might have arrived at the perfect moment.'[470]

The good condition of the warheads suggested that they may have been handled recently, although no traces of chemical weapons or chemical agents nearby were found, as noted by Loren Thompson, a Pentagon consultant at the Lexington Institute in Arlington, Virginia. 'This is not the proverbial smoking gun. A real smoking gun would be an armed weapon,' she observed. Their good condition, however, 'doesn't draw one to think they are old weapons that were simply overlooked.' But as the London *Guardian* reported, the White House 'manna from heaven' was not as it seemed:

> Matthew Meelson, a weapons expert at Harvard's International Security Program, said that the US had in the past lost track of chemical and biological weapons from abandoned programs and that warheads had turned up from time to time. 'If these canisters are new and show signs of recent machine-shop work, then that is one thing, but if not, it's less than trivial,' he said. 'It would be unfortunate if they go to war over bad bookkeeping.'

Meelson further commented:

> Whether they are of recent origin or not, we do not believe they justify war. The Government has not presented any evidence that Iraq intends to use whatever weapons it does possess, and the success of the inspectors in finding the warheads merely reinforces the case for allowing the inspectors to continue their work in peace.[471]

The London *Daily Telegraph* further elaborated citing another military intelligence expert that the Iraqi Government's official explanation was perfectly credible:

> Charles Heyman, the editor of *Jane's World Armies*, said that given the state of the Iraqi armed forces, the official response from Baghad that the missile warheads had been forgotten was entirely credible. In the reports on stocks of chemical weapons that it was forced to compile at the end of the 1991 Gulf War, Iraq reported that it had 2500 122 mm Saqr-30 warheads filled with sarin which were buried under the rubble of a building destroyed by the allies' bombing raids.[472]

Similarly, former Executive Chairman of UNSCOM Rolf Ekeus described the discovery of the warheads as 'militarily insignificant'. According to UNMOVIC chief Blix, the discovery amounted to 'no big deal': 'This discovery is interesting and obviously the warheads have to be destroyed. But it's not something that's so important, because we're talking about empty warheads.'[473] In conclusion, Blix observed: 'Some 12 empty shells have been forgotten and that, evidently, is not very good. But it is not a very big quantity. It's not a smoking gun.'[474]

There are other important issues that should be understood. Although the majority of media commentators have described the weapons discovered as empty 'chemical warheads', in reality they were nothing of the sort. As described by US expert on Iraq

William Rivers Pitt, author of the *New York Times* bestseller *War on Iraq*:

> In the Iraqi arsenal, a warhead is a warhead – an empty ordnance space strapped to a missile. What matters is the payload, be it explosive or chemical or nuclear ... The item placed in the warhead denotes the designation. These warheads were stone-cold empty, so by definition they are not 'chemical warheads'. They are, in fact, nothing, because they were loaded with no payload. Furthermore, the word 'warhead' is in itself misleading, as these were artillery munitions.

Pitt goes further in dissecting the manner in which the discovery of the warheads has been distorted by the Anglo-American governments and media:

> Iraq is allowed by UN resolutions to have a variety of weapons, including the Al-Samoud missile. We did not want to pull Iraq's fangs completely after the Gulf War, considering the neighborhood they live in. We allowed them to keep missiles that fly only a certain distance (150 km most often). Many people will not know this, and will think the presence of these munitions will represent a breach of the UN resolution. This is not the case ... [Former chief UN weapons inspector] Scott Ritter informed me [on 16 January 2003] that these munitions were part of Iraq's declaration last December ... This [discovery] is absolutely a vindication of the inspections regime. They found the stuff, and it will be destroyed, and no American soldiers or Iraqi civilians died in the process. Inspections work.[475]

A further example illustrates how the Bush administration consistently attempted to exaggerate the implications of even the most minor discovery in order to generate an image of an out-of-control weapons program being pursued by an Iraqi regime intent on refusing to disarm. When UN inspectors visited the home of Iraqi scientist Faleh Hassan Hamza on 18 January

2003, they discovered a 3000-page document on how to produce material for nuclear weapons by enriching uranium using laser technology. Immediately, Western officials claimed the documents were recent 'and relate to on-going work taking place in Iraq to develop nuclear weapons'.[476] While the documents should have been declared, as Hans Blix noted, 'documents are not weapons of mass destruction', nor are they 'evidence of a weapon of mass destruction'. Indeed, being 'all pre-1990', the documents related to long-dead Iraqi weapons programs that had been either destroyed by Iraq or dismantled by UNSCOM.[477]

As was done with former Executive Chairman of UNSCOM Richard Butler, intense pressure was applied by the US Government on UNMOVIC chief Hans Blix to manipulate his findings in order that the US could claim Iraq's non-compliance with relevant UN resolutions. The *Los Angeles Times* reported in mid-February 2003 that:

> Behind the scenes, the United States has been pressing the case for a tough report from Blix. National security advisor Condoleezza Rice made an unannounced trip Tuesday to see Blix in New York, where she urged him to underscore Iraq's failures to meet several obligations outlined in numerous UN resolutions, US officials said.

Among the issues seized upon by the American and British administrations to justify military action was the conclusion of 'a team of international missile experts, who told Blix this week that an ongoing Iraqi missile program violates UN restrictions...

> Based on repeated tests, the Al-Samoud 2 missile exceeds the 90-mile limit imposed by the United Nations by about 25 miles, which would make it more than a defensive weapon, the experts

concluded. Blix is likely to point to the missile violation in his report Friday.

Iraq will not destroy the missiles, Iraq's UN ambassador, Mohammed Douri, countered Wednesday. The range discrepancy is attributable to the fact that the missiles weren't weighted during tests with payload guidance systems and fuel that would have limited their range, he said.[478]

This sort of range discrepancy is a technicality with no meaningful military significance. Indeed, Iraq had already declared the discrepancy in May 2002. As one weapons expert noted, 'Iraq declared almost a year ago that it had tested missiles beyond the range permitted by the United Nations...'

Douglas Richardson, editor of *Jane's Missiles and Rockets*, said the missiles criticized by UN diplomats on Wednesday appear to have been mentioned in Iraq's March 2002 declaration to UN weapons inspectors. Iraq is permitted to have missiles with a range of 150 km (93 miles). Richardson said Iraq told the UN last March that 'a couple of their missiles had been tested beyond that range' to just over 180 km (112 miles).

He said those appeared to be the Al-Samoud 2 rockets referred to ... when UN diplomats said experts had concluded that Iraqi missiles in some tests exceeded the maximum range allowed under Security Council resolutions in place since the 1991 Gulf War ... Richardson said firing the missiles past their allowed range offered Iraq little military advantage. Even with the lightest possible warhead the Al-Samouds – liquid propellant 'mini-Scud' ballistic missiles – would have nowhere near the reach of the Scud missiles used to attack Israel during the Gulf War in 1991.

'It's roughly the equivalent of you or I driving at 36 miles an hour rather than the permitted 30 miles an hour through my village,' Richardson said. 'You'd expect the constable to stop you, but you wouldn't expect to be in the magistrates' court with the pickpockets.'[479] While the US and Britain were keen to characterize what amounted to a technical accident as a serious material breach of UN resolutions, in reality the range discrepancy could not grant Iraq any particular military advantage, let alone amount to a weapon of mass destruction that threatens Iraq's neighbors and the world. Nor did this technicality illustrate Iraq's refusal to cooperate with inspections or disarm its weapons of mass destruction. On the contrary, having declared the range discrepancy in the first place, the Ba'athist regime made the effort to avoid deceiving the international community. Indeed, citing Blix, the *LA Times* noted that: 'Iraq has increased its cooperation with inspectors in the past week by allowing spyplane overflights, offering to let the monitors drill for soil samples at locations where they say chemical and biological weapons were destroyed and allowing a few private interviews with scientists.'[480] By mid-February 2003, Blix issued his interim report amidst a flurry of controversy over whether the US would finally be able to prove Iraqi non-compliance. The results were extremely displeasing for the British and American governments who had been hoping that intensifying US pressure on Blix might have worked. Summarizing Blix's report, the Associated Press stated:

> Chief UN weapons inspector Hans Blix said Friday that inspectors hadn't found any weapons of mass destruction, interviews with scientists have been useful and he cast doubt on evidence provided by Secretary of State Colin Powell indicating Iraq may have cleaned up sites before inspectors arrived.[481]

By March, Blix issued perhaps his most anticipated report on the progress of UN inspections as the US and Britain were gearing up their war plans. He noted that the Iraqi regime had finally destroyed its Al-Samoud 2 missiles, an example of significant progress: 'The destruction undertaken constitutes a substantial measure of disarmament. We are not watching the

destruction of toothpicks. Lethal weapons are being destroyed.'
Iraq's cooperation with the inspections process was described as
'active, or even proactive'. He noted that additional documentation on anthrax and VX nerve agent had been provided,
most of which had 'been found to restate what Iraq had already
declared'. Blix was also decidedly optimistic, concluding that
Iraq would be fully disarmed in a matter of months under the
UN inspections process. 'It will not take years, nor weeks, but
months.' Most significantly, Blix asserted that UN inspectors
had been unable to verify American and British claims about
hidden Iraqi weapons, asking for further data on suspect sites.
But CIA Director George Tenet had already confirmed that all
relevant information had been passed on. IAEA Director-General
Mohamed El-Baradei also refuted Anglo-American claims
regarding alleged Iraqi nuclear weapons programs. Citing
investigations by UN and independent experts, El-Baradei noted
that suspect aluminium tubes were not destined for equipment
that could be used to refine uranium for nuclear weapons:

> Extensive field investigation and document analysis have failed to
> uncover any evidence that Iraq intended to use these 81mm tubes
> for any project other than the reverse engineering of rockets ...
> Based on thorough analysis, the IAEA has concluded, with the
> concurrence of outside experts, that documents which formed the
> basis for the reports of recent uranium transactions between Iraq
> and Niger are in fact not authentic. We have therefore concluded
> that these specific allegations are unfounded ... After three
> months of intrusive inspections, we have to date found no evi-
> dence or plausible indication of the revival of a nuclear weapons
> program in Iraq.[482]

Indeed, it appears that the documents presented by the American and British governments to support their claims amounted
to 'faked evidence', in the words of the *Washington Post*:

Knowledgeable sources familiar with the forgery investigation described the faked evidence as a series of letters between Iraqi agents and officials in the central African nation of Niger. The documents had been given to the UN inspectors by Britain and reviewed extensively by US intelligence. The forgers had made relatively crude errors that eventually gave them away – including names and titles that did not match up with the individuals who held office at the time the letters were purportedly written, the officials said ... The discovery was a further setback to US and British efforts to convince reluctant UN Security Council members of the urgency of the threat posed by Iraq's weapons of mass destruction.[483]

The most glaring example of the absurd and immoral lengths to which the US and UK governments were willing to go to manufacture justification for war is the infamous Iraq dossier published and distributed by the office of British Prime Minister Tony Blair. The 'British intelligence' dossier titled *Iraq – Its Infrastructure of Concealment, Deception and Intimidation* was used by US Secretary of State Colin Powell to make his case for war before the UN in February 2003. To support his claim that 'Iraq today is actively using its considerable intelligence capabilities to hide its illicit activities', Powell called attention to 'the fine paper the United Kingdom distributed yesterday, which describes in exquisite detail Iraqi deception activities'. As *The Nation* reported, however, 'much of that "fine paper" ... was not a fresh accounting of information based on new "intelligence" about Iraqi attempts to thwart UN weapons inspections. Rather, the document has been exposed by Britain's ITN television network as a cut-and-paste collection of previously published academic articles, some of which were based on dated material.'

The report plagiarized almost entirely three separate previously published academic papers, including one 'written by a postgraduate student [Ibrahim al-Marashi] who works not in

Baghdad but in Monterey, California'. That piece, published in the *Middle East Review of International Affairs*, primarily described the state of Iraq during the 1991 Gulf War period, and drew heavily from the work of former UN inspector Scott Ritter who opposes the Anglo-American war drive against Iraq.

> So sweeping was the plagiarism that, according to British journalists who reviewed the materials, typographical errors – including a misplaced comma – that appeared in al-Marashi's article were reproduced in the official dossier that was posted on Blair's 10 Downing Street website ... To the extent that changes were made, they appear to have been inserted to increase the shock value of the information ... In addition to the sections taken from al-Marashi's article, according to the *Guardian*, 'The content of six more pages (of the dossier) relies heavily on articles by Sean Boyne and Ken Gause that appeared in *Jane's Intelligence Review* in 1997 and last November. None of these sources is acknowledged.'

Cambridge University political scientist Glen Rangawala, who first discovered the plagiarism, commented that: 'Apart from passing this off as the work of its intelligence services, it indicates that the UK really does not have any independent sources of information on Iraq's internal policies. It just draws upon publicly available data.'[484] This, of course, is an understatement. Neither the US, which relied on the British dossier, nor the UK governments possessed any intelligence or evidence regarding Iraq proving the existence of weapons of mass destruction or programs for their development. All that was available was a concoction of falsities, baseless speculation and outdated irrelevant material designed to manufacture public support for an illegitimate military intervention motivated not by humanitarian or security concerns, but by mounting economic and strategic interests in the Middle East. That perhaps is made even clearer by Dr Rangawala's detailed critical analyses of British and

American claims regarding Saddam's proscribed weapons and alleged weapons programs, which he boldly dissects using official UN data.[485]

The Grand Strategy

Several commentators have accurately outlined the clearly anti-humanitarian objectives of the US-led war drive against Iraq of 2002/2003, based on an amalgamation of various economic and military strategies — sanctions, 'no-fly zones', and full-scale invasion — to secure regional interests. It is quite evident that there has never been any sort of humanitarian motivation behind Western policy in the Persian Gulf. On the contrary, policy appears to be formulated specifically to consolidate regional military hegemony. As IAC analyst Sara Flounders concluded:

> The sanctions are really part of an overall destabilization strategy. This same strategy has been used by the Pentagon and CIA many times in the past: from 1950 to 1953 against the elected government of Mossadegh in Iran, leading to its overthrow and the bloody reign of the Shah; in 1954 against the democratically elected government of Arbenz in Guatemala, leading to a US-engineered military coup and the subsequent slaughter of over 100,000 Indian people; from 1970 to 1973 against a democratically elected government of Salvador; against Allende in Chile which ended in the coming to power of the dictatorship of General Pinochet and the murder of 30,000 Chileans.

'The US policy of economic destabilization and overthrow in Iraq,' Flounders concluded prophetically, 'will not lead to a democratic government, but rather to a dictatorship compliant to US bidding, as has been shown time and again.'[486]

In the case of Iraq, the specific interest has always been unimpeded access to, and control over, Middle East oil and other resources. A preliminary answer to the question of why the US and UK have wished to remove Saddam Hussein from power since the first Gulf War lies in his domestic policies combined with his emerging tendencies towards independence. Although his regime had always been an exceedingly brutal dictatorship, 'in his pre-war period' Saddam Hussein 'did more than most rulers in that part of the world to meet the basic material needs of his people in terms of housing, health care, and education', reports Professor Stephen Zunes, Chair of the Peace and Justice Studies program at the University of San Francisco.

> In fact, Iraq's impressive infrastructure and strongly nationalistic ideology led many Arabs to conclude that the overkill exhibited by American forces and the post-war sanctions was a deliberate effort to emphasize that any development strategy in that part of the world must be pursued solely on terms favourable to Western interests. Saddam Hussein was also able to articulate the frustrations of the Arab masses concerning the Palestinian question, sovereignty regarding natural resources, and resistance to foreign domination. He was certainly opportunistic and manipulative in doing so, but it worked.[487]

As similarly pointed out by Director of the Middle East Project at the Institute for Policy Studies in Washington, DC, Phyllis Bennis, before the 1991 Gulf War 'the majority of Iraqi civilians enjoyed an almost First World-level standard of living, with education and health-care systems that remained free, accessible to every Iraqi and among the highest quality in the developing world'.[488] This domestic development strategy was combined with a strongly nationalistic ideology that appeared to be intensifying with time. As previously noted, in February 1990, Saddam made a speech before an Arab summit that certainly seemed to show that his days of subservience to the West could be ending. Condemning the ongoing US military presence in the

Persian Gulf, Saddam warned: 'If the Gulf people and the rest of the Arabs along with them fail to take heed, the Arab Gulf region will be ruled by American will,' and that the United States would dictate the production, distribution and price of oil, 'all on the basis of a special outlook which has to do solely with US interests and in which no consideration is given to the interests of others'.[489] Having propped up the dictator and his brutal regime for so long while he remained subservient to Western interests, it was his growing drive for anti-Western independence – rather than his ongoing savage policies of domestic repression – that caused the West, and now the US and UK, to embark on a new crusade to destroy his regime and replace it with another suitably subservient dictatorship.

The centrality of the energy factor (i.e., oil and gas) is beyond reasonable doubt. Iraq possesses the world's second largest proven oil reserves, an estimated 112.5 billion barrels, and 110 trillion cubic feet of natural gas. Experts believe that further undiscovered oil reserves could raise the total to over 250 billion barrels, far above other oil-producing countries, and possibly even larger that Saudi reserves. The other advantages of Iraq are that while its oil is inexpensive to produce, it is also of high quality. As one oil industry source put it, Iraq is 'a boom waiting to happen ... There is not an oil company in the world that doesn't have its eye on Iraq.'[490] Control of Persian Gulf reserves is a longstanding US policy. As General Anthony C. Zinni – Commander-in-Chief of the US Central Command – testified before Congress in 1999, the Persian Gulf is a 'vital interest' of 'longstanding' for the US, which 'must have free access to the region's resources'.[491]

Ultimately then, a key objective of the Anglo-American war drive of 2003 was to establish absolute control over the profits that flow from Middle East oil. As the Associated Press observes: 'The [US/UK] military's success in holding Iraq in check ensures a continued flow of oil from the Persian Gulf.'[492] Indeed, according to Pentagon sources, US military planners by January 2003 had 'crafted strategies that will allow us to secure and protect those fields as rapidly as possible in order to then preserve those prior to destruction'. The London *Guardian* elaborated that 'the prospect of British and US commandos claiming key oil installations around Basra by force has pushed global oil diplomacy into overdrive. International oil companies have been jockeying position to secure concessions before "regime change"', the result being that 'Saddam has offered lucrative contracts to companies from France, China, India and Indonesia as well as Russia'. Ironically, 'the oil majors based in Britain and America – now the leading military hawks' were the only ones 'that don't have current access to Iraqi contracts', which of course only strengthened their desire to reverse the situation.[493]

That the Anglo-American alliance certainly intended to reverse the status of Iraqi oil contracts is clear from the observation of Richard Lugar, Chairman of the Senate Foreign Relations Committee, who confirms that reluctant Europeans risk losing out on oil contracts. 'The case he had made is that the Russians and the French, if they want to have a share in the oil operations or concessions or whatever afterward, they need to be involved in the effort to depose Saddam as well.' Indeed, one leaked oil analyst report from Deutsche Bank confirmed that ExxonMobil would be in 'pole position in a changed-regime Iraq'. The State Department and Vice-President Dick Cheney's staff have also sponsored two sets of meetings 'attended by representatives of ExxonMobil, ChevronTexaco, ConocoPhilips and Halliburton, the company that Cheney ran before his election'. Grant Aldonas, Under-Secretary at the US Department of Commerce, explained the implications that the war 'would open up this spigot on Iraqi oil which certainly would have a profound effect in terms of the performance of the world economy for those countries that are manufacturers and oil consumers'. The *Guardian* concludes that the 'war stands to give control over the oil price to 'new Iraq' and its [Anglo-American] sponsors, with Saudi Arabia losing its capacity to control prices by altering productive capacity'.[494]

Of course, a further question remains regarding why the British and American governments had been so desperate to invade Iraq in the aftermath of 9/11. As already noted, US plans consisted of replacing Saddam with a more subservient military dictatorship run by occupying US forces, thus establishing US control over one of the world's biggest oil reserves. The urgency of this grab for Middle East oil, following hot on the heels of the grab for central Asian resources, was exacerbated by the 2000/2001 peak in world oil production. As documented by oil industry expert Colin J. Campbell – Trustee of the London-based Oil Depletion Analysis Centre – conventional oil production appears to have already peaked in the year 2000. Campbell demonstrates that almost half the oil that is available has already been produced, leaving only an estimated 150 Gb (billion barrels) still to be found. Oil reserves are now being depleted at the rate of about 2 per cent each year, and thus it seems clear that conventional oil production has peaked. However, the actual consequent decline of production will probably take a few more years to sink in.[495] Structural geologist Dave Allen Pfieffer describes the potential impact of this coming decline of oil production:

> As oil and natural gas production decline, so will the economy and our technological civilization. Without oil and natural gas modern agriculture will fail, and people will starve. Without oil and natural gas, industry will grind to a halt, transportation will be grounded, and people in northern climes will freeze in the winter.

Scientist Richard Duncan has created a model that has so far gone unrefuted. His model states that technological civilization cannot outlast its resource base, particularly its energy resource base. Once this resource base is exhausted, technological civilization will be forever beyond the grasp of life on a particular planet. Duncan makes his model readily available to anyone who wishes to test it in the hope that someone will be able to successfully refute the model. To date, no one has done so.[496]

The scientific model produced by Richard Duncan – Director of the Institute on Energy and Man – was presented to the Summit 2000 of the Geological Society of America. It elaborates in detail on the alarming implications of the peak of world oil production for the fate of industrial civilization without urgent appropriate measures to reduce oil-dependency and transfer to renewable energy resources.[497]

Unfortunately, Western governments do not seem to be interested in implementing such measures, perhaps due to the corresponding consequence in terms of the decentralization of power, since control over renewable resources such as solar energy etc. is harder to concentrate in the hands of a few by their very nature. US/Western elites appear to be more concerned with maintaining their immediate investments and profits, while establishing grand plans to consolidate their control over the world's remaining energy reserves. Colin Campbell observes that as a result, US foreign policy seems to be fundamentally directed at racing to grab these reserves:

> We may look back and find that the year 2000 was the peak: a turning-point when the prosperity of the past, driven by an abundant supply of cheap oil-based energy, gave way to decline in the future. A discontinuity of this magnitude is hard to grasp. The poor countries of the world will bear most of the burden. But the United States will be in serious difficulties. There is a danger of some ill-considered military intervention to try to secure oil.[498]

Indeed, it is a matter of record that US policy planners have acknowledged the crucial implications of these facts in formulating its new national security strategy. In 2001, a report on 'energy security' – commissioned by Vice-President Dick Cheney and sponsored by two leading government-influenced US think-tanks, the Council on Foreign Relations and the James Baker Institute for Public Policy, concluded ominously that: 'The world is currently precariously close to utilizing all of its available global oil production capacity.' The impending crisis is increasing 'US and global vulnerability to disruption' and now leaves the US facing 'unprecedented energy price volatility', already leading to electricity blackouts in areas like California. The report warns of 'more Californias' ahead. The 'central dilemma' for the Bush administration is that 'the American people continue to demand plentiful and cheap energy without sacrifice or inconvenience'. But if the global demand for oil continues to rise, world shortages could reduce the status of the US to that of 'a poor developing country'. With the 'energy sector in critical condition, a crisis could erupt at any time [which] could have potentially enormous impact on the US ... and would affect US national security and foreign policy in dramatic ways'. The growing energy crisis thus demands 'a reassessment of the role of energy in American foreign policy ... Such a strategy will require difficult trade-offs, in both domestic and foreign policy. But there is no alternative. And there is no time to waste.' The US will only be able to prevent other powers from exploiting its dependency by seizing the strategic initiative to adopt 'a leadership role in the formation of new rules of the game', otherwise 'US firms, US consumers and the US Government [will be] in a weaker position'. One of the key 'consequences' of the fact that 'the United States remains a prisoner of its energy dilemma' is the 'need for military intervention'. The report thus recommends that energy and security policy be integrated to prevent 'manipulations of markets by any state'.

The principal source of disruption to the existing energy system, the report concludes, lies in 'Middle East tension'. The growing decline of the Anglo-American system of regional control by proxy means that the 'chances are greater than at any point in the last two decades of an oil supply disruption'. The Middle East seems to be facing a rise in anti-American sentiment, particularly the oil-rich states of the Persian Gulf:

> Gulf allies are finding their domestic and foreign policy interests increasingly at odds with US strategic considerations, especially as Arab-Israeli tensions flare. They have become less inclined to lower oil prices ... A trend towards anti-Americanism could affect regional leaders' ability to cooperate with the US in the energy area. The resulting tight markets have increased US vulnerability to disruption and provided adversaries undue political influence over the price of oil.

The threat posed by Iraq is highlighted as a particularly crucial focus of US foreign policy. During the year 2000, the report observes, Iraq had 'effectively become a swing producer, turning its taps on and off when it has felt such action was in its strategic interest to do so'. There was a 'possibility that Saddam Hussein may remove Iraqi oil from the market for an extended period of time' in order to damage prices.

> Iraq remains a destabilizing influence to ... the flow of oil to international markets from the Middle East. Saddam Hussein has also demonstrated a willingness to threaten to use the oil weapon and to use his own export program to manipulate oil markets. This would display his personal power, enhance his image as a pan-Arab leader ... and pressure others for a lifting of economic sanctions against his regime. The United States should conduct

an immediate policy review toward Iraq including military, energy, economic and political/diplomatic assessments.

The United States should then develop an integrated strategy with key allies in Europe and Asia, and with key countries in the Middle East, to restate goals with respect to Iraqi policy and to restore a cohesive coalition of key allies.[499]

This focus on reintegrating Iraq into the regional framework of order under US hegemony was no doubt heightened by the fact that Iraq challenged the US monopoly over the oil trade, maintained through the fact that oil transactions occur in US dollars. Since 1971, all oil has been traded in US dollars under OPEC. The dollar has thus become the *de facto* world reserve currency, accounting for two-thirds of all official exchange reserves. More than four-fifths of all foreign exchange transactions and half of all world exports are in dollars. Overall, since the world economy is fundamentally oil-dependent, this not only lends the US a dominant trading advantage, it also grants the US dominance over the world economy.

In November 2000, Iraq began trading its oil in euros, and profited handsomely in the process. Iran, Venezuela and Russia – all key oil-producers – have also considered and/or moved towards switching to the euro. This growing trend represented a significant obstacle to the maintenance of US economic preeminence, threatening to bring an absolute end to the US economy's dominance of world trade via the dollar. As one former US government macro-economist observed of the 2003 war drive against Iraq: 'The Federal Reserve's greatest nightmare is that OPEC will switch its international transactions from a dollar standard to a euro standard...'

Iraq actually made this switch in November 2000 (when the euro was worth around 82 cents), and has actually made off like a bandit considering the dollar's steady depreciation against the euro. (Note: the dollar declined 17% against the euro in 2002.)

The real reason the Bush administration wants a puppet government in Iraq — or more importantly, the reason why the corporate-military-industrial network conglomerate wants a puppet government in Iraq — is so that it will revert back to a dollar standard and stay that way (while also hoping to veto any wider OPEC momentum towards the euro, especially from Iran, the second largest OPEC producer who is actively discussing a switch to euros for its oil exports).[500]

The urgency of the initiative outlined here was exacerbated by the fact that 'US crude-oil inventories have fallen to the lowest level since 1975 — below what the industry considers essential for smooth operation,' as reported by the Associated Press. The continued decline was 'expected to prompt renewed calls for drawing on some of the 600 million barrels of oil in the government's emergency Strategic Petroleum Reserve'. Analysts, however, predicted that 'an easing of the supply crunch may come soon' in the form of a temporarily increased output of crude oil from the Middle East. 'There's some crude oil from the Middle East arriving soon that could help build up stocks,' observed John Lichtblau, Chairman of the New York-based Petroleum Industry Research Foundation.[501] It so happens that the key country to which the US had turned to alleviate its 'chronic oil shortage' was Iraq. 'Weeks before a prospective invasion of Iraq, the oil-rich state has doubled its exports of oil to America, helping US refineries cope with a debilitating strike in Venezuela...'

> ... [O]il giants such as Chevron, Exxon, BP and Shell saved the day by doubling imports from Iraq from 0.5 m barrels in November to over 1 m barrels per day to solve the problem. Essentially, US importers diverted 0.5 m barrels of Iraqi oil per

day heading for Europe and Asia to save the American oil infrastructure . . .

[The trade] shows the unspoken aim of military action in Iraq,
which has the world's second largest proven reserves – some 112
billion barrels, and at least another 100 billion of unproven
reserves, according to the US Department of Energy. Iraqi oil is
comparatively simple to extract – less than $1 per barrel, com-
pared with $6 a barrel in Russia. Soon, US and British forces
could be securing the source of that oil as a priority in the war
strategy. The Iraqi fields south of Basra produce prized 'sweet
crudes' that are simpler to refine.[502]

Iraq is thus an indispensable pivot in the invigorated US foreign
policy scheme of energy control. The *San Francisco Chronicle*
observes that: 'The world's biggest oil bonanza in recent memory
may be just around the corner, giving US oil companies huge
profits and American consumers cheap gasoline for decades to
come. And it all may come courtesy of a war with Iraq . . .

While debate intensifies about the Bush administration's policy,
oil analysts and Iraqi exile leaders believe a new, pro-Western
government – assuming it were to replace Saddam Hussein's
regime – would prompt US and multinational petroleum giants to
rush into Iraq, dramatically increasing the output of a nation
whose oil reserves are second only to that of Saudi Arabia.

There already is a stampede, with the Russians, French and
Italians already lined up,' said Lawrence Goldstein, president of
the Petroleum Industry Research Foundation, a New York think-
tank funded by large oil companies. Until now, debate over the
economic impact of a US-led attack on Iraq has focused mostly on
short-term dangers . . .

Iraq has 113 billion barrels of proven reserves, second worldwide
only to Saudi Arabia, which has 262 billion barrels. But because of
its two decades of war, Iraq's oil potential remains relatively
unexplored. The US Energy Department estimates that Iraq has as

much as 220 billion barrels in undiscovered reserves, bringing the Iraqi total to the equivalent of 98 years of current US annual oil imports.[503]

Many oil analysts predicted that the successful return of Iraqi oil to the international market would in the long term drastically lower oil prices, providing US corporations with unhindered access. Michael T. Klare, Professor of Peace and World Security Studies at Hampshire College in Amherst, reported that:

> The administration doesn't want oil to be part of the war discussion because it undercuts the reasoning that the rush to war is because of an imminent (Iraqi) military threat. If the real motives were made clear − that this is a grab for oil and an attempt to break the back of OPEC − it would make our motives look more predatory than exemplary.[504]

There were also specifically strategic reasons for enforcing the sanctions and the 'no-fly zones' against Iraq: the maintenance of the flow of Western weapons of mass destruction to regional client states. The *New Statesman* noted that:

> Both Richard Butler and Scott Ritter, late of UNSCOM, the weapons inspections agency, have said that Saddam Hussein has been disarmed of his weapons of mass destruction. With all non-military sanctions lifted, Baghdad has indicated that the inspectors can return. What alarms the US and Britain is a section of the original Resolution 687 on Iraq, which they never mention. This calls for the downgrading of weapons of mass destruction throughout the region, meaning the nuclear-armed Israeli invaders of Lebanon and the Turkish invaders of Iraqi Kurdistan. It would also mean the scaling down of the West's arming of countries like Saudi Arabia, upon which much of Britain's weapons trade depends.[505]

US policy in Iraq was thus inseparable from a wider regional policy designed to maintain the overall framework of regional order under US domination. Indeed, the 2003 war drive against Iraq, in much the same vein, has brought to fruition a much contemplated master-plan for the Middle East that was formulated as long as over 30 years ago, designed not simply to maintain that order, but to consolidate it through direct military occupation. In 1975, an article titled 'Seizing Arab Oil' was published in *Harpers' Magazine*, authored under the pseudonym Miles Ignotis – identified as 'a Washington-based professor and defence consultant with intimate links to high-level US policy-makers'. The article's implications, its author's true identity and its relationship to the 2003 war drive have been revealed by James Akins who served as US envoy in Iraq and Kuwait, and ultimately as US ambassador to Saudi Arabia during the oil crisis of 1973–4. As he puts it, the article – released during his diplomatic career in Saudi Arabia – outlines 'how we could solve all our economic and political problems by taking over the Arab oilfields [and] bringing in Texans and Oklahomans to operate them'. Noting that a large number of similar articles were simultaneously published in other respected magazines and newspapers, he observes: 'I knew that it had to have been the result of a deep background briefing. You don't have eight people coming up with the same screwy idea at the same time, independently.'

Akins soon appeared on television asserting that 'anyone who would propose that is either a madman, a criminal or an agent of the Soviet Union', a statement he now describes as a 'fatal mistake' costing him his position. Not long after his television statement, he learned that there had indeed been a background briefing – conducted by his boss, then-US Secretary of State Henry Kissinger. Later that year, Akins was fired. Although Kissinger has not acknowledged authoring any such briefing, in an interview with *Business Week* that year, he openly threatened to bring down oil prices through 'massive political warfare against countries like Saudi Arabia and Iran to make them risk their political stability and maybe their security if they did not cooperate'.[506]

US national security expert and senior correspondent for the *American Prospect*, Robert Dreyfuss, reports that 'starting with the Miles Ignotis article, and a parallel one by conservative strategist and Johns Hopkins University professor Robert W. Tucker in commentary', what has been described by former ambassador Akins as 'the Kissinger plan' began to 'gain favour among a feisty group of hardline, pro-Israeli thinkers, especially the hawkish circle aligned with Democratic senators Henry Jackson of Washington and Daniel Patrick Moynihan of New York...'

> Eventually, this amalgam of strategists came to be known as 'neo-conservatives', and they played important roles in President Reagan's Defense Department and at think-tanks and academic policy centres in the 1980s. Led by Richard Perle, chairman of the Pentagon's influential Defense Policy Board, and Deputy Secretary of Defense Paul Wolfowitz, they now occupy several dozen key posts in the White House, the Pentagon, and the State Department. At the top, they are closest to Vice-President Cheney and Defense Secretary Donald Rumsfeld, who have been closely aligned since both men served in the White House under President Ford in the mid-1970s. They also clustered around Cheney when he served as Secretary of Defense during the Gulf War in 1991. Throughout those years, and especially after the Gulf War, US forces have steadily encroached on the Gulf and the surrounding region, from the Horn of Africa to Central Asia ... Removing Saddam Hussein could be the final piece of the puzzle, cementing an American imperial presence.[507]

Indeed, according to Robert Kagan, founder of the Project for the New American Century – the neo-conservative think-tank that is heavily wired into the Bush Cabinet: 'We will probably need a major concentration of forces in the Middle East over a long period of time ... When we have economic problems, it's been caused by disruptions in our oil supply. If we have a force in Iraq, there will be no disruption in oil supplies.' As noted in the Introduction to this study, the members of the Bush adminis-tration closely affiliated with the Project include I. Lewis Libby, the Vice-President's Chief of Staff; Elliott Abrams, Middle East director at the National Security Council; Zalmay Khalilzad, White House liaison to Iraqi opposition groups; and perhaps most prominently, Dick Cheney, Donald Rumsfeld and Paul Wolfowitz. Describing the 2003 war drive against Iraq in this context, former ambassador Akins observed: 'It's the Kissinger plan. I thought it had been killed, but it's back ... It'll be easier once we have Iraq. Kuwait, we already have. Qatar and Bahrain, too. So it's only Saudi Arabia we're talking about, and the United Arab Emirates falls into place.'[508]

It is not surprising then that former Assistant Defense Secre-tary under Reagan, Richard Perle — Chairman of the Defense Policy Board that advises the Pentagon — held a private Pentagon briefing on 10 July 2002 where RAND analyst Laurent Murawiec was invited to argue that Saudi Arabia should cease the financial support of Islamic fundamentalists — and that a failure to comply must be met with an invasion to 'target' its oilfields and financial assets. The briefing also referred to a 'Grand Strategy for the Middle East' listing 'Iraq' as 'the tactical pivot', 'Saudi Arabia' as 'the strategic pivot', and 'Egypt' as the end-goal of the strategy, 'the prize'.[509]

The broad agenda behind this regional 'grand strategy' is nothing less than the expansion and consolidation of US global pre-eminence. Former mid-level CIA official Robert E. Ebel — Director of the Energy Program at the Washington DC-based Center for Strategic and International Studies (CSIS) whose advisers include prominent policy-makers such as Kissinger,

James Schlesinger and Zbigniew Brzezinski – warned that: 'If something happens in Saudi Arabia, if the ruling family is ousted, if they decide to shut off the oil supply, we have to go in.' The simple reason for this, and for the 'grand strategy', is that:

> Oil is high-profile stuff. Oil fuels military power, national treasuries, and international politics. It is no longer a commodity to be bought and sold within the confines of traditional energy supply and demand balances. Rather, it has been transformed into a determinant of well-being, of national security, and of international power.

Western Europe, Japan, the developing industrial powers of Asia and China are all increasingly dependent on Persian Gulf oil. Thus, control of Persian Gulf oil is a matter of securing US hegemony over its rivals, as Professor Michael Klare points out: 'Controlling Iraq is about oil as power, rather than oil as fuel. Control over the Persian Gulf translates into control over Europe, Japan and China. It's having our hand on the spigot.'[510] The 2003 war drive was thus not merely about unimpeded access to regional energy reserves, but fundamentally about world control through unrivalled domination of such reserves.

One must therefore conclude that the various Persian Gulf crises were in many ways contrived and provoked to legitimize a continued Western military presence in the Persian Gulf region, buttressed by a brutal and illegal sanctions regime in accord with strategic, political and economic interests. Included in these interests is the aim to demonstrate to the Third World what happens when a country in a strategic region acts independently: its entire population is ruthlessly punished, its infrastructure is devastated, and its government is eventually overthrown. The Anglo-American military alliance continued with its campaign of punishing and prostrating Iraq in the hope that Saddam would be eliminated, to be replaced by a pliant US puppet regime. Furthermore, as the ruthless nature of the US-UK military-economic strategy in Iraq exemplified, a pretext for dramatic increases in military spending – by which to strengthen US-led Western military hegemony over the world and further enrich arms contractors and other corporations – was successfully manufactured. Most importantly, the possibility that Iraq may develop into an independent regional power has been decisively cut short. It is thus clear that the variety of threats that the Ba'athist regime was alleged to pose were merely propaganda exercises designed to deflect public attention from the facts, distort and limit public discourse over Western policy, and establish legitimacy for an unjustifiable anti-humanitarian program of military-economic atrocities designed to return to a policy of regional imperialism. Throughout this escapade, the United Nations has been exploited as an instrument to support a genocidal array of policies that are in fact thoroughly opposed to the principles enshrined within this very same international body. The stark contradictions of world order under US hegemony are apparent.

Experts had predicted that the 2003 war drive against Iraq would bring these policies to bloody fruition by creating an unprecedented humanitarian catastrophe. Such predictions, however, did not curb the American and British governments from their 'grand strategy'. One such prediction worth citing is a confidential UN report from December 2002 whose authenticity was confirmed by UN officials, and elements of which were posted on the website of Cambridge University's Campaign Against Sanctions on Iraq (CASI). The report detailed how: 'As many as half a million Iraqis could require medical treatment as a result of serious injuries suffered in the early stages of a war on Iraq...'

The total includes some 100,000 expected to be injured as a direct result of combat and a further 400,000 wounded as an indirect result of the devastation, according to estimates prepared by the World Health Organization, the document said ... UN officials confirmed the authenticity of the document, which assumes that unlike the 1991 Gulf War, a new war in Iraq would develop beyond an initial aerial bombardment into a large-scale and protracted ground offensive.

'The resultant devastation would undoubtedly be great,' the UN planners concluded. The estimates were based on material from several different UN organizations ... The confidential assessment assumes that ... the Iraqi electricity network, railway and road transportation systems would be significantly damaged.

UN officials had previously disclosed that as many as 4.5 million to 9.5 million of Iraq's 26.5 million people could quickly need outside food to survive once an attack began ... War would also produce a huge refugee problem, driving some 900,000 Iraqis into neighboring countries, with about 100,000 of those requiring immediate assistance as soon as they arrived, according to the UN estimate.

Another 2 million could be driven from their homes but remain inside Iraq, where access by relief agencies would be a particular problem due to the fighting, the planners say ... Children under five, pregnant women and mothers who are breast-feeding their infants 'will be particularly vulnerable because of the likely absence of a functioning primary health-care system in a post-conflict situation,' it said.

'Furthermore, the outbreak of diseases in epidemic if not pandemic proportions is very likely ... Diseases such as cholera and dysentery thrive in the environment ... When determining the requirement for pharmaceuticals and medical supplies, these factors must be considered.'[511]

This UN emergency planning assessment granted a clear insight into the Holocaust-like proportions of the impact of the planned

Anglo-American invasion, long before its commencement. Yet on 15 February 2003, the day when 2 million British citizens marched in London to protest against the war drive, Prime Minister Blair declared that a British and American sponsored 'regime change' in Baghdad would constitute an 'act of humanity'. How the potential death and injury of over 10 million civilians could amount to an example of Anglo-American humanitarianism is, of course, inexplicable, unless we conclude that world order is structured on the basis of more familiar imperial values, such as power and profit. The contrast between government propaganda and harsh reality suffices to illustrate the fundamentally anti-humanitarian nature of Anglo-American foreign policy, reminiscent of the cold-blooded brutality of the colonial era when British and European empire-building was depicted as 'civilizing the natives'.

The parallels between the current and the colonial eras are unnerving. Colonialism was legitimized as a benevolent crusade designed to bring the noble values and practices of Western civilization to indigenous peoples who were characterized as primitive savages incapable of self-government. Colonial atrocities were justified as attempts to defend colonists from spontaneous and barbaric attacks upon them by such ungrateful savages. Little has changed in the 'new' world order, when the American Empire legitimizes the same brand of imperial values as a benevolent crusade designed to 'export democracy' to backward and helpless 'failed-states'. The atrocities undertaken in this vein are justified as 'pre-emptive' or even 'preventive' strikes against evil tyrannies intent on destroying the ever-innocent Western pinnacles of democracy. It would be fair in this context to see Anglo-American policy in the Persian Gulf as being modelled on essentially the same imperial value-system as adopted by the British Empire in the colonial era.

Conclusions: Subjugation or Hope

Based on our detailed examination of Western interventions in one key Middle East hot-spot, Iraq, it is clear that Western policy, pursuing the control of strategic regions to dominate the world's key energy resources, has consistently violated the basic humanitarian principles that Western civilization purports to define itself by. It is important to emphasize that in doing so Western policy has systematically engaged in state terrorism, both indirectly by sponsoring regimes indulging in terrorism and directly by conducting military operations that utilize terrorism. This, of course, fundamentally refutes the integrity of the new 'War on Terror' being pursued in the aftermath of 9/11. Furthermore, at the root of Western policy in the Middle East is a capacity to manufacture and/or provoke conflicts in order to manipulate the regional political and geo-strategic fabric to concord with Western interests, reminiscent of the traditional 'divide-and-rule' strategy of the colonial era. In this respect, Western policy in the Middle East has at no time undergone any sort of drastic or fundamental reversal, following a consistent pattern of intervention and interference that amounts to an unbroken continuum of empire-building since colonialism.

Decolonization, rather than signalling a reversal of this continuum of empire-building in reality signified its rehabilitation in accounting for new national and international conditions, and moreover its development into a new more sophisticated and effective world-system under US/Western hegemony. The occurrence of decolonization, however, was symptomatic of the inherent instability of this imperial order. The British Empire was suffering from costly military overstretch and facing increasing indigenous protests against colonial rule. But under decolonization, domestic social, political and economic structures in the fledgling post-colonial states remained fundamentally unchanged, governed now not by the British, but by the most wealthy and powerful sectors of those states. But imperialism continued nevertheless in indirect form, with the Western powers, particular the United States, forging close alliances (and often sponsoring quite directly) ruling cliques in the post-colonial states. This development in the imperial system was perhaps more efficient and effective in securing Western interests than before. In this manner, imperialism became at once more subtle and entrenched: subtle because it continued not through direct control, but through the external manipulation and influence of regional surrogates, often established through covert (and overt) interventions; entrenched because the appearance of independence through decolonization veiled the extent to which domestic structures were still ordered to meet Western interests.

But it is crucial to note that the transition of the imperial system from a colonial to a surrogate method of organization – although rehabilitating and consolidating that system – certainly signified that system's inevitable decline due to its intrinsic contradictions, evidenced by the massive almost simultaneous unrest and uprisings against colonialism. Such a brutal system of unashamed repression and profiteering was thus unsustainable, and decolonization allowed the basic social, political and economic structures of colonial states to be essentially maintained through Western alliances with regional surrogates.

The inherent instability of this imperial system – now governed primarily by the United States and secondarily by other powers through international multilateral institutions such as the United Nations, regional coalitions and regional surrogates – and its tendency to decline has again become increasingly apparent. Undoubtedly, the historical continuum of Western imperialism has repeatedly and directly impacted on Western security by predictably exacerbating anti-Western sentiment throughout the region, which for a few (e.g. al-Qaeda) has translated into devastating reactionary terrorist attacks against Western targets. In particular, ongoing Western hostility in the region only serves to fuel motivations on the part of various Middle East states to acquire and proliferate conventional weapons and weapons of mass destruction in anticipation of military intervention. Thus it is clear that in general terms the phenomena of non-state international terror networks and states developing weapons of mass destruction are a very product of the imperial system, illustrative of its intrinsic self-destructive tendency.

Regarding Iraq, the unprecedented schism in the UN over the US-led 2003 war drive from prominent Security Council members and other UN members – including key US allies such as France, Germany and Russia – rendered that institution completely unworkable for the implementation and/or legitimization of US policy, leaving the US unable to secure the desired UN resolution for the war on Iraq despite enlisting propaganda assistance from Britain, and despite extensive pressure.[512] Meanwhile, indigenous unrest and opposition to US global designs as well as to the repression of US client-regimes is reaching crisis proportions in highly strategic areas. In Saudi Arabia, a key Middle East ally, there were credible reports of the potential toppling of the ruling royal family amidst rising dissatisfaction with tyrannical Saudi domestic and foreign policies. 'Saudi Arabia is teetering on the brink of collapse, fuelling Foreign Office fears of an extremist takeover of one of the West's key allies in the war on terror,' reported the London *Observer* in 2002.

Anti-government demonstrations have swept the desert kingdom in the past months in protest at the pro-American stance of the *de facto* ruler, Prince Abdullah. At the same time, Whitehall officials are concerned that Abdullah could face a palace coup from elements within the royal family sympathetic to al-Qaeda. Saudi sources said the Pentagon had recently sponsored a secret conference to look at options if the royal family fell.[513]

Such indications of a possible coup therefore certainly influenced the formulation of urgent contingency plans for the US invasion of Saudi Arabia. Similarly, fervent US attempts to lobby its crucial (and normally compliant) ally Turkey to allow the country to be used as a springboard for launching US invasion forces against Iraq were, it seemed, facing significant obstacles when the Turkish Government, under unavoidable domestic opposition to the war drive, rebuffed US demands. The *Los Angeles Times* reported that the Grand National Assembly, Turkey's parliament, 'refused to authorize a deployment of 62,000 American soldiers'. The Assembly's top political leader, Recep Tayyip Erdogan, 'balked at a backup proposal to open Turkish airspace to US missiles and warplanes for a bombing campaign in Iraq. But with Turkey's mostly Muslim populace strongly opposed to war and with the country's politics in turmoil, US officials ran out of hope for a reversal of parliament's surprise decision on March 1.'[514] Although Turkey's decision thereafter remained uncertain due to continuing pressure to acquiesce to US demands, the fact remained that a strategic US ally bore extreme reluctance to participate in US regional designs.

Throughout the Middle East, there has been a tangible rise in popular opposition to US policies, threatening the stability of US client-regimes, particularly the Gulf States. As the *Chicago Tribune* observed, the 'same influential voices in Saudi Arabia, Kuwait, Jordan and other Arab states' that once supported US policy 'are openly suspicious of American ambitions in the

Middle East and increasingly pessimistic about the effect of an Iraq War on stability, security and economic growth...'

> Opinion polls show growing opposition to the United States in Arab states with close strategic and economic ties. A December survey by the Pew Research Center found that 75 per cent of Jordanians hold an unfavourable view of the United States, as do 69 per cent of Egyptians and 59 per cent of Lebanese. Even in Qatar, the tiny Gulf state that has risked the ire of its Arab neighbors by welcoming US military forces, there are ripples of resentment toward the United States.
>
> ... A dozen years after US forces liberated Kuwait from Iraqi president Saddam Hussein, Kuwait still holds strong affinity for US visitors and products. But there also is widespread scepticism of American strategic goals, say political observers ... the tide of anti-Americanism is forcing Arab governments to downplay cooperation with the US military build-up. Busloads of troops arriving in Kuwait have been shuttled quietly to remote bases, without press coverage or official comment. Saudi leaders have refused for weeks to say if American forces will be permitted to attack Iraq with the benefit of the Prince Sultan Air Base, home to 4000 American troops.[515]

This inevitable escalating dissent and protest is directed against the crushingly repressive, destructive and unjust impact of Western (specifically Anglo-American) policy in the region, including of course the support of repressive regimes. Such escalating political turmoil fermenting across the region (and beyond) is symptomatic, once again, of the worsening deterioration of the imperial system generally and of the regional framework of order under US hegemony in the Middle East specifically, especially in the Persian Gulf. That systemic deterioration is fatally compounded by the depletion of oil reserves and the decline in oil production in the coming years following on from the 2000/2001 peak. With the world economy structured in a manner that is fundamentally oil-dependent, this peak threatens to eventually bring Anglo-American power – contingent as it is on dominant control of hydrocarbon energy reserves – to an end.

The Bush administration is attempting to counter this overall systemic deterioration by applying its new doctrine of military action. The 'new' doctrine – which in reality builds upon a strategy that has been contemplated by top US strategists over at least a decade if not longer – has been aptly summarized in *Foreign Affairs* by G. John Ikenberry, Peter F. Krogh Professor of Geopolitics and Global Justice at Georgetown University:

> In the shadows of the Bush administration's war on terrorism, sweeping new ideas are circulating about US grand strategy and the restructuring of today's unipolar world. They call for American unilateral and pre-emptive, even preventive, use of force, facilitated if possible by coalitions of the willing.
>
> [T]hese notions form a neo-imperial vision in which the United States arrogates to itself the global role of setting standards, determining threats, using force, and meting out justice ... America's nascent neo-imperial grand strategy threatens to rend the fabric of the international community and political partnerships ... It is an approach fraught with peril and likely to fail. It is not only politically unsustainable but diplomatically harmful. And if history is a guide, it will trigger antagonism and resistance that will leave America in a more hostile and divided world ...
>
> According to this new paradigm, America is to be less bound to its partners and to global rules and institutions while it steps forward to play a more unilateral and anticipatory role ... The United States will use its unrivalled military power to manage the global order ... The neo-imperial thinkers ... seek a radical reordering of America's role in the world. America's commanding unipolar power and the advent of frightening new terrorist threats feed this imperial temptation.[516]

The 'new' imperial doctrine establishes the same unil right to 'pre-emptive' or 'preventive' war employed by Hitler in 1941 against the Soviet Union, and by Japan that year against the US in Pearl Harbor. In doing so, the doctrine destroys one of the most fundamental principles of international law created through the 1648 Treaty of Westphalia, which stipulated that one sovereign state does not intervene in the internal affairs of another. Washington's adoption of the imperial doctrine as *official* national security strategy therefore unambiguously signals the end of the international order constructed since 1945 through the United Nations.[517]

The potential impact of this imperial doctrine can be discerned from elements of US planning *vis-à-vis* the war on Iraq. As far as the Bush administration is concerned, the military operation in Iraq is hoped to be the inception of a regional plan – in the vein of the new imperial doctrine – to control, carve up and restructure the Middle East in accordance with regional interests, particularly the Bush administration's new energy-obsessed national security strategy. The Bush plan envisages that this new grand strategy amounts to the next stage in the historical continuum of Western imperialism, of which Iraq is merely the beginning, the principal aim being to firm up the collapsing international system under US hegemony. Former British Cabinet Minister Mo Mowlam, who was in Prime Minister Tony Blair's government from 1997 to 2001, has described the broad strategic objectives behind the drive for a war on Iraq: 'The key country in the Middle East, as far as the Americans are concerned, is Saudi Arabia: the country with the largest oil reserves in the world, the country that has been prepared to calm the oil markets, producing more when prices are too high and less when there is a glut...'

The Saudi royal family has been rewarded with best friend status by the West for its cooperation. There has been little concern that the government is undemocratic and breaches human rights, nor that it is in the grip of an extreme form of Islam. With American support it has been believed that the regime can be protected and will do what is necessary to secure a supply of oil to the West at reasonably stable prices.

Since September 11, however, it has become increasingly apparent to the US administration that the Saudi regime is vulnerable. Both on the streets and in the leading families, including the royal family, there are increasingly anti-Western voices. Osama bin Laden is just one prominent example. The love affair with America is ending. Reports of the removal of billions of dollars of Saudi investment from the United States may be difficult to quantify, but they are true. The possibility of the world's largest oil reserves falling into the hands of an anti-American, militant Islamist government is becoming ever more likely – and this is unacceptable.

The Americans know they cannot stop such a revolution. They must therefore hope that they can control the Saudi oilfields, if not the government. And what better way to do that than to have a large military force in the field at the time of such disruption. In the name of saving the West, these vital assets could be seized and controlled. No longer would the US have to depend on a corrupt and unpopular royal family to keep it supplied with cheap oil. If there is chaos in the region, the US armed forces could be seen as a global saviour. Under cover of the war on terrorism, the war to secure oil supplies could be waged.[518]

There is good reason to believe that at least in terms of initial planning, the Bush administration hoped that Israel would be heavily involved in this strategy. High-level elements of Israeli governmental, military and intelligence agencies under the Sharon administration have for some time planned to implement an unprecedented invasion of the Occupied Territories by

Israeli forces to 'transfer' a substantial number of the Palestinian population to neighboring Jordan. Elaborating on the probable outcomes of this operation, the authoritative Israeli military historian Professor Martin van Creveld of the Hebrew University in Jerusalem reports that Sharon's near-term goal is the 'transfer' or forcible expulsion of the Palestinian people. 'I think Mr Sharon is waiting for the day when he can throw out all the Palestinians. It is not so very difficult. I think these attacks are playing straight into his hands,' he observed in an interview with the London *Guardian*. 'I think he wants to escalate the situation because he feels there is no way Israel can make peace with the Palestinians, and he is just waiting for the opportunity to throw them all out.' *Guardian* correspondent Suzanne Goldenberg further reported that this notion of 'transfer' was once 'the preserve of the far right. But it has gained greater currency in recent months. Opinion polls last month [April 2002] showed that 44% of the Jewish Israeli population endorsed the mass expulsion of the Palestinians.' With almost half the population backing Sharon's ethnic cleansing strategy, he argues, it could be only a matter of time before the IDF begins to carry it out. 'Israel is becoming desperate,' comments van Creveld, 'and people who even a few months ago would never dream of such a solution are beginning to think it is the only possibility.'[519]

Writing in the London *Telegraph*, Professor Martin van Creveld recounts how Sharon has often alleged that Jordan, having a Palestinian majority even now, amounts to the real Palestinian state, thus advocating that Jordan is the proper destination to which Palestinians must be forcefully 'transferred' – ethnically cleansed. Van Creveld admits that the idea of driving out the entirety of the Palestinian population has always been nurtured by Sharon. All that is required is a pretext, and a cover; US and Israeli military planners, according to Van Creveld, have explored the possibility of exploiting the US assault on Iraq as a

cover for an Israeli 'transfer' operation in the Occupied Territories. Van Creveld recalls, for instance, how Sharon himself
insisted to US Secretary of State Colin Powell that nothing
happening in Israel should delay a US attack on Iraq. Van Creveld also explains that Israel would be able to launch a massive
attack within mere hours if it deems necessary, and outlines one
such scenario:

> First, the country's three ultra-modern submarines would take up
> firing positions out at sea. Borders would be closed, a news
> blackout imposed, and all foreign journalists rounded up and
> confined to a hotel as guests of the government. A force of 12
> divisions, 11 of them armoured, plus various territorial units
> suitable for occupation duties, would be deployed: five against
> Egypt, three against Syria, and one opposite Lebanon. This would
> leave three to face east, as well as enough forces to put a tank
> inside every Arab-Israeli village just in case their populations get
> any funny ideas ... The expulsion of the Palestinians would
> require only a few brigades. They would not drag people out of
> their houses but use heavy artillery to drive them out; the damage
> caused to Jenin would look like a pinprick in comparison.

Egypt, Syria, Lebanon or Iraq would not be able to respond
effectively at all – indeed, any reaction by the entire international community would fail to deter the Sharon administration if it chooses to implement such a plan:

> Saddam Hussein may launch some of the 30 to 40 missiles he
> probably has. The damage they can do, however, is limited.
> Should Saddam be mad enough to resort to weapons of mass
> destruction, then Israel's response would be so 'awesome and
> terrible' (as Yitzhak Shamir, the former prime minister, once said)
> as to defy the imagination ... If Mr Sharon decides to go ahead,
> the only country that can stop him is the United States. The US,
> however, regards itself as being at war with parts of the Muslim

world that have supported Osama bin Laden. America will not necessarily object to that world being taught a lesson – particularly if it could be as swift and brutal as the 1967 campaign; and also particularly if it does not disrupt the flow of oil for too long. Israeli military experts estimate that such a war could be over in just eight days … If the Arab states do not intervene, it will end with the Palestinians expelled and Jordan in ruins. If they do intervene, the result will be the same, with the main Arab armies destroyed. Israel would, of course, take some casualties, especially in the north, where its population would come under fire from Hizbollah. However, their number would be limited, and Israel would stand triumphant, as it did in 1948, 1956, 1967 and 1973.[520]

There is a significant possibility – if not probability – that the course of the Sharon plan, if implemented, would lead to a nuclear conflict with potentially devastating implications for the region and the world. American Pulitzer Prize-winning journalist Seymour Hersh, for instance, observes in a study of Israeli nuclear policy: '… the size and sophistication of Israel's nuclear arsenal allows men such as Ariel Sharon to dream of redrawing the map of the Middle East aided by the implicit threat of nuclear force … Should war break out in the Middle East again … or should any Arab nation fire missiles against Israel, as the Iraqis did, a nuclear escalation, once unthinkable except as a last resort, would now be a strong probability.'[521]

There is little doubt that the ultimate goal of the 'transfer' policy planned by the right-wing Sharon administration is to expand the borders of the state of Israel to engulf the entirety of Palestine and, if possible, beyond. In May 1993 Sharon had proposed at the Likud Convention that: 'Israel should adopt the "Biblical borders" concept as its official policy. There were rather few objections to this proposal, either in the Likud or outside it, and all were based on pragmatic grounds.' The most far-reaching interpretation of these borders include the following areas: 'in the south, all of Sinai and a part of northern Egypt up to the environs of Cairo; in the east, all of Jordan and a large chunk of Saudi Arabia, all of Kuwait and a part of Iraq south of the Euphrates; in the north, all of Lebanon and all of Syria together with a huge part of Turkey (up to lake Van); and in the west, Cyprus.'[522] Although the Sharon plan has been gaining popularity within Israel, there is no doubt that it amounts to a dangerous extremist trend with little legitimacy within the mainstream of authentic Jewish discourse.

Notably, *Jane's Foreign Report* has thrown further light on the joint Bush-Sharon military plan *vis-à-vis* the two theatres of war, Iraq and Palestine. Citing the *Jane's* report, *Ha'aretz* suggests, like Israeli military expert Professor Van Creveld, that the Bush and Sharon administrations were coordinating their respective plans for Iraq and the Occupied Territories, including the possibility that the two planned operations be conducted simultaneously:

> There was something familiar in the story: the prime minister has a 'grand plan' for war with the Palestinians. It will break out at the same time as the US attack on Iraq, about which Israel will receive advance warning. After defeating the Palestinians, Sharon will make them a generous political offer. Is there secret coordination between Sharon and the Bush administration over such a horrifying scenario, like there was over Lebanon 20 years ago?[523]

These sources strongly suggest that the Bush and Sharon administrations — or at least powerful high-level elements thereof — have planned simultaneous operations in the Middle East, namely, Iraq and the Occupied Territories. This, of course, does not guarantee that they will be capable of conducting those plans, and indeed our purpose in analysing these plans here is not to consider the probability of their implementation, but rather their implications regarding the practical connotations of the new imperial doctrine.

The sheer existence of such planning is very revealing with regards to the overall objective and design behind the US war drive in Iraq. The planning behind the military operation in Iraq and the other operations to follow was, it seems, clearly motivated by a fundamental desire to extend and consolidate the mutual economic hegemonies of the United States and Israel, with the latter operating within a strategic framework directed by the former. It was planned that this would be achieved by establishing military control over the resource-rich Middle East, and by implementing a carefully planned carve-up of the region to feed the interests of their respective military-corporate complexes. The US, of course, intended from the beginning to lead the way as the primary hegemon at this current historical conjuncture, with Britain and Israel playing their traditional roles – the former as a junior partner in the American orbit of global power, and the latter as a key regional proxy force in the Middle East.

Elements of the Bush-Sharon carve-up plan were revealed towards the end of 2002 in several reports, including most prominently by Strategic Forecasting (Stratfor), a private US intelligence firm staffed by former US intelligence officials. Stratfor reports on how the US and Israel have planned to manipulate the political fabric of Iraq after the war:

> An idea to unite Jordan and Iraq in a pro-US Hashemite kingdom after a US war is being floated in diplomatic and opposition circles. The plan could be Washington's best scenario for ensuring a stable post-war Iraq ... As a US war against Iraq appears to be nearing, both Washington and Middle Eastern players also are working to make sure the expected American victory will result in strategic long-term gains. The idea of a central Iraq populated by Sunni Arabs joining with Jordan to form one Hashemite kingdom

is being considered as one way to secure such gains. Such a plan reportedly was discussed at an unusual meeting between Crown Prince Hassan of Jordan and pro-US Iraqi Sunni opposition members in London last July. In September, Israeli paper *Yedioth Ahronoth* stated that the US goal in Iraq was to create a united Hashemite kingdom embracing Jordan and Iraq's Sunni areas. Israeli terrorism expert Ehud Sprinzak recently echoed this sentiment on Russian television September 24.[524]

Chairman and founder of Stratfor Dr George Friedman – an internationally recognized expert in national security and intelligence issues who founded the Center for Geopolitical Studies at Louisiana State University – provided in even more detailed analysis of how the Bush administration has hoped to use the military occupation of Iraq as a stepping-stone to the expansion of the US empire throughout the region. 'The 2003 war with Iraq,' he observes, 'is about redefining the status quo in the region. Geopolitically, it will leave countries like Syria and Saudi Arabia completely surrounded by US military forces and Iran partially surrounded.' If successful, 'Washington intends to occupy Iraq militarily, and it officially expects to remain there for at least 18 months – or to be more honest, indefinitely.' To prevent the disintegration of Iraq in the post-war period and prolong its occupation, the US will 'build air bases and deploy substantial ground forces' as well as 'create a puppet government underwritten by US power'.

Thereafter, 'the entire geopolitics of the region will be redefined. Every country bordering Iraq will find not the weakest formations of the Iraqi army along their frontiers, but US and British troops...'

The United States will be able to reach into any country in the region with covert forces based in Iraq, and Washington could threaten overt interventions as well. It would need no permission from regional hosts for the use of facilities, so long as either Turkey or Kuwait will permit transhipment into Iraq. In short, a US victory will change the entire balance of power in the region, from a situation in which the United States must negotiate its way to war to a situation where the United States is free to act as it will. ... The conquest of Iraq will not be a minor event in history. It will represent the introduction of a new imperial power to the Middle East and a redefinition of regional geopolitics based on that power. The United States will move from being an outside power influencing events through coalitions to a regional power that is able to operate effectively on its own.[525]

This would be a significant step towards the consolidation of US global pre-eminence, or in other words, a 'Pax Americana' (as described by the Bush Cabinet think-tank, the Project for the New American Century). Once again, there is considerable evidence that the Bush plan includes a key role for the Sharon administration in a joint regional design that has been formulated over a period of years by various US and Israeli policy planners. Reporting for *Time Magazine* in February 2003, leading US political commentator Joe Klein — a member of the Council on Foreign Relations — observed that: 'Israel is very much embedded in the rationale for war with Iraq. It is part of the argument that dare not speak its name, a fantasy quietly cherished by the neo-conservative faction in the Bush administration and by many leaders of the American Jewish Community.' The US war on Iraq is intended to be the beginning of a whole new era in the Middle East, designed to 'send a message to Syria and Iran about the perils of support for Islamic terrorists', bring an end to the Palestinian problem, and shake the 'wobbly Hashemite monarchy in Jordan'.[526] An authoritative 1996 strategy paper authored by David Wurmser, Director of Middle East Studies at the American Enterprise Institute, published by the Institute for Advanced Strategic and Political Studies (IASPS) based in Jerusalem and Washington DC – a highly influential Israeli think-tank – illustrates how such sentiments are the result of years of intensive planning, referring to how 'Iraq's future will profoundly affect the strategic balance in the Middle East...'

> The battle to dominate and define Iraq is, by extension, the battle to dominate the balance of power in the Levant over the long run ... The United States and Israel can use this competition over Iraq to improve the regional balance of power in favour of regional friends like Jordan ... *Ha'aretz* reported that in Peres' December meetings with top American officials, he even proposed the creation of NATO-style alliance among Israel, Jordan, a post-Saddam Iraq, and Turkey ... The United States must support moves to challenge Syria's position in Lebanon, to undermine Iran, to ensure Turkey's long-term pro-Western tilt and integration into Europe, to support Jordan's efforts in Iraq, and to understand better the dynamics of Saudi succession as they relate to its foreign policy.[527]

Richard Perle, who heads the prominent Pentagon advisory group, the Defense Policy Board, issued a briefing for Pentagon officials in September 2002 that essentially recommended this strategy for US policy in the Middle East. In summary, the goal is: 'all of Palestine as Israel, Jordan as Palestine, and Iraq as the Hashemite kingdom.' US Secretary of Defense Rumsfeld appears to have adopted the strategy, having at around the same time described the West Bank and Gaza as the 'so-called occupied territories' – thereby characterizing all of Palestine as Israeli territory. Describing the virtually indivisible confluence of interests driving this joint Bush-Sharon strategy in the Middle East, former CIA political analyst Kathleen Christison and former Director of the CIA's Office of Regional and Political Analysis Bill Christison record that:

... [T]wo strains of Jewish and Christian fundamentalism have dovetailed into an agenda for a vast imperial project to restructure the Middle East, all further reinforced by the happy coincidence of great oil resources up for grabs and a president and vice-president heavily invested in oil. All of these factors – the dual loyalties of an extensive network of policymakers allied with Israel, the influence of a fanatical wing of Christian fundamentalists, and oil – probably factor in more or less equally to the administration's calculations on the Palestinian-Israeli situation and on war with Iraq.

Kathleen and Bill Christison have offered a detailed review of this rising trend within the US policy-making establishment over the years based on analysing the backgrounds of key figures in the Bush administration.[528] Many other US military intelligence experts have provided further details about the strategic objectives of the Bush-Sharon plan. According to Vincent Cannistraro, former chief of counter-terrorism operations of the CIA: 'Clearly Iraq is not the last phase of what the administration intends to do in the Middle East ... Syria is to be the next target.' The Bush administration thereby plans to 'wean the Jewish lobby away from the Democrats', something which has 'already pretty much happened'.[529]

Former State Department and CIA counter-terrorism expert Larry Johnson also agreed that: 'The administration may be working on the theory that by taking care of a secondary target like Syria, you bring tremendous pressure on primary targets' such as Iran, which may force changes in behaviour 'without resorting to force.' Johnson continues: 'By rights [Iran] should be the next target.'[530]

Former CIA official Robert Baer, who worked in the CIA's Directorate of Operations for over two decades spending most of his career in the Middle East, further observed of the Bush-Sharon master-plan that the Bush cabinet wanted 'to divide up Syria, give part of Iraq to Turkey, overthrow the monarchy in

Saudi Arabia, restore the Hashemites to the Hijaz', a very centre of Saudi Arabian culture. 'The underlying motivation [for this] is Israel. They think the demographics are going badly for Israel, for the US.'[531]

Another State Department official and Middle East expert directly acquainted with White House policy discussions has said that she 'first heard of the plan from ultra-conservative think-tanks...'

> They talked about how the Turks are our friend – let's have Turks invade northern Iraq. Turkey has an alliance with Israel and has difficult relations with Arab states and wants to maintain good relations with Tel Aviv, but it doesn't want to take part in dis-memberment of an Arab state. That's a step too far ... [But] There have been discussions to that effect in the administration. We go back to Hopkirk and the Great Game.

Peter Hopkirk was a British historian who documented the nineteenth-century colonial struggle to control central Asia by Russia and Britain. It is worth noting here that the above testi-monials clearly indicate that one element of the Bush plan from the beginning was to consider allowing Turkey to invade northern Iraq in some manner. As Turkish army chief confirmed near the end of March 2003, 'Turkey will send extra troops into northern Iraq in coordination with the United States, if forces currently there are unable to cope with security concerns.'[532] The State Department official continues:

> It's very romantic, very silly. It's madness I think that they [Douglas Feith, a Defense Department planner and Vice-President Richard Cheney] are living in some sort of nineteenth-century imperial phase where Britain did these things. It was before CNN too. If we try to do these kinds of things we won't be able to travel anywhere in the world. I have heard a lot of horrifyingly scary things from people in the administration who just want to do

things for the sake of pure power, as if there is not a price to pay for it, in taking over the world.[533]

According to one Western diplomat, Syria seems to have caught on to the plan:

> Syria fears Washington would restructure the region in line with its new vision … This vision sees Israeli hegemony as possible after the liquidation of the Palestinian cause and the acceptance of Israel continuing to occupy Syria's Golan Heights and the Shabaa farms. The latter is territory on the Israeli border that Syria says belongs to Lebanon but Israel insists is part of Syria.[534]

Another Bush administration official told the *Washington Post* that opinion on Saudi Arabia is changing rapidly within the US Government, noting that many people recognize that 'Saudi Arabia is a problem'. He further argued that a US invasion of Iraq would eventually lead to a regional transformation, similar to what the US achieved after the Second World War with Germany and Japan. Summarizing the essence of the Bush plan he observed: 'The road to the entire Middle East goes through Baghdad.'[535]

The intervention in Iraq was thus hoped by its planners to signal the commencement of a strategy to establish a new order in the Middle East based on direct military control. Such a strategy might be described as a form of 'post-modern colonialism', packaged deceptively and appealingly as it is in humanitarian slogans focusing public consciousness on the noble ideals of fighting terrorism and securing world peace. Notably, the strategy amounts ultimately not to a new policy, but rather to a return to the method of direct control employed during the colonial era.

The general strategy has perhaps been most bluntly described in a paper delivered in 2000 at the Atlanta Conference by Richard Haass, who in 2001 became Director of Policy Planning at the US State Department. Haass observes that the international system 'is and will likely remain a world of distinct American primacy. No country or group of countries will be in a position to balance American economic, military, and cultural power for the foreseeable future.' But US foreign policy is still confronted with a fundamental question, 'what to do with a surplus of power and the many and considerable advantages this surplus confers on the United States'. One of the key 'building-blocks' of Haass's vision for the future of world order under US primacy is the erosion of the concept of state sovereignty. According to the traditional notion of sovereignty, 'what goes on within the borders of a nation-state is its business and its business alone'. This definition, however, is unsuited to the times. Over the past half century, 'and especially over the past decade, the idea that sovereignty should not be absolute has gained strength'. State sovereignty, Haass argues, should be 'conditional,' i.e., 'linked to how a government treats its own citizens'. When the US decides that a 'government is unable or unwilling to safeguard its citizens' or that 'the inherent contract between the government and the governed is violated' then it falls upon the international community, under US leadership of course, 'to act – be it diplomatically, with sanctions, with aid, or with military force – under the banner of humanitarian intervention'.

But the principal objective of any such international action against a state is not the promotion of democracy or, conversely, the undermining of tyranny. Haass argues that 'mature democracies' act with 'relative restraint towards both their own citizens and their neighbors'. He then concedes that 'promoting democracy' should be a 'consideration' for US foreign policy, 'but not a fundamental one, given that other vital interests often must take precedence'. If considered at all, US foreign policy should target 'immature democracies' that are 'all too prone to being captured by nationalist forces', a term he uses dis-approvingly, perhaps revealing that his concept of 'democracy' precludes 'nationalist' sentiments such as independence, self-determination or control over one's own resources. Citing unjust 'local economic, political, social, and cultural realities' – the structures of which were deliberately established by the Western powers during and after the colonial era – as obstacles to any attempt at democratization, Haass emphasizes that the US should instead focus on 'helping to build ... markets'. Thus, while Haass advocates international action – including military intervention – to counter governments that do not 'safeguard their citizens', at the same time he admits that democracy – defined as acting with 'restraint towards ... [its] own citizens' is not in reality a central concern of US foreign policy. Haass further concludes that 'ambitious objectives, such as promoting multi-ethnic societies or democracy, should normally be avoided'. Rather, other 'vital interests' take precedent, namely, what Haass calls 'economic openness', which is 'defined not only by the movement of goods, capital and services across national lines but also by openness within states, i.e., transparent markets that favour private sector activities', and thus of course the profitable activities of private US corporations and investors. The logical conclusion is that if in securing such 'vital interests in the Persian Gulf or north-east Asia' democracy is undermined, then this is not a problem. Indeed, if 'nationalist forces' repre-senting indigenous interests are caught in the cross-fire of US foreign policy, that is only to the advantage of US interests.

Despite Haass's attempts to veil this strategy in humanitarian jargon designed to lend US goals a benevolent appearance, he summarizes the essence of the strategy in very revealing terms. '[B]uilding and maintaining such an order,' he notes, 'would require sustained effort by the world's most powerful actor, the United States.' This requires Americans to 're-conceive their role from one of a traditional nation-state to an imperial power'. Haass goes on to call for the establishment of an 'informal' American empire, informal because it is to be maintained when possible indirectly, and only through direct means when necessary to stabilize the informal system of indirect control. Referring to the nineteenth-century British Empire as a model, Haass argues that direct coercion or force should be normally used as a last resort to protect this informal system:

> To advocate an imperial foreign policy is to call for a foreign policy that attempts to organize the world along certain principles affecting relations between states and conditions within them. The US role would resemble nineteenth-century Great Britain. Influence would reflect the appeal of American culture, the strength of the American economy, and the attractiveness of the norms being promoted as much as any conscious action of US foreign policy ... Coercion and the use of force would normally be a last resort; what was written by John Gallagher and Ronald Robinson about Britain a century and a half ago, that 'The British policy followed the principle of extending control informally if possible and formally if necessary,' could be applied to the American role at the start of the new century. Indeed, an American empire would have to be informal if it were to succeed if only because American democracy could not underwrite an imperial order that required constant, costly applications of military power.[536]

In the new American century then, according to the State Department's chief policy planner, military power is to be employed to 'extend control formally' when 'informal control' is threatened, a policy considered necessary in the Middle East in particular due to the systemic deterioration already discussed. In other words, post-modern colonialism must be applied when surrogate imperialism fails. The new imperial doctrine is bound to fail, since it is designed to shore up the repressive social, political and economic structures of an imperial system that is collapsing under the weight of its own inherent instability. That collapse began to reach crisis-point decades ago in the middle of the twentieth century, and was temporarily forestalled by the transition to a system of surrogate imperialism managed by the establishment of new international institutions, designed to maintain those structures by proxy. With the system of surrogate imperialism sliding into deepening chaos and decline, it is clear that any attempt to return to a traditional form of imperialism through direct control – in effect a return to British-style colonialism – is bound to fail for the same reasons it failed early in the twentieth century. Here, we are faced with the paradoxical logic of an imperial world order, which of course explains why it is unsustainable and doomed to decline. As noted in *Foreign Policy* in 2002 by Immanuel Wallerstein, Senior Research Scholar at Yale University, 'the United States has been fading as a global power since the 1970s, and the US response to the terrorist attacks has merely accelerated this decline ...'

> The economic, political, and military factors that contributed to US hegemony are the same factors that will inexorably produce the coming US decline ... The hawks believe the United States should act as an imperial power for two reasons. First, the United States can get away with it. And second, if Washington doesn't exert its force, the United States will become increasingly marginalized.
>
> Today, this hawkish position has three expressions: the military assault in Afghanistan, the *de facto* support for the Israeli attempt to liquidate the Palestinian Authority, and the invasion of Iraq ... The hawks' reading of recent events emphasizes that opposition to US actions, while serious, has remained largely verbal ...
>
> But hawk interpretations are wrong and will only contribute to the United States' decline, transforming a gradual descent into a much more rapid and turbulent fall ... there is little doubt that the

United States will continue to decline as a decisive force in world affairs over the next decade. The real question is not whether US hegemony is waning but whether the United States can devise a way to descend gracefully, with minimum damage to the world, and to itself.[537]

There is no doubt that the 11 September terrorist attacks provided the trigger by which the US could pave the way to prop up its declining empire, assisted at first by its principal allies. The Middle East operations, however, are likely to spark unprecedented uprisings in protest throughout the region, and indeed throughout the world; other major world powers such as China, Russia and Europe already view the drive for US global pre-eminence with extreme distaste verging on firm opposition, implicating the prospect of their fevered attempts to counter US policy. If the US-led plan is successful, Europe and Russia will be permanently sidelined from the frontiers of world control, with the latter reserved as a comfortable source of raw materials and markets. Meanwhile, the US stranglehold on China and Japan will be immeasurably strengthened. However, the invasion of Iraq and subsequent interventions will certainly aggravate the decades-long grievances in regions of the world such as the Middle East and elsewhere that have been subject to Western imperialism, and which have contributed to the socio-economic repression that lies at the core of terrorism's psychological mindset. Furthermore, they will once and for all signal the irrelevance of the normative institutions of world order since 1945 (i.e., international law and the United Nations), giving rise to a new world dis-order of international anarchy consisting of new arms races, unprecedented proliferation and the em-boldening of new and existing terrorist networks. It is also probable that such invasions would result in an irreversible and potentially fatal split within the Western alliance, pitting state against state in the race to grab diminishing energy reserves in order to survive in an oil-dependent world economy. In these respects, US and Western security will be further immeasurably endangered.

The Bush-Sharon plan could also lead to a regional nuclear holocaust that could have immediately devastating implications for civilization. The US could end up left to administer Iraq with minimal international cooperation under threat of indigenous resistance and international terror attacks from Al-Qaeda, amidst a regional nuclear war open to exacerbation or intervention from other powers – including North Korea, which might exploit the opportunity to export (as well as use) its nuclear weapons. According to Rtd. Col. Michael Turner: 'These are not remote possibilities, but in my view reasonable, possibly even likely outcomes.'[538]

It is worth emphasizing that as a direct consequence of such operations in the Middle East, international terrorism against Western targets – particularly American, British and Israeli – would certainly rocket to a hitherto unprecedented scale dwarfing the 9/11 atrocities, as shocking and unprecedented as they were. Indeed, American, British and Israeli policy planners no doubt foresee this, but interpret the rise of terrorism as an incidental byproduct of their plans which is of little import compared to the potential strategic, political and economic gains. In this regard, the predictable terror backlash on Western targets, including of course civilians and civilian structures, is seen to be worth tolerating as far as the elite establishment is concerned. While the public thus bears the brunt of policy, the private sector – the elite hopes – will reap the riches. Indeed, elements of this international elite already view terrorism as providing a somewhat useful pretext for the militarization of foreign and domestic policy in the name of fighting terror.[539] This general mindset of indifference, verging on tacit consent, towards the rising trend of terrorism as a direct result of policy has been described well by Stratfor's George Friedman regarding the Bush administration:

> The United States is, of course, well aware that its increased presence in the region will result in greater hostility and increased paramilitary activity against US forces there. However, the US view is that this rising cost is acceptable so long as Washington is able to redefine the behaviour of countries neighboring Iraq. In the long run, the Bush administration believes, geopolitical power will improve US security interests in spite of growing threats. To be more precise, the United States sees Islamic hostility at a certain level as a given, and does not regard an increase in that hostility as materially affecting its interests.[540]

In other words, the powers-that-be are convinced that escalating hostility and terrorist activity as a consequence of their aggressive military posture in the Middle East is irrelevant, since while it may result in increasing civilian deaths and casualties on the part of both Western soldiers and citizens it nevertheless is not seen to be 'materially affecting' their considerable regional 'interests'.

This catastrophic direction of world affairs in the aftermath of (and including) 9/11 is indicative of systemic institutional and ideological flaws at the core of the structure of world order. To divert this direction will require a variety of drastic fundamental transformations in this structure, institutional, ethical and ideological. Such structural change must of course be initiated through intensive grassroots activities designed to transform social interaction and understanding at a local and community level, but nevertheless be constantly oriented towards national and international reform. Perhaps one of the most urgent such changes that must be immediately considered is the necessity of a transition from reliance on fossil fuels to innovative, more environmentally responsible, and more sustainable energy sources. Given the inevitable overall decline of world oil production in the coming years indicating the effective climax of the Oil Age in a few decades, such a transition is a matter of sheer survival for current civilization. The world must move away from oil-dependence towards new forms of technology.

There are many new and viable renewable energy alternatives to hydrocarbons such as conventional oil and gas, implementation of which will accompany ingenious new forms of technology and social organization. Many of these alternative technologies are already being developed. Citing endless academic studies and other authoritative sources documenting the viability – and ultimate superiority – of renewable resources, physicist Fritjof Capra of the University of California, Berkeley, reports that these technologies 'tend to be small-scale and decentralized, responsive to local conditions and designed to increase self-sufficiency, thus providing a maximum degree of flexibility...'

> Solar energy collectors, wind generators, organic farming, regional and local food production and processing, and recycling of waste products are examples ... Such a redirection of technology offers tremendous opportunities for human creativity, entrepreneurship, and initiative. The new technologies are by no means less sophisticated than the old ones, but their sophistication is of a different kind...
> The only way out of the energy crisis is to follow a 'soft energy path', which ... has three main components: conservation of energy by more efficient use, intelligent use of present non-renewable energy sources as 'bridging fuels' during the transition period, and rapid development of soft technologies for energy production from renewable sources. Such a threefold approach would not only be environmentally benign and ecologically balanced; it would also be the most efficient and cheapest energy

policy. A recent Harvard Business School study has stated authoritatively that efficiency improvements and soft technologies are the most economical of all available energy sources, besides providing more and better jobs than any of the other options.[541]

Capra refers specifically to the potentially revolutionary invention of hydrogen fuel cells in explaining the feasibility of a genuinely sustainable and secure economy: 'In particular, the recent development of efficient hydrogen fuel cells promises to inaugurate a new era in energy production – the 'hydrogen economy'.

> ... A fuel cell is an electrochemical device that combines hydrogen with oxygen to produce electricity and water – and nothing else! This makes hydrogen the ultimate clean fuel. At present, several companies around the world are racing to be the first to produce fuel cell systems to supply electricity for our homes and commercial buildings.
>
> At the same time, car companies are developing hydrogen-powered hybrid-electric cars that will revolutionize the automobile industry. The gradual replacement of the US car fleet with these 'hypercars' would eventually save all the oil OPEC now sells and, in addition, would reduce America's CO_3 emissions by about two-thirds![542]

The shift in energy dependence must correspond to a broad transformation of the global patterns of production, consumption and distribution of wealth that ultimately lie behind the rise of poverty and economic instability worldwide. Reviewing the conclusions of former Vice-President of the World Bank and Nobel Prize-winning economist Professor Joseph Stiglitz, *Human Nature Review* observes:

> For most of the world's people, globalization has not worked out as advertised. The fall of the Iron Curtain brought great hopes for development of the Third World, but the reality has been far

crueller. Poverty has increased. The global distribution of wealth has grown more unequal. War and social upheaval have intensified, infectious disease and famine have persisted, and environmental destruction threatens human welfare on a global scale.[543]

Indeed, as Capra rightly and eloquently points out, the concept of security 'needs to be broadened to include considerations such as food security, the security of a healthy environment, social justice, and cultural integrity. In our globally interconnected world, the concept of 'national security' is outdated; there can only be global security...

> A global economic system based on inequity, over-consumption, waste, and exploitation is inherently violent and insecure. An economy based on local self-sufficiency, decentralized renewable energy sources, and the continual cycling of materials will be ecologically and socially sustainable and thus globally secure.[544]

A broad economic transformation designed to tackle such issues will inevitably be the consequence of an ideological shift in the value-system underlying social relations. The profit-oriented materialism that dominates policy-making and the cultural norms of both Western and non-Western societies must give way to a new sensitivity to other individuals and to the environment in which we are situated. That can only occur on the basis of a fundamental re-evaluation of the human condition that recognizes the overarching pre-eminence of moral and spiritual values.[545]

All these paths out of our current civilization impasse briefly alluded to here have already been explored in depth by various academics, scientists and experts around the world. It remains up to us to develop the public pressure necessary to implement urgent programs of research, development and practice in these fields in order to truly tackle and solve the multiple crises facing humanity at this critical historical conjuncture. This, indeed, would be a fitting memorial for those who were so tragically murdered on 11 September 2001.

Postscript: The 'Liberation' of Iraq

As the US military began preparing for the new war on Iraq in January 2003, President George W. Bush rallied US troops with the declaration that 'you will be fighting not to conquer anybody but to liberate people.'[546] Henceforth, the Anglo-American military invasion was characterized by the mass media as a humanitarian intervention designed to bring democracy to the Iraqi people in the process of saving not only them, but the entire civilized world, from the imminent threat of weapons of mass destruction posed by Saddam Hussein's Ba'athist regime.

The First Casualty

Perhaps the first indication that something was amiss in this glorious narrative was the startling testimony of veteran BBC war correspondent Kate Adie on Irish Radio in March 2003, revealing that the Pentagon had threatened to fire on the satellite uplink positions of independent journalists in Iraq (an uplink is a satellite telephone and television method of distributing information). Adie, who covered the 1991 Gulf War, told Irish national broadcaster Tom McGurk on the RTE1 Radio *Sunday Show* that non-embedded journalists could be targeted by the Pentagon:

> I've seen a complete erosion of any kind of acknowledgment that reporters should be able to report as they witness... The Americans ... and I've been talking to the Pentagon ... [which] take[s] the attitude which is entirely hostile to the free spread of information...

I was told by a senior officer in the Pentagon, that if uplinks – that is the television signals out of ... Baghdad, for example – were detected by any planes ... electronic media ... mediums, of the military above Baghdad ... they'd be fired down on. Even if they were journalists... 'Who cares!' They would be 'targeted down,' said the officer... He said: 'Well ... they know this ... they've been warned.' This is threatening freedom of information, before you even get to a war...

The second thing is there was a massive news blackout imposed ... this time the Americans are (a) Asking journalists to go with them, whether they ... have feelings against the war. And therefore if you have views that are skeptical, then you are not to be acceptable. Secondly, they are intending to take control of the Americans' technical equipment ... those uplinks and satellite phones I was talking about. And control access to the airwaves.

And then on top of everything else, there is now a blackout (which was imposed, during the last war, at the beginning of the war) ... ordered by one Mr. Dick Cheney, who is in charge of this. I am enormously pessimistic of the chance of decent on-the-spot reporting, as the war occurs.

Award-winning investigative journalist Phillip Knightley, who was special correspondent for the *Sunday Times* for 20 years, joined Adie on the show, adding that the Pentagon had threatened they 'may find it necessary to bomb areas in which war correspondents are attempting to report from the Iraqi side.'[547]

As the war progressed, the substance of Adie's testimony was increasingly confirmed as journalists were systematically killed, injured and/or mistreated by US forces. The alarming death toll, along with the specific circumstances of the killings, led the international agency Reporters Without Borders (reporters sans frontiérs) to accuse the US military of 'deliberately firing upon journalists.' The agency was referring to the US targeting in Baghdad of the offices of the pan-Arab TV station al-Jazeera and the Palestine Hotel housing foreign journalists, which resulted in the death of three journalists. In an official statement, secretary-general of Reporters Without Borders, Robert Menard, observed that:

> ... it was known that both places contained journalists... Film shot by the French TV station France 3 and descriptions by journalists show the neighbourhood was very quiet at that hour and that the US tank crew took their time, waiting for a couple of minutes and adjusting its gun before opening fire...
>
> This evidence does not match the US version of an attack in self-defence and we can only conclude that the US army deliberately and without warning targeted journalists. US forces must prove that the incident was not a deliberate attack to dissuade or prevent journalists from continuing to report on what is happening in Baghdad.
>
> We are concerned at the US army's increasingly hostile attitude towards journalists, especially those non-embedded in its military units. Army officials have also remained deplorably silent and refused to give any details about what happened when a British ITN TV crew was fired on near Basra on 22 March, killing one journalist and leaving two others missing.
>
> Very many non-embedded journalists have complained about being refused entry to Iraq from Kuwait, threatened with withdrawal of accreditation and being held and interrogated for several hours. One group of non-embedded journalists was held in secret for two days and roughed up by US military police.[548]

Foreign correspondent for the London *Independent*, Robert Fisk, similarly asks: 'Is there some element in the US military that wants to take out journalists?' He cites al-Jazeera journalist Maher Abdullah's recollection that: 'The plane was flying so low that those of us downstairs thought it would land on the roof — that's how close it was. We actually heard the rocket being launched. It was a direct hit — the missile actually exploded against our electrical generator. Tariq died almost at once. Zuheir was injured.'

But far more disturbing, notes Fisk, is the fact that 'the al-Jazeera network – the freest Arab television station, which has incurred the fury of both the Americans and the Iraqi authorities for its live coverage of the war' – had already given the Pentagon the precise co-ordinates locating its Baghdad office two months prior to the attack. al-Jazeera had furthermore been explicitly assured that the bureau would not be attacked:

> Then on Monday, the US State Department's spokesman in Doha, an Arab-American called Nabil Khouri, visited al-Jazeera's offices in the city and, according to a source within the Qatari satellite channel, repeated the Pentagon's assurances. Within 24 hours, the Americans had fired their missile into the Baghdad office.

Referring to the assault on Reuters via the Palestine Hotel 'where more than 200 foreign journalists were staying to cover the war from the Iraqi side' – which occurred only four hours after the al-Jazeera attack – Fisk reports that the US explanation amounted to 'a straightforward lie...'

> General Buford Blount of the US 3rd Infantry Division – whose tanks were on the bridge – announced that his vehicles had come under rocket and rifle fire from snipers in the Palestine Hotel, that his tank had fired a single round at the hotel and that the gunfire had then ceased. The general's statement, however, was untrue. I was driving on a road between the tanks and the hotel at the moment the shell was fired – and heard no shooting. The French videotape of the attack runs for more than four minutes and records absolute silence before the tank's armament is fired. And there were no snipers in the building. Indeed, the dozens of journalists and crews living there – myself included – have watched like hawks to make sure that no armed men should ever use the hotel as an assault point.[549]

The testimony of two Portuguese journalists, Luis Castro and Victor Silva, who work for RTP Portuguese television, perhaps throws some light on the US army policy. The two correspondents entered Iraq in March 2003, traveling to Umm Qasr and Basra with the appropriate 'Unilateral Journalist' accreditation granted by coalition forces' Central Command. On the way to Najaf, they were stopped by the US army's military police to have their accredited identification checked. After being given the all clear to proceed, Castro reports that:

> Suddenly, for no reason, the situation changed... We were ordered down on the ground by the soldiers. They stepped on our hands and backs and handcuffed us...
>
> We were put in our own car. The soldiers used our satellite phones to call their families at home. I begged them to allow me to use my own phone to call my family, but they refused. When I protested, they pushed me to the ground and kicked me in the ribs and legs... A lieutenant in charge of the military police told me, 'My men are like dogs, they are trained only to attack, please try to understand'...
>
> The Americans in Iraq are totally crazy and are afraid of everything that moves. I would have expected this to happen to us at the hands of the Iraqis, but not at the hands of the Americans... The attitude is 'shoot first and ask questions later.'

After four days of being beaten up and deprived of water and food, Castro and Silva were eventually transported to the 101st Airborne Division where they were escorted out of Iraq. Luis Castro commented:

> I have covered 10 wars in the past six years – in Angola, Afghanistan, Zaire, and East Timor. I have been arrested three times in Africa, but have never been subjected to such treatment or been physically beaten before...
>
> I believe the reason we were detained was because we are not

embedded with the US forces. Embedded journalists are always escorted by military minders. What they write is controlled and, through them, the military feeds its own version of the facts to the world. When independent journalists such as us come around, we pose a threat because they cannot control what we write.[550]

The narrative of the war broadcast by the mass media has thus largely failed to report the reality of events in Iraq as a consequence of US invasion and occupation. To derive a glimpse of the truth, it is necessary to dig deeper into the few revelations that have surfaced despite US attempts to establish total information control.

Shock and Awe

The *Washington Post* notes that:

The 'Shock and Awe' aerial bombardment of Baghdad launched by U.S. and British forces today is based on concepts first developed in an obscure 1996 Pentagon publication...

In 'Shock and Awe: Achieving Rapid Dominance,' former military officers Harlan K. Ullman and James Wade sought to formulate a new military strategy that could 'so destroy or so confound the will to resist that an adversary will have no alternative except to accept our strategic aims and military objectives'... The concept appealed to Donald H. Rumsfeld before he became secretary of defense in 2001.[551]

The concept of 'Shock and Awe' as a way of war was meticulously espoused in a dense tome published by the Pentagon-funded National Defence University (NDU) in 1996. Shock and Awe was proposed as a 'revolutionary' new doctrine designed to defeat an adversary's will itself, or in other words, to rapidly overwhelm the adversary with destruction and fear in order to render him demoralized, confused, and hopeless, to the extent that he loses all determination to resist. Thus, the new way of war, rather than focusing on the physical destruction of the enemy's military forces, instead aims at the psychological destruction of the enemy's will to fight by applying huge levels of destruction against selected targets. The principal NDU document on the concept explains that:

> Shock and Awe are actions that create fears, dangers, and destruction that are incomprehensible to the people at large, specific elements/sectors of the threat society, or the leadership. Nature in the form of tornadoes, hurricanes, earthquakes, floods, uncontrolled fires, famine, and disease can engender Shock and Awe. The ultimate military application of Shock and Awe was the use of two atomic weapons against Japan in WW II.[552]

The NDU document further lists specific aspects of civilian infrastructure to be targeted in order to achieve the doctrine's objectives:

> [Options for targeting] could include means of communication, transportation, food production, water supply, and other aspects of infrastructure... (Introduction)

> Shutting the country down would entail both the physical destruction of appropriate infrastructure and the shutdown and control of the flow of all vital information and associated commerce so rapidly as to achieve a level of national shock akin to the effect that dropping nuclear weapons on Hiroshima and Nagasaki had on the Japanese. (Chapter 1)

> ... it would be vitally important to give the appearance that there are no safe havens from attack, and that any target may be attacked at any time with impunity and force. (Chapter 4)

> ... the appropriate balance of Shock and Awe must cause the perception and anticipation of certain defeat and the threat and fear of action that may shut down all or part of the adversary's

society or render his ability to fight useless short of complete physical destruction. (Chapter 5)[553]

Indeed, a Pentagon official briefed on the Shock and Awe plan for Iraq remarked that as a result: 'There will not be a safe place in Baghdad.' Moreover, the principal author of the Shock and Awe doctrine, Harlan Ullman – a military analyst at the Center for Strategic and International Studies – explicitly emphasized that the Shock and Awe doctrine is designed to 'have this simultaneous effect, rather like the nuclear weapons at Hiroshima, not taking days or weeks but in minutes... You also take the city down. By that I mean you get rid of their power, water. In 2, 3, 4, 5 days they are physically, emotionally, and psychologically exhausted.'[554]

In an interview with the *Christian Science Monitor*, Ullman continued:

> You'll see simultaneous attacks of hundreds of warheads, maybe thousands, so that very suddenly the Iraqi senior leadership, or much of it, will be eviscerated...
> At the same time, you'll see forces put into Iraq ... [to] make the situation look virtually hopeless for Saddam Hussein and the leadership... The pressure will continue until we run out of targets... The Japanese quit [in World War II], because they couldn't appreciate that one bomb could do what 500 planes did in a night. That was shock. Now, can you take that level of shock and apply it with conventional weapons? We thought you could.[555]

In a White House press conference, American journalist Russell Mokhiber, concerned about the implication of Operation Shock and Awe for civilian life in Iraq, pointedly asked administration spokesman Ari Fleischer:

> You said last week that, 'Every step will be taken to protect civilian and innocent life in Iraq.' But Pentagon officials have said that

under a battle plan called 'Shock and Awe,' 'there will not be a safe place in Baghdad when we attack.' Baghdad is a city the size of Paris, with five million residents. If there will not be a safe place in Baghdad when we attack, then how do you plan to protect every civilian life?

Ironically, Fleischer was unable to respond except to insist that Mokhiber maintain faith in the Pentagon's sincerity: 'It's well-known how the United States conducts itself in military affairs. We are very proud of the fact that any time force is reluctantly used, the force is applied to military targets and innocents are protected.'[556]

There is no doubt in light of all this that the Shock and Awe war plan for Iraq aimed to rapidly target significant aspects of civilian infrastructure combined with overwhelming force, in a manner that would inevitably create a humanitarian catastrophe designed to subjugate the Iraqi will. Joseph C. Wilson, former Political Advisor to the Commander-in-Chief of United States Armed Forces, Europe (1995–1997), former Deputy Chief of Mission at the U.S. Embassy in Baghdad (1988–91), and acting Ambassador during Operation Desert Shield responsible for the freeing of several hundred American hostages, admitted the following:

> ... before our ground forces get there, there will be the so-called shock and awe air attack, and there have been some military officials who have said that it will be dangerous to be in Baghdad during that time, so we should anticipate ... lots of Iraqi civilian casualties ... you can't drop that much ordinance on a city of four million people without having a lot of civilian casualties. It just can't be done.[557]

But to date, the actual number of civilian casualties has been obfuscated and minimized both by coalition forces, keen to avoid revelations that may damage the war's clean humanitarian image, and by Saddam's administration, desperate to boost its military's flagging morale.

Blood and Tears

Coalition forces under the leadership of the US army managed to successfully invade and occupy Iraq through a combination of policies derived from the Shock and Awe concept: launching more bombs and missiles in the first few days of 'Operation Iraq Freedom' than were used during the first Gulf War, in a massive show of military power; laying siege to key cities by cutting off water and power supplies to the entire population and targeting other elements of civilian infrastructure; instigating numerous indiscriminate massacres of civilians and soldiers, some of which were immense in scale; exploiting the prospects for establishing ties with the entire Ba'athist political-military establishment, except of course Saddam Hussein and his close leadership.

Within 48 hours of the official commencement of the war on Iraq, as many as 800 Tomahawk cruise missiles fell on Baghdad – more than during the entire 1991 Gulf War. US political commentator Professor Ira Chernus of the University of Colorado noted that the 'moral implications' of this strategy 'are horrifying… It's amazing how little talk you hear in the main-stream debate about the number of people who would be killed.' Chernus rightly observed that the two-day bombing campaign would not only cause massive destruction, but would also eliminate sources of power and clean drinking water.[558] Given that the 1991 war resulted in the wholesale destruction of Iraq as a country – described by one UN official as bombing Iraq into the stone age – the untold impact of such an intense bom-bardment within such a short period of time is hard to imagine. There is no doubt that large numbers of Iraqi civilian and military targets were wiped out during this period, although reports emanating from US army-approved 'embedded' journalists obviously ignore – and indeed obviate – the extent of this carnage.

The second noteworthy element is the immediate impact of the initial bombing campaign on the destruction of power and water supplies, which has affected many key cities including Basra and Baghdad. In the London *Guardian*, Arundhati Roy described the siege of Basra in gruesome detail:

> About a million and a half people, 40 per cent of them children. Without clean water, and with very little food ...
>
> After days of enforcing hunger and thirst on the citizens of Basra, the 'Allies' have brought in a few trucks of food and water and positioned them tantalisingly on the outskirts of the city. Desperate people flock to the trucks and fight each other for food. (The water we hear, is being sold. To revitalise the dying economy, you understand.)...
>
> ...[U]nder the loving caress of live TV, 450 tonnes of humanitarian aid – a minuscule fraction of what's actually needed (call it a script prop) – arrived on a British ship, the *Sir Galahad*. Its arrival in the port of Umm Qasr merited a whole day of live TV broadcasts ... Nick Guttmann, head of emergencies for Christian Aid ... said that it would take 32 *Sir Galahads* a day to match the amount of food Iraq was receiving before the bombing began.[559]

UN and relief agencies consequently issued dire warnings of a humanitarian crisis, as 1.2 million people in Basra were at risk due to the Anglo-American siege. The crisis was not alleviated in the aftermath of a US declaration of victory. Towards the end of April 2003, aid agencies were describing basic infrastructure conditions in Baghdad as 'appalling'. With food aid barely trickling into the city, children were seen digging in the street for untreated water, and power had largely yet to be restored. The prolongation of such alarming conditions was instrumental in throwing Iraq into almost complete chaos, as starving civilians desperate to survive began fighting one another and looting over scarce valuables. The predictable anarchy, of course, only exacerbated the humanitarian crisis as the US-led coalition bombing campaign resulted in increasing numbers of civilian deaths and injuries.

The International Committee of the Red Cross (ICRC) reported at the beginning of April that hospitals in Baghdad were 'in danger of being overwhelmed by the huge numbers of wounded people brought in for treatment.' An average of '100 patients an hour' were being taken to the Yarmouk hospital alone, one of around five in the city equipped to treat the war wounded. The situation was worse in the south of the city 'where smaller hospitals were unable to cope with an influx of injured people.' The Red Cross noted that many attacks 'were so close to the hospitals that the wounded were walking in for treatment. The ICRC said they had not kept figures for those injured because emergency admissions had kept coming in.' Indeed, one 48 year old doctor, Osama Saleh al-Duleimi, who has witnessed two previous wars, commented on the huge numbers, stating: 'I've been a doctor for 25 years and this is the worst I've seen in terms of casualty numbers and fatal wounds.'[560]

Casualty figures were so immense that hospitals simply stopped trying to keep count of the escalating numbers of people being treated. The Red Cross stated: 'No one is able to keep accurate statistics of the admitted and transferred war wounded any longer as one emergency arrival follows the other in the hospitals of Baghdad.'[561] When looting broke out throughout the city, however, the situation became extremely grave as the entire medical system began to collapse. The ICRC reported that as a consequence of 'combat damage, looting and fear of anarchy,' there were probably no more hospitals functioning.

'The medical system in Baghdad has virtually collapsed,' stated the Red Cross. 'The ICRC is profoundly alarmed by the chaos currently prevailing in Baghdad and other parts of Iraq. Lawless persons, sometimes armed, have been ransacking and looting even essential public facilities such as hospitals.' Although US-led coalition forces had by now already established control over most of the capital, they did nothing to restore order – although it was US policy that had created the grave conditions conducive to anarchy – a fact criticized by the ICRC noting that this was their duty under the Geneva Conventions: 'In areas under their control, the coalition forces have specific responsibilities as occupying powers under international humanitarian law.'[562] The impact of all this on civilian death and injury tolls is incalculable.

Outside of the major cities of Baghdad and Basra where many embedded journalists were operating, it appears that the crisis is even worse. Red Cross doctors, for instance, reported witnessing 'incredible' levels of civilian casualties in southern Iraq. International Red Cross worker Roland Huguenin confirmed that doctors were 'horrified' by casualties in a hospital in Hilla, 160 kilometres south of Baghdad. 'There has been an incredible number of casualties with very, very serious wounds in the region of Hilla,' he observed. 'We saw that a truck was delivering dozens of totally dismembered dead bodies of women and children. It was an awful sight. It was really very difficult to believe this was happening.'

The dead and injured in Hilla – apparently the result of 'bombs, projectiles' – came from the village of Nasiriyah, where US forces were reportedly involved in heavy fighting. At least 400 people were taken to the Hilla hospital over a period of only two days, far more than the hospital could treat. 'At this stage we cannot comment on the nature of what happened exactly at that place,' noted Dr Huguenin. He continued:

... but it was definitely a different pattern from what we had seen in Basra or Baghdad. There will be investigations I am sure. In the case of Hilla, everybody had very serious wounds and many, many of them small kids and women. We had small toddlers of two or three years of age who had lost their legs, their arms. We have called this a horror... The city is no longer accessible.

Other cities subject to heavy US fighting were soon similarly impossible to access. 'We do not know what is going on in Najaf and Karbala,' stated Huguenin. 'It has become physically impossible for us to reach out to those cities because the major road has become a zone of combat.'[563] A reasonable inference from the context of such reports is that the actual Iraqi civilian death toll as a direct result of the bombing campaign is at a minimum of several thousand, but likely to be many times higher, with an even larger number of injuries. Any realistic assessment of civilian deaths due to war must, however, take into account not only the number of civilians killed through injuries incurred due to a military operation, but also the number of civilians who die in the aftermath of war as a consequence of the long-term impact of a military operation on civilian infrastructure. The death toll directly due to bombing must therefore be examined in tandem with the long-term effects of infrastructural destruction — in terms of the collapse of healthcare, water supplies, power supplies, etc. — compounding the country's already devastated condition due to the first Gulf War, continual Anglo-American bombing, and UN sanctions. Expert projections of *overall* civilian deaths due to the war refer first to deaths caused directly by the coalition bombing campaign, and second to deaths caused by the collapse of essential infrastructure produced by the bombing campaign. In this respect, estimates suggesting a total death toll of several hundred thousand as an overall result of the war are entirely probable. To demonstrate this, we may assess these two aspects of estimating the death toll separately.

On the first aspect, an independent research group, Iraq Body Count (IBC), has conducted one the most systematic surveys of Iraqi civilian casualties as a direct consequence of the war. Since the beginning of the war, the IBC – whose research staff consists of an international network of professors, scholars and journalists – has established a meticulous and exhaustive compilation of every reported civilian death in Iraq caused by coalition military action, based on corroborated reports in credible mainstream media sources worldwide. By mid-June 2003, the IBC found that at a bare minimum, the number of civilian deaths due to coalition intervention in Iraq amounts to 5,546. At a maximum, the IBC concluded, the number of civilian deaths based on media reports is 7,219.[564]

In its mid-June report, *Counting the Human Costs*, the IBC conducted a critical review of all projects to calculate the Iraqi death toll, concluding that, as more evidence is collated, 'the figure could reach 10,000.' John Sloboda, Professor of Psychology at Keele University and an IBC researcher, observed that:

> One of the things we have been criticised for is quoting journalists who are quoting other people. But what we are now finding is that whenever the teams go into Iraq and do a detailed check of the data we had through the press, not only is our data accurate but [it is] often on the low side. The totality is now producing an unassailable sense that there were a hell of a lot of civilian deaths in Iraq.[565]

Similarly, the *Christian Science Monitor* reports that:

> Evidence is mounting to suggest that between 5,000 and 10,000 Iraqi civilians may have died during the recent war, according to researchers involved in independent surveys of the country...
> Such a range would make the Iraq war the deadliest campaign for

noncombatants that US forces have fought since Vietnam. Though it is still too early for anything like a definitive estimate, the surveyors warn, preliminary reports from hospitals, morgues, mosques, and homes point to a level of civilian casualties far exceeding the Gulf War... 'Thousands are dead, thousands are missing, thousands are captured,' says Haidar Taie, head of the tracing department for the Iraqi Red Crescent in Baghdad. 'It is a big disaster.'[566]

These figures should now be put in perspective. Based solely on the reporting of civilian deaths from mainstream media agencies, the IBC calculation inevitably omits civilian deaths that occurred unreported. This problem is compounded by the fact illustrated previously here that media reporting was subject to the US military's attempt to secure total information control. It is made all the worse by the result that many zones of combat in Iraq were lacking – if not utterly devoid of – media access. This increases the possibility that actual figures for civilian deaths could be several times higher.

At this stage, it is essential to further consider the second crucial aspect of estimating total civilian deaths due to the war in terms of the long-term impact of the bombing. This impact includes the breakdown of critical infrastructure leading to increased starvation, impoverishment and disease throughout the country, all of which will lead, as with the first Gulf War, to tens of thousands more deaths over time. Independent surveys of the 1991 war found that 'about 3,500 Iraqi civilians were killed during the war, and another 110,000 died from the after-effects on the country's health and sanitation system', bringing the total to approximately 113,500 overall civilian deaths due to the war.[567] This ratio can be applied to our attempt to estimate overall civilian deaths due to the 2003 war on Iraq, considering that it was clearly far more ferocious in its intensity than the 1991 war: If the number of civilians killed during the 2003 war is far higher – verging on 10,000 – then a realistic projection estimating the *overall* number of deaths including those caused by the 'after-effects on the country's health and sanitation system' of the 2003 war, should amount to approximately several hundred thousand:

	Civilians Killed During War Due to Direct Injury	Civilian Deaths in Aftermath Due to Impact of War on Infrastructure	TOTAL
1991 Gulf War	3,500 (confirmed)	110,000 (confirmed)	113,500 (confirmed)
2003 Gulf War	10,000 (confirmed)	314,300 (probable projection)	324,300 (probable projection)

The above table estimates the number of civilian deaths due to the impact of the war on civilian infrastructure during the 2003 war, based on the proportionality between this figure and the number of civilian deaths during the conflict in the 1991 Gulf War. It assumes that this proportionality is accurate, based on the notion that the 2003 war occurred with at least the same ferocity as the 1991 Gulf War. Based on the facts presented here illustrating that the 2003 war had an even worse impact than the 1991 war, however, this indicates that the above projection of total civilian deaths due to the 2003 war is a reasonably accurate estimate, with the actual figure being probably higher. It is noteworthy that the above projection corresponds with other pre-war projections such as those conducted by the UN.

Regime Change?

Another key element of the US victory was the co-opting of the same Ba'athist regime which the US was purportedly removing.

The leadership of Saddam Hussein and his cabinet was nullified not by abolishing the Ba'athist regime, but by buying it off. As reported in detail by London's *Daily Express*, 'Republican Guard generals betrayed Saddam Hussein in return for huge payments in cash and gold ... In so doing, they allowed the Allies to seize Baghdad virtually without a fight.' Indeed, the head of Saddam's Republic Guard, General Maher Sufyan — who of course played a crucial role in the Ba'athist regime's military repression — was befriended by coalition forces in order to pave the way for the US control of Baghdad. 'Resistance around the capital from six Republican Guard divisions just melted away because the senior commander of Saddam's elite troops defected and ordered his men to give up or go home,' noted the Express. 'He was spirited away by a United States Apache helicopter to a secret location,' one among many from 'the heart of Saddam's inner circle' bought off by coalition forces. 'Working hand-in-hand with MI6 and CIA paramilitaries,' undercover squads of SAS special forces 'were responsible for buying off factions of Saddam's henchmen' and had begun operations before the war, 'contacting Iraqi military, intelligence and secret police leaders to make them change sides ...' The *Daily Express* further reported that:

> The teams carried suitcases full of gold bullion, US dollars, Swiss francs and euros to buy off regime leaders, and threatened to kill those who refused to cooperate ... Intelligence sources have told strategic analysts Stratfor that senior Republican Guard generals and commanders from the Special Republican Guard and the Iraqi security services betrayed Saddam and revealed his location on two occasions, leading to the 'decapitation' raids designed to assassinate him and his senior men. They then cut a secret deal agreeing to surrender in the second week of the war.

Most crucially, these former 'factions of Saddam's henchman,' many of whom belonged to 'the heart of Saddam's inner circle,' were to be doubly rewarded for their defection by remaining in positions of authority within the post-war Iraqi administration. 'US Brigadier-General Vince Brooks ... hinted that those who had cooperated with the coalition may not lose their jobs. 'There will be former military members who will have a role to play in a future Iraq', he said.'[568] In other words, Saddam's Ba'athist regime, including its most prominent and powerful murderers, was to be maintained with US connivance, the only difference being the elimination of the anti-Western leadership of Saddam Hussein.

This was further confirmed by *The Observer*, which interviewed British Defence Secretary Geoff Hoon, who admitted (in the newspaper's words), that: 'Members of the Ba'ath Party who were loyal to Saddam Hussein are to be used to restore order in major Iraqi cities as looting and mob violence threatens to undermine coalition attempts to paint military action against the dictator as a success.' Hoon characterized this policy as allowing the Iraqi people to 'build from the bottom,' and further justified it as follows: 'The administration, although Ba'athist in that anyone who worked for the government had to be a member of the party, [contained] many perfectly decent people who are party members but have not participated in any atrocities and will want to go back to their teaching, medicine or administrative work.'[569]

That, of course, did not explain why the coalition had decided to indiscriminately restore to power Ba'athists likely to have been involved in huge levels of corruption and/or repression, including the re-installation of several notoriously oppressive figures. As Suzanne Goldenberg reported from Baghdad, less than two weeks after the collapse of Saddam's regime:

> ... thousands of members of the Arab Ba'ath Socialist party, the all-too-willing instrument of Saddam, are resuming their roles as the men and women who run Iraq ...

Two thousand policemen – all cardholding party members – have put on the olive green, or the grey-and-white uniforms of traffic wardens, and returned to the streets of Baghdad at America's invitation. Dozens of minders from the information ministry, who spied on foreign journalists for the security agencies, have returned to the Palestine Hotel where most reporters stay, offering their services as translators to unwitting new arrivals. Seasoned bureaucrats at the oil ministry – including the brother of General Amer Saadi, the chemical weapons expert now in American custody – have been offered their jobs back by the US military… [T]he Ba'ath party – whose neighbourhood spy cells were as feared as the state intelligence apparatus – will survive in some form.[570]

There are myriad other examples, such as the appointment of Brigadier-General Zuheir Al-Nuami, 'one of the Hussein regime's top police officers' who headed the police force at Saddam's Interior Ministry, to the post of 'new chief of the city police' in Baghdad;[571] or the installment of Sheikh Muzahim Mustafa Kanan Tamimi as leader of Basra, a former Brigadier-General in Saddam Hussein's army and member of the Ba'ath party.[572] As rightly noted by British military analyst Dan Plesch, senior research fellow at the Royal United Services Institute in London: 'The use of the former regime's police … puts them in the position of sort of starting de-Nazification by rehiring the Gestapo' – a contradiction in terms, of course, which makes clear that the 'de-Nazification' project in Iraq is non-existent.[573]

Meanwhile, popular indigenous opposition to this 'Gestapoization' of Iraq has been put down by US forces with extreme brutality. Agence France Press (AFP) reported, for instance, that in the northern city of Mosul in mid-April, the US responded to protests against the installation of new governor Mahshaan al-Juburi by simply firing indiscriminately into the crowd, massacring large numbers of civilians. 'United States troops have opened fire on a crowd opposed to the US-installed governor in the northern Iraqi city of Mosul, killing at least 10 people and injuring as many as 100, witnesses and doctors said,' reported AFP. The report continued:

> The incident overshadowed the start of US-brokered talks aimed at sketching out a post-Saddam Hussein Iraq... Witnesses reported that US troops had fired into a crowd which was becoming increasingly hostile towards the new governor, Mashaan al-Juburi, as he was making a pro-US speech in the northern oil city... 'There are perhaps 100 wounded and 10 to 12 dead,' Dr Ayad al-Ramadhani said at the city hospital.

The incident was initially completely denied by US authorities: 'US forces in Mosul refused to comment to AFP,' while US Central Command denied military reports of the event and refused to confirm it.[574] Eventually, the incident was admitted, with the qualification by Brigadier-General Vince Brooks that US forces 'fired at demonstrators ... after they came under attack from people shooting guns...'[575] The qualification, however, contradicts credible eye-witness testimony indicating that the US army fired first. One witness, 50-year old Marwan Mohammed told AFP:

> We were at the market place near the government building, where Juburi was making a speech. He said everything would be restored — water, electricity, and that democracy was with the Americans. As for the Americans, they were going through the crowd with their flag. They placed themselves between the civilians and the building. The people moved toward the government building, the children threw stones, the Americans started firing. Then they prevented the people from recovering the bodies.

Another, 37-year-old Ayad Hassun, testified that the crowd interrupted Juburi's speech with cries of 'There is no God but

God, and Muhammad is his prophet.' When Juburi retorted, 'You are with Saddam's fedayeen,' the crowd began to chant, 'The only democracy is to make the Americans leave,' where-upon, according to Hassun, 20 US soldiers escorted Juburi back inside before firing from the building's roof. 'They (the soldiers) climbed on top of the building and first fired at a building near the crowd, with the glass falling on the civilians. People started to throw stones, then the Americans fired at them. Dozens of people fell.'

According to a third witness, 49-year old Abdulrahman Ali, the US soldiers opened fire when they saw the crowd running at the government building.[576]

The testimony of US soldiers further confirms the reality of the war and the ensuing occupation. The London *Evening Standard* observed that: 'By their own admission these American soldiers have killed civilians without hesitation, shot wounded fighters and left others to die in agony.'

Sergeant First Class John Meadows told the Standard: 'You can't distinguish between who's trying to kill you and who's not. Like, the only way to get through s*** like that was to con-centrate on getting through it by killing as many people as you can, people you know are trying to kill you. Killing them first and getting home.'

Specialist (Corporal) Michael Richardson, 22, said: 'There was no dilemma when it came to shooting people who were not in uniform, I just pulled the trigger. It was up close and personal the whole time, there wasn't a big distance. If they were there, they were enemy, whether in uniform or not. Some were, some weren't.'

Specialist Anthony Castillo added: 'When there were civilians there we did the mission that had to be done. When they were there, they were at the wrong spot, so they were considered enemy.'

The GIs also shot civilians at checkpoints. According to Sgt Meadows:

> When they used white flags we were told to stop them at 400 metres out and then strip them down naked then bring them through. Most obeyed the order...
> We knew about others who had problems with [Iraqis] carrying white flags and then opening up on our guys. We knew about every trick they were trying to do. Then they'd use cars to try and drive at us. They were men, women and children. That day we shot up a lot of cars.
> We'd shoot warning shots at them and they'd keep coming, so we'd kill them. We'd fire a warning shot over the top of them or on the road. When people criticize us killing civilians they don't know that a lot of these civilians were combatants, they really were . And they still are.[577]

The use of massacres as a means to crush indigenous protest in order to consolidate a US occupation buttressed through a revamped Ba'athist puppet-regime, illustrates the extent to which 'Operation Iraqi Freedom' was designed to 'liberate' the Iraqi people. Coalition forces under US leadership, it seems, were liaising with the very same hated representatives of the Ba'athist establishment in order to secure US control.

Who will benefit? According to the *Wall Street Journal*, giant US oil companies and their political-military associates, who intend to give themselves 'a large degree of leeway in managing the country's oil fields,'[578] while sidelining the UN to ensure an Anglo-American monopoly on the structure of the post-war Iraqi administration in order to guarantee this 'leeway.'[579] Even worse, in late May, the US and UK governments abruptly reversed their professed plan to 'allow Iraqi opposition forces to form a national assembly and an interim government by the end of the month', according to the *New York Times*. Rather, 'top American and British diplomats leading reconstruction efforts here told exile leaders ... that allied officials would remain in charge of Iraq for an indefinite period.'[580]

Curiously enough, the principal company awarded the contract to manage Iraq's oil industry is the giant American conglomerate Halliburton Corp. – the same company once chaired by Vice-President Dick Cheney. Interviews with Halliburton's most senior executives reveal that Halliburton was recommended as early as October 2002 by the Department of Defence to fulfill the tasks of 'assessing the condition of oil-related infrastructure; cleaning up oil spills or other environmental damage at oil facilities; engineering design and repair or reconstruction of damaged infrastructure; assisting in making facilities operational; distribution of petroleum products; and assisting the Iraqis in resuming Iraqi oil company operations.'[581] Ironically, Halliburton's Brown & Root division also happens – through a 10-year deal signed on December 2001 – to be the main supplier of logistical support to the US military worldwide, in the form of housing, food, water, mail, laundry and heavy equipment, for which the company has to date been paid $3 billion.[582]

Meanwhile, the primary alleged pretext for the war – disarming Saddam's weapons programs – has been discredited by none other than UNMOVIC chief Hans Blix:

> There is evidence that this war was planned well in advance. Sometimes this raises doubts about their attitude to the (weapons) inspections ... I now believe that finding weapons of mass destruction has been relegated, I would say, to fourth place, which is why the United States and Britain are now waging war on Iraq ... you ask yourself a lot of questions when you see the things they did to try and demonstrate that the Iraqis had nuclear weapons, like the fake contract with Niger.[583]

As *The Independent* observed on the tired WMD pretext, the

coalition has found nothing to substantiate their allegations: 'Not one illegal warhead. Not one drum of chemicals. Not one incriminating document. Not one shred of evidence that Iraq has weapons of mass destruction in more than a month of war and occupation.'[584] Indeed, in his final report to the UN Security Council, Hans Blix castigated the American and British governments for assuming that 'something exists' just because it is unaccounted for. He emphasized that the UN inspections team had 'not at any time during the inspections in Iraq found evidence of the continuation or resumption of programs of weapons of mass destruction or significant quantities of pro-scribed items – whether from pre-1991 or later.' Blix also poured scorn on intelligence tip-offs his team received from the West: 'Only in three of those cases did we find anything at all, and in none of these cases were there any weapons of mass destruction, and that shook me a bit, I must say.' Noting that UN inspectors had been promised the best information available, he added: 'I thought – my God, if this is the best intelligence they have and we find nothing, what about the rest?'[585] In an interview with the German daily *Der Tagesspiegel*, Blix went even further in debunking the possibility of weapons of mass destruction in Iraq:

> I am obviously very interested in the question of whether or not there were weapons of mass destruction – and I am beginning to suspect there possibly were none... The fact that [Lt. Gen Amer] al-Saadi [head of Iraq's unconventional weapons pro-grams] surrendered [to US forces] and said there were no weapons of mass destruction has led to me to ask myself whether there actually were any. I don't see why he would still be afraid of the regime, and other leading figures have said the same.[586]

Anglo-American Deception and the Propaganda System

In early June 2003, numerous reports emerged from authoritative intelligence sources confirming that the American and British governments had deliberately deceived their publics in order to generate a pretext for the war on Iraq.

For instance, when Lt. Gen. James Conway, US commander of the 1st Marine Expeditionary Force, was asked about the failure of his Marines to find Iraqi weapons of mass destruction on the basis of claims made by US intelligence, he responded with damning honesty:

> We were simply wrong. It was a surprise to me then, it remains a surprise to me now, that we have not uncovered [nuclear, chemical or biological] weapons [in Iraq] . . . Believe me, it's not for lack of trying. We've been to virtually every ammunition supply point between the Kuwait border and Baghdad, but they're simply not there.[587]

According to retired US military intelligence official Greg Thielmann, director of the Strategic, Proliferation and Military Issues Office in the State Department's Bureau of Intelligence and Research during the months leading up the 2003 war, the Bush administration distorted intelligence and presented conjecture as evidence to justify a US invasion of Iraq. 'What disturbs me deeply is what I think are the disingenuous statements made from the very top about what the intelligence did say. The area of distortion was greatest in the nuclear field,' observed Thielmann, whose office was privy to classified intelligence gathered by the CIA and other agencies about Iraq's chemical, biological and nuclear programs. 'When the administration did talk about specific evidence,' he continued, 'it was basically declassified, sensitive information — it did it in a way that was also not entirely honest.' Thielmann further noted that although the Bush administration frequently suggested that Saddam supported Osama bin Laden's al-Qaeda network, he himself '... was similarly unconvinced of a strong link between al-Qaida and Saddam's government.'[588]

In other words, the administration pressured the US intelligence community to produce disinformation which would create the image of an Iraqi regime posing an imminent nuclear, chemical and biological threat to the entire world. According to *Knight-Ridder Tribune News*, reporting as early as October 2002, over a dozen US military and intelligence sources confirmed that:

> ... administration hawks have exaggerated evidence of the threat that Iraqi leader Saddam Hussein poses – including distorting his links to the al-Qaida terrorist network, have overstated the amount of international support for attacking Iraq and have downplayed the potential repercussions of a new war in the Middle East... [US intelligence officials] charge that the administration squelches dissenting views and that intelligence analysts are under intense pressure to produce reports supporting the White House's argument that Saddam poses such an immediate threat to the United States that pre-emptive military action is necessary. 'Analysts at the working level in the intelligence community are feeling very strong pressure from the Pentagon to cook the intelligence books,' said one official, speaking on condition of anonymity. A dozen other officials echoed his views in interviews. No one who was interviewed disagreed.[589]

The government propaganda campaign was coordinated via the Pentagon's Office of Special Plans (OSP). Larry Johnson, former deputy director of the State Department's Office of Counter Terrorism (1989–93) and former analyst in the CIA's Directorate of Intelligence (1985–1989), described the OSP as 'dangerous for US national security and a threat to world peace,' adding that it 'lied and manipulated intelligence to further its agenda of removing Saddam...' Johnson continued:

> It's a group of ideologues with pre-determined notions of truth and reality. They take bits of intelligence to support their agenda and ignore anything contrary. They should be eliminated... We've entered the world of George Orwell. I'm disgusted. The truth has to be told. We can't allow our leaders to use bogus information to justify war.

Johnson described the idea that Saddam was an 'imminent threat' to the West as 'laughable and idiotic,' noting that many CIA officers were in 'great distress' over the administration's manipulation and distortion of intelligence.[590]

Similar revelations surfaced concerning the Blair government. According to British and US intelligence sources, the UK Defence Intelligence Staff established 'Operation Rockingham' in the Ministry of Defence in 1991 to 'cherry-pick' intelligence that could be used to construe an active Iraqi unconventional weapons program while quashing intelligence proving the very opposite. MI6 and Operation Rockingham supplied skewed information to the Joint Intelligence Committee (JIC), which produced the intelligence dossiers published by the British government to galvanize parliamentary and public opinion in support of war, reported intelligence sources. The sources added that the JIC is essentially a British equivalent of the Pentagon's OSP, explicitly 'following political instructions.' A former US military intelligence officer similarly confirmed that 'this policy was coming from the very highest levels.'[591]

The Bush and Blair administrations must be held to account for such efforts to deliberately deceive both political representatives and the public at large. As the *New York Times* observes:

The problem lay not with intelligence professionals, but with the Bush and Blair administrations...

They wanted a war, so they demanded reports supporting their case, while dismissing contrary evidence... The public was told that Saddam posed an imminent threat. If that claim was fraudulent, the selling of the war is arguably the worst scandal in American political history – worse than Watergate, worse than Iran-contra.

If President Bush and his colleagues are 'not held accountable for its deceptions', continues the NY Times, it is absolutely clear that the US 'political system has become utterly, and perhaps irrevocably, corrupted.'[592] One could say the same for the UK. As British military historian and former newspaper editor Sir Max Hastings remarked, Prime Minister Blair's case for war was 'fraudulent... It is irrelevant that [coalition forces] won the war. The prime minister committed British troops and sacrificed British lives on the basis of a deceit, and it stinks.'[593]

But perhaps the most stinging criticism, equally applicable to the Bush administration, came from Ann Nichol, whose 36-year old son John Cecil – a Royal Marine – died when his helicopter crashed in Kuwait early on in the war. Responding to the US Defence Secretary Donald Rumsfeld's belated admission that weapons of mass destruction might never be found in Iraq, Nichol responded:

If this [WMD pretext] turns out to be a lie, then Tony Blair should resign. He should also be prosecuted under international law as a war criminal. If they don't find any weapons of mass destruction, then this war has been based on a pack of lies, and they have put all of our sons' and daughters' lives on the line for a lie.[594]

The failure of the mass media to have properly critiqued the baseless claims of the Bush and Blair governments in the months leading up to – and even in the aftermath of – the war (despite mountains of facts to the contrary available from open sources) is indicative of the extent to which media institutions have become servile to political propaganda. Furthermore, both the Bush and Blair governments must be held accountable and prosecuted under international law for war crimes and crimes against humanity in Iraq. Indeed, the failure on the part of the US and UK political systems to hold Bush and Blair accountable in this manner is indicative of the corruption of our democratic institutions.[595] If Western publics do not address this matter, then there will only be more humanitarian catastrophes, terrorism and global insecurity in store.

* * *

An objective assessment of the 2003 war on Iraq thus shows clearly that it was nothing less than a brazen colonial enterprise, fundamentally opposed to elementary humanitarian principles, and motivated by longstanding imperial values. Neither the flagrant lies of American and British political leaders, nor the web of distortions woven by a largely subservient mass media, can ultimately gloss over the horrifying reality of what has been wrought in a country that was once the cradle of civilization. The reality, indeed, will not be fully understood as long as US forces continue to brutally police the region and ruthlessly control information. But what has been documented here suffices to prove that it is a moral imperative to not merely oppose the new imperial doctrines espoused and practiced by the Bush administration and its global lackeys, but to endeavor to find viable and just alternatives to these doctrines, as well as to the overarching imperial structure of international relations from which they spring.

5th July 2003

Notes

1. Huntington, Samuel, *Clash of Civilizations: Remaking of World Order*, Simon & Schuster, New York, 1996.
2. *The Times*, 12 September 2001.
3. Huntington, Samuel P., 'The Age of Muslim Wars', *Newsweek*, January 2002, http://www.msnbc.com/news/672440.asp.
4. Policy Planning Staff, 'Review of current trends: US foreign policy', 24 February, 1948, *Foreign Relations of the United States (FRUS)*, Vol. 1, Part 2, pp. 510–29.
5. Cited in Gifford, Prosser, and Louis, W. Roger, (eds.), *The Transfer of Power in Africa: Decolonization 1940–1960*, Yale University Press, London, 1982, p. 261.
6. Cited in ibid., pp. 42, 51.
7. Cited in Kiernan, V. G., *European Empires from Conquest to Collapse, 1815–1960*, Fontana, London, 1982, p. 205.
8. Nkrumah, Kwame, *Neo-Colonialism: The Last Stage of Imperialism*, Thomas Nelson and Sons, London, 1965.
9. Spoken by John Balfour of the British Embassy in Washington to then British Foreign Secretary Ernest Bevin, 9 August 1945, *Documents on British Foreign Policy (DBFP)*, London, 1954, Ser. 2, Vol. 2, pp. 244–5. For an extensive overview of how the US and British powers developed the colonial system into a new order of indirect control, see Curtis, Mark, *The Great Deception: Anglo-American Power and World Order*, Pluto Press, London, 1998.
10. From the series of memoranda of the War and Peace Studies Project of the Council on Foreign Relations (CFR) during the Second World War, whose participants included top government planners and members of the foreign policy establishment; this and the following comments made in the next three paragraphs rely on Shoup, Laurence H., 'Shaping the Postwar World', *Insurgent Sociologist*, Vol. 5, No. 3, Spring 1975, which includes references for the quotes in the next three paragraphs; see also, Shoup, L. and Minter, W., *Imperial Brains Trust*, Monthly Review Press, New York, 1977; Chomsky, Noam, *Towards a New Cold War: Essays on the Current Crisis and How We Got There*, Sinclair Brown, London, 1982.
11. State Department Memorandum, 'Petroleum Policy of the United States', April 1944.

12. Cited in Kolko, Gabriel, *The Politics of War*, Random House, New York, 1968, pp. 302f.

13. See Blair, John, *The Control of Oil*, Pantheon, New York, 1976.

14. See 'Multinational Oil Corporations and US Foreign Policy (MNOC)', Report to the Committee on Foreign Relations, US Senate, 2 January 1975, Government Printing Office, Washington, DC, 1975.

15. Cited in Chomsky, Noam, *Towards a New Cold War*, op. cit., p. 100; for further analyses of the design and execution of US imperial planning as documented in the Pentagon Papers, see Du Boff, Richard B., 'Business Ideology and Foreign Policy', in Chomsky, Noam, and Zinn, Howard, (eds.), *Critical Essays*, published as Volume 5 of the Gravel edition of the Pentagon Papers (Beacon Press, Boston, 1972); see also Dower, John, 'The Superdomino in Postwar Asia' in the same volume; and Chomsky, Noam, 'The Pentagon Papers and US Imperialism in South East Asia', *The Spokesman*, Winter 1972/3; Chomsky, Noam, *For Reasons of State*, op. cit. As Chomsky comments, the central aim espoused in the Pentagon Papers involved the integration of southeast Asia into a US dominated global system that would ensure American 'access to resources', by preventing any possibility of independent domestic utilization of resources. This provided the primary basis for policies towards, for example, Vietnam, under the guise of self-defence against the Communist threat — in actuality the only 'threat' was to American economic hegemony.

16. Kennan, George F., *Memoirs*, Little, Brown, Boston, 1967, p. 361.

17. Cited in Talbott, Strobe, 'Rethinking the Red Menace', *Time*, 1 January 1990.

18. Record of a meeting of the State-Defense Policy Review Group, 16 March 1950, *FRUS*, 1950, Vol. 1, p. 198.

19. Zinn, Howard, *A People's History of the United States*, Harper & Row, New York, 1980, Chapter 16.

20. Bacevich, Andrew J., *American Empire: The Realities and Consequences of US Diplomacy*, Harvard University Press, 2002.

21. Blum, William, 'A Brief History of US Interventions: 1945 to the Present', *Z Magazine*, June 1999. For a thoroughly documented review of such interventions, see Blum, William, *Killing Hope: US Military and CIA Interventions Since World War II*, Common Courage Press, Monroe, Maine, 1995.

22. Bacevich, Andrew, *American Empire*, op. cit.

23. Hadar, Leon T., 'The "Green Peril": Creating the Islamic Fundamentalist Threat', *Policy Analysis*, Cato Institute, No. 177, 27 August 1992.

24. *The Guardian*, 3 February 1995. Similar such quotes from the Western press and academia are cited copiously in Said, Edward, *Covering Islam*, op. cit.

25. Fandy, Mamoun, 'In Focus: Islamists and US Policy', *Foreign Policy In Focus*, Vol. 1, No. 21, December 1996.

26. Mackay, Neil, 'Bush planned Iraq "regime change" before becoming President', *Sunday Herald*, 15 September 2002, http://www.sundayherald.com/27735.

27. Bookman, Jay, 'The president's real goal in Iraq', *Atlanta-Journal Constitution*, 29 September 2002, http://www.accessatlanta.com/ajc/opinion/0902/29bookman.html.

28. For full document, see PNAC Report, *Rebuilding America's Defenses: Strategies, Forces and Resources for a New Century*, Project for the New American Century, Washington, DC, September 2000, http://www.newamericancentury.org/RebuildingAmericasDefenses.pdf.

29. Mackay, Neil, 'Bush planned Iraq "regime change" before becoming President', op. cit.

30. These documents are as follows: *Defense Planning Guidance for the 1994–1999 Fiscal Years* (Draft), Office of the Secretary of Defense, 1992; *Defense Planning Guidance for the 1994–1999 Fiscal Years* (Revised Draft), Office of the Secretary of Defense, 1992; *Defense Strategy for the 1990s*, Office of the Secretary of Defense, 1993; *Defense Planning Guidance for the 2004–2009 Fiscal Years*, Office of the Secretary of Defense, 2002.

31. Armstrong, David, 'Dick Cheney's Song of America: Drafting a plan for global dominance', *Harpers Magazine*, October 2002, Vol. 305, No. 1892.

32. Memorandum by the Acting Chief of the Petroleum Division, 1 June 1945, *FRUS*, 1945, Vol. VIII, p. 54.

33. Introductory paper on the Middle East by the UK, undated [1947], *FRUS*, 1947, Vol. V, p. 569.

34. NSC 5401, quoted in Heikal, Mohammed, *Cutting the Lion's Tail; Suez Through Egyptian Eyes*, Andre Deutsch, London, 1986, p. 38. It is essential to note in this connection that the ongoing Western desire to control Middle East oil has nothing to do with security, and everything to do with the simple maximization of corporate profits. Michael Shuman of the Institute for Policy Studies (IPS) based in Washington, DC, points out in an important study of the subject that 'greater energy efficiency could enable the United States to reduce its dependence on foreign oil supplies and the associated military risks of the Persian Gulf'. For example, 'before the United States sent its troops to Saudi Arabia, it was calculated that investing *a single year's* budget for the Rapid Deployment Force in efficiency improvements could eliminate the United States' need for Middle East oil, as well as the risks posed by the force itself'. In other words, 'had the United States invested as much as a quarter of the price it is paying for the war against Iraq on

energy savings, the country could have permanently unplugged itself from Persian Gulf oil. Just increasing the efficiency of American cars by three miles per gallon could replace all US oil imports from Iraq and Kuwait.' (Shuman, Michael, 'Participatory peace policies', in Hartman, Chester, and Vilanova, Pedro, *Paradigms Lost: The Post Cold War Era*, Pluto Press, London, 1992, p. 133).

35. Spoken by John Balfour of the British Embassy in Washington, to Bevin, 9 August 1945, *DBFP*, Ser. 2, Vol. 2, pp. 244–5.

36. By Orme Sargent, 'Stocktaking after VE Day', 11 July 1945; refer to Ross, Graham, (ed.), *The Foreign Office and the Kremlin: British documents on Anglo-Soviet relations 1941–45*, Cambridge University Press, Cambridge, 1984, p. 211.

37. File FO 371/132 779. 'Future Policy in the Persian Gulf', 15 January 1958, FO 371/132 778.

38. Aburish, Said K., *A Brutal Friendship: The West and the Arab Elite*, Indigo, London, 1998.

39. Ibid.

40. Greer, Edward, 'The Hidden History of the Iraq War', *Monthly Review*, May 1991.

41. Stivers, William, *Supremacy and Oil: Iraq, Turkey, and the Anglo-American World Order, 1918–1930*, Cornell University Press, Ithaca, 1982, p. 28, 34.

42. Cited in Curtis, Mark, *The Great Deception*, op. cit., p. 147.

43. Public Statement, 'Do Not Bomb Iraq', Committee On the Middle East (COME), December 1997.

44. Also see Aburish, Said K., *A Brutal Friendship*, op. cit., for an analysis of the West's self-interested infiltration and manipulation of the Middle East, continuing to this day, including the creation and subsequent control of impotent but repressive Arab states such as Saudi Arabia, Iraq, Lebanon, Syria, Egypt, etc. Also of some relevance in this regard is Kayali, Hasan, *Arabs and Young Turks: The Ottoman Empire 1908–1918*, University of California Press, Berkeley, 1997.

45. Cited in Curtis, Mark, *The Great Deception*, op. cit., p. 127.

46. Fandy, Marmoun, 'US Policy in the Middle East', *Foreign Policy In Focus*, Vol. 2, No. 4, January 1997.

47. COME, 'Towards a New Middle East', Washington, DC, January 1998, http://www.MiddleEast.Org/come.htm.

48. Smith, J. W., *World's Wasted Wealth II: Save Our Wealth, Save Our Environment*, Institute for Economic Democracy, Cambria, CA, 1994, p. 294.

49. Curtis, *The Great Deception*, op. cit., p. 128–9.

50. For first-hand accounts of the Anglo-American backed coup by the MI6 and CIA officials responsible for it, see Woodhouse, C. M., *Something Ventured*, Granada, London, 1982; Roosevelt,

Kermit, *Countercoup: The struggle for the control of Iran*, McGraw Hill, London, 1979.

51. Pike, John, 'Minister of Security SAVAK', Federation of American Scientists Intelligence Resource Program, 16 January 2000, http://www.fas.org/irp/world/iran/savak.

52. For a more detailed refutation of this notion based on declassified documents, see Curtis, Mark, *The Ambiguities of Power: British Foreign Policy Since 1945*, Zed, London, 1995.

53. G. Middleton to A. Eden, 23 September 1952, PRO, FO 248/ 1531.

54. US Embassy Tehran dispatch, 19 May 1953, PRO, FO 371/ 104566. These two documents cited in Curtis, *The Ambiguities of Power*, op. cit.

55. Cited in Blum, William, *The CIA: A forgotten history*, Zed, London, 1986.

56. *New York Times*, 6 August 1954. See Chomsky, *Towards a New Cold War*, op. cit. where this report is cited with useful commentary.

57. Armstrong, Karen, *The Battle for God: Fundamentalism in Judaism, Christianity and Islam*, HarperCollins, London, 2001, p. 245.

58. Curtis, *The Ambiguities of Power*, op. cit.

59. Armstrong, Karen, *The Battle for God*, op. cit., p. 299.

60. Curtis, *The Ambiguities of Power*, op. cit.

61. Foran, John, *Fragile Resistance: Social Transformation in Iran from 1500 to the Revolution*, West View Press, Oxford, 1993. This book won awards from the Middle East Studies Association, the American Sociological Association, and the Pacific Sociological Association.

62. Pishevar, Shervin, *Centralization of Power and Dictatorship in Modern Iran: Prelude to Collapse*, LeaderNet, http://www.leadernet.org/Articles/pishevar1.htm. Shervin Pishevar is founder and editor-in-chief of the peer-reviewed research journal *Berkeley Scientific* and is the Director of Global Outreach, and Co-founder and Chair of the Board of Directors of the American scholarly research group LeaderNet.

63. Cited in ibid., p. 95; Pishevar, Shervin, *Centralization of Power and Dictatorship in Modern Iran: Prelude to Collapse*, op. cit.

64. Rubin, Barry, *Paved with Good Intentions: The American experience and Iran*, Oxford University Press, Oxford, 1980, p. 67.

65. Cited in Curtis, *The Ambiguities of Power*, op. cit., p. 95.

66. Ibid., p. 96.

67. Pike, John, 'Minister of Security SAVAK', op. cit.

68. Baraheni, Reza, *The Crowned Cannibals: Writings on Repression in Iran*, Vintage Books, New York, 1977.

69. Armstrong, Karen, *The Battle for God*, op. cit., p. 246.

70. Cited in Kolko, Gabriel, *Confronting the Third World: United States foreign policy 1945–1980*, Pantheon, New York, 1988.

71. Kissinger, Henry, *The White House Years*, Little, Brown & Co., Boston, 1979.
72. Cited in Sick, Gary, *All Fall Down: America's Fateful Encounter with Iran*, London, 1985, p. 30.
73. Cited in Milani, Mohsen M., *The Making of Iran's Islamic Revolution: From Monarchy to Islamic Republic*, Westview Press, Boulder, 1988, p. 77.
74. Cited in Curtis, *The Great Deception*, op. cit., p. 129.
75. See especially Aburish, Said K., *A Brutal Friendship*, op. cit., for an extensive and well-documented review of this process.
76. Curtis, *The Ambiguities of Power*, op. cit.
77. Cited in Chomsky, Noam, *Deterring Democracy*, Vintage, London, 1995, p. 55.
78. Armstrong, *The Battle for God*, op. cit., p. 248.
79. Shariati studied at the University of Mashad and at the Sorbonne, where he had studied the work of French orientalist Louis Massignon, existentialist Jean-Paul Sartre, and anti-imperialist Frantz Fanon.
80. Momen, Moojem, *An Introduction to Shii Islam: The History and Doctrines of Twelver Shiism*, London, 1985, p. 254.
81. Fischer, Michael J., 'Imam Khomeini: Four Levels of Understanding', in Esposito, John, (ed.), *Voices of Resurgent Islam*, Oxford, 1983, p. 159.
82. Keddie, Nikki R., *Roots of Revolution: An Interpretive History of Modern Iran*, London, 1981, p. 243.
83. Sick, *All Fall Down*, op. cit., p. 51; Keddi, *Roots of Revolution*, op. cit., p. 250.
84. Sick, *All Fall Down*, op. cit., p. 51.
85. *Washington Post*, 25–30 October 1980; cited in Chomsky, *Towards a New Cold War*, op. cit.
86. Armstrong, *The Battle for God*, op. cit., p. 323. Also see Fischer, 'Imam Khomeini: Four Levels of Understanding', op. cit., p. 171.
87. Armstrong, *The Battle for God*, op. cit., pp. 325–6.
88. President Jimmy Carter, State of the Union Address, 23 January 1980.
89. Keane, John, 'Power-Sharing Islam?', in Tamini, Azzam, (ed.), *Power-Sharing Islam?*, Liberty for Muslim World Publications, London, 1993.
90. Pilger, John, 'Squeezed to death', *The Guardian*, 4 March 2000.
91. Cited in editorial, 'An Open Eye on Baghdad', *New York Times*, 5 May 1980.
92. Timmerman, Kenneth R., *The Death Lobby: How the West Armed Iraq*, Houghton Mifflin, Boston, 1991, pp. 76–7.
93. *Saddam's War: The Origins of the Kuwait Conflict and the International Response*, Faber and Faber, London, 1991, pp. 75–6.
94. Former Assistant Secretary of Defense Noel Koch, cited in 'At

War, Iraq Courted US into Economic Embrace', *Washington Post*, 16 September 1990.

95. Wright, Robin, 'Hypocrisy Seen in US Stand on Iraqi Arms', *Los Angeles Times*, 16 February 1998.

96. Ibid.

97. See 'The War Machine', International Broadcasting Trust (IBT), 1994.

98. Hartung, William D., 'US Weapons at War: US Arms Deliveries to Regions of Conflict', World Policy Institute, May 1995. Also see discussion of these matters in Pilger, John, *Hidden Agendas*, Vintage, London, 1998.

99. Jentleson, Bruce W., *With Friends Like These: Reagan, Bush and Saddam, 1982–1980*, W.W. Norton & Company, London, 1994.

100. US Congress, House of Representatives, Committee on Government Operations, 'US Government Controls on Sales to Iraq', hearing before the Commerce, and Monetary Affairs Subcommittee', 101st Congress, 2nd Session, 27 September 1990, p. 386.

101. Timmerman, *The Death Lobby*, op. cit., pp. 157–60.

102. Congressman Henry Gonzalez (D-Texas) statement in the *Congressional Record*, 10 August 1992, pp. H 7871–82.

103. Gonzalez, *Congressional Record*, 21 July 1992, pp. H 6338–46.

104. Jentleson, Bruce W., *With Friends Like These*, op. cit.

105. 'US Documents Dispute Bush on Iraq A-Arms', *Los Angeles Times*, 2 July 1992; *Congressional Record*, 21 July 1992, p. H6341; 'Iraq Got US Technology After CIA Warned Baker', *Los Angeles Times*, 22 July 1992.

106. Testimony of David Kay, Gary Milhollin and Kenneth Timmerman in US Congress, Senate Committee on Banking, Housing, and Urban Affairs, 'United States Export Policy Toward Iraq Prior to Iraq's Invasion of Kuwait', Hearing, 102nd Congress, 2nd Session, 27 October 1992, p. 81.

107. 'Dozens of US Items Used in Iraqi Arms', *Washington Post*, 22 July 1992.

108. Shultz, George P., *Turmoil and Triumph: My Years as Secretary of State*, Charles Scribner's Sons, New York, 1993, p. 238.

109. UN, Security Council, Document S/16433, 'Report of the Specialists Appointed by the Secretary-General to Investigate Allegations by the Islamic Republic of Iran Concerning Use of Chemical Weapons', 26 March 1984.

110. Axelgard, Frederick W., *A New Iraq? The Gulf War and Implications for US Policy*, Praeger, New York, 1988, p. 41.

111. US Congress, Senate, Committee on Foreign Relations, 'War in the Persian Gulf: the US Takes Sides', Staff Report 100–160, 100th Congress, 1st Session, 1987, p. 16.

112. 'Poison Gas Attack Kills Kurds', *Washington Post*, 24 March 1988.

113. US Congress, Senate, Committee on Foreign Relations, 'Civil War in Iraq', Staff Report (S. Rpt. 102–27), 102nd Congress, 1st Session, May 1991, p. 13.

114. US State Department Memorandum, 'US-Iraqi Relations: Implications of Passage of Economic Sanctions Bill', 18 October 1988.

115. 'Approved Licenses to Iraq, 1985–1990', US Department of Commerce.

116. US Congress, House of Representatives, Committee on Ways and Means, 'Adminstration and Enforcement of US Export Control Programs', hearing before the Subcommittee on Oversight, 102nd Congress, 1st Session, 18 April and 1 May 1991, p. 466.

117. 'US Gave Iraq Bacteria, Sen. McCain Charges', *Washington Post*, 26 January 1989.

118. US Congress, House of Representatives, Committee on Ways and Means, 'Adminstration and Enforcement of US Export Control Programs', hearing before the Subcommittee on Oversight, 102nd Congress, 1st Session, 18 April and 1 May 1991, p. 466.

119. US Congress, Senate, Committee on Foreign Relations, 'United States Policy Toward Iraq: Human Rights, Weapons, Proliferation and International Law', Hearing, 121st Congress, 2nd Session, 15 June 1990, p. 60.

120. US Congress, General Accounting Office, 'Iraq's Participation in US Agricultural Export Programs', GAO/NSIAD–91–76, November 1990.

121. US Department of Energy, 'Petroleum Supply Annual', Energy Information Administration, Office of Oil and Gas, 1981–90; 'Discount Prices on Imports of Iraqi Oil, 1988–1990', document provided by US Congress, House of Representatives, Committee on Energy and Commerce, Subcommittee on Energy and Power to Bruce W. Jentleson.

122. US Department of Energy, 'Imports from Iraq', 26 August 1992; US Congress, House of Representatives, 'Discount Prices on Imports of Iraqi Oil, 1988–1990', Committee on Energy and Commerce, Subcommittee on Energy and Power.

123. US General Accounting Office, 'Iraq's Participation in US Agricultural Export Programs', p. 15.

124. US State Department Memorandum, 'US-Iraqi Relations: Implications of Passage of Economic Sanctions Bill', 18 October 1988.

125. Canason, Joe, 'The Iraq Lobby', *The New Republic*, 1 October 1990; Waas, Murray, 'What We Gave Saddam for Christmas', *Village Voice*, 18 December 1990, included in US Congress, House of Representatives, Committee on Government Operations, 'US Government Controls on Sales to Iraq', hearing before the Commerce, Consumer and Monetary Affairs Subcommittee, 101st Congress, 2nd Session, 27 September 1990, pp. 300–310; Timmerman, *The Death Lobby*, pp. 219–23, 305–08.

126. Many of the internal US documents cited in this section can be found in Jentleson, Bruce W., *With Friends Like These: Reagan, Bush and Saddam, 1982–1980*, W.W. Norton & Company, London, 1994, See this book for more on US policies towards Iraq up to the Gulf War. Jentleson chooses not to draw conclusions about the structure of US democracy in light of the systematically anti-humanitarian nature of US policies; subsequently, I would argue that his advice concerning US policy changes is solely oriented towards finding a better way of appeasing US interests. However, Jentleson hardly ever compromises on facts, and his study therefore suffices as a most lucid documentation of US policies towards Iraq. In his failure to comprehend the implications of his own analysis, however, in regard to the inherent orientation of US policies towards corporate interests – or rather, in his failure to see this as a genuine flaw in need of drastic change – Jentleson betrays his effectively pro-elite standpoint. His conclusions are therefore conditioned by this standpoint. Also see Aburish, Said K., *A Brutal Friendship*, op. cit., pp. 98–102; Rezun, Miron, *Saddam Hussein's Gulf Wars*, Praeger, 1992; Phythian, Mark, *Arming Iraq: How the US and Britain Secretly Built Saddam's War Machine*, Northeastern University, 1997. For a further insight into the horrifying policies of repression and torture that the West supported by propping up Saddam, see Al-Hilli, Walid, *Human Rights in Iraq 1968–1988*, London, 1990.

127. Bennis, Phyllis, 'And They Called It Peace: US Policy on Iraq', Iraq: A Decade of Invasion, *Middle East Report 215*, Middle East Research and Information Network (MERIP), Washington, DC, Summer 2000, http://www.merip.org/mer/mer215/mer215.html.

128. Dreyfuss, Robert, 'The Thirty Year Itch', *Mother Jones Magazine*, March/April 2003, http://www.motherjones.com/news/feature/2003/10/ma_273_01.html.

129. Aburish, Said K., *A Brutal Friendship: The West and the Arab Elite*, op. cit.

130. Morris, Roger, 'A Tyrant 40 Years in the Making', *New York Times*, 14 March 2003.

131. Ibid.

132. Aburish, Said K., *A Brutal Friendship: The West and the Arab Elite*, op. cit.

133. Ibid.

134. Morris, Roger, 'A Tyrant 40 Years in the Making,' op. cit.

135. Cited in Curtis, *The Great Deception*, op. cit., p. 129.

136. See especially Frank, Andre Gunder, *Third World War: A Political Economy of the Gulf War and the New World Order*, The Andre Gunder Frank Archive, 20 May 1991, http://rrojasdatabank.info/agfrank/gulf_war.html.

137. *Washington Post*, 12 February 1990.

138. *Washington Post*, 16 June 1990.
139. *Los Angeles Times*, 11 July 1990.
140. Gallup, Alec M., 'The Gallup Poll: Public Opinion 1990', in *The Gallup Poll Cumulative Index: Public Opinion, 1935–1997*, Scholarly Resources, Wilmington, DE, 1999.
141. Webster, William, 'Threat Assessment; Military Strategy; and Operational Requirements', Testimony to Senate Committee on Armed Services, 23 January 1990, 60. Credit to Blum, William, *Killing Hope: US Military and CIA Interventions Since World War II*, op. cit., Chapter 52 for his data and analysis on this topic.
142. Schwarzkopf, H. Norman, 'Threat Assessment; Military Strategy; and Operational Requirement', Testimony to Senate Committee on Armed Services, 8 February 1990, 577–9.
143. United States Army, 'A Strategic Force for the 1990s and Beyond', January 1990, by General Carl E. Vuono, US Army Chief of Staff, 1–17.
144. Mathews, Tom, et al., 'The Road to War', *Newsweek*, 28 January 1991.
145. Blackwell, Major James, *Thunder in the Desert: The Strategy and Tactics of the Persian Gulf War*, Bantam Books, New York, 1991, pp. 86–7.
146. Ibid., pp. 85–6. Also see *Newsweek*, 29 January 1991; 'Triumph Without Victory: The Unreported History of the Persian Gulf War', *US News and World Report/Times Books*, 1992, pp. 29–30; *Air Force Magazine*, Arlington, March 1991, p. 82.
147. *Los Angeles Times*, 5 August 1990. Credit to Blum, *Killing Hope*, op. cit. for his data on war simulations.
148. Boyle, Francis A., 'International War Crimes: The Search for Justice', symposium at Albany Law School, 27 February 1992; reprinted as 'US War Crimes During the Gulf War', *New Dawn Magazine*, September–October 1992, No. 15.
149. See Frank, op. cit., Blum, op. cit. and Clark, Ramsey, *The Fire This Time: US War Crimes in the Gulf*, Thunder's Mouth Press, New York, 1992, for further documentation on this subject.
150. Dreyfuss, Robert, 'The Thirty Year Itch', op. cit.
151. Schuler, G. Henry, 'Congress Must Take a Hard Look at Iraq's Charges Against Kuwait', *Los Angeles Times*, 2 December 1990.
152. Salinger, Pierre, and Laurent, Eric, (Howard Curtis [trans.]), *Secret Dossier: The Hidden Agenda Behind the Gulf War*, Penguin Books, New York, 1991.
153. Pelletiere, Stephen C., et al., *Iraqi Power and US Security in the Middle East*, Strategic Studies Institute, US Army War College, Carlisle, PA.
154. Salinger and Laurent, *Secret Dossier*, op. cit.
155. Clark, Ramsey, *The Fire This Time: US War Crimes in the Gulf*, Thunder's Mouth Press, New York, 1992.

156. Royce, Knut, 'A Trail of Distortion Against Iraq', *Newsday*, 21 January 1991.

157. Hayes, Thomas, 'Big Oilfield is at the Heart of Iraq-Kuwait Dispute', *New York Times*, 3 September 1990. Also see Schuler, G. Henry, 'Congress Must Take a Hard Look at Iraq's Charges Against Kuwait', op. cit.

158. Graz, Liesi, *Middle East International*, 3 August 1990; energy specialist Henry Schuler cited in Hayes, Thomas, *New York Times*, 3 September 1990.

159. 'Note from the Iraqi Minister of Foreign Affairs, Mr Tariq Aziz, to the Secretary-General of the Arab League, July 15, 1990', in Salinger, Pierre and Laurent, Eric, *Secret Dossier*, op. cit., Appendix 1, pp. 223–4.

160. *San Francisco Chronicle*, 13 March 1991.

161. Frankel, Glenn, 'Imperialist Legacy; Lines in the Sand', *Washington Post*, 31 August 1990.

162. Kuwaiti Intelligence Memorandum, labelled top secret, from Brigadier General Fahd Ahmad Al-Fahd, Director-General of the State Security Department, to Sheikh Salem Al-Sabah, Minister of the Interior, November 1989. Iraq claimed that its forces had discovered the document from Kuwait's Internal Security Bureau.

163. *Los Angeles Times*, 1 November 1990.

164. *Washington Post*, 19 August 1990.

165. Clark, Ramsey, *The Fire This Time*, op. cit.

166. *Christian Science Monitor*, 5 February 1991.

167. Viorst, Milton, 'A Reporter at Large: After the Liberation', *The New Yorker*, 30 September 1991.

168. *Village Voice*, 5 March 1991. Also cited in *International Viewpoint*, 15 April l991.

169. Emery, Michael, 'How Mr Bush Got His War', in Ruggiero, Greg, and Sahulka, Stuart, (eds.), *Open Fire*, The New Press, New York, 1993, pp. 39–40, 52, based on Emery's interview with King Hussein, 19 February 1991, in Jordan.

170. Viorst, Milton, 'A Reporter At Large: After the Liberation', op. cit.

171. Cited in Clark, Ramsey, *The Fire This Time*, op. cit.

172. Viorst, Milton, 'A Reporter At Large: After the Liberation', op. cit., p. 66.

173. Boyle, Francis A., 'International War Crimes: The Search for Justice', op. cit.

174. *New York Times*, 23 September 1990, 17 July 1991; *The Independent*, 30 December 2000.

175. As the highest ranking CIA official to go public, Stockwell is the founding member of Peaceways and the Association for Responsible Dissent (ARDIS – an organization of former CIA and US government officials who are openly critical of the CIA's activities). A former US Marine Corps major, he was

hired by the CIA in 1964, spent six years working for the CIA in Africa, and was later transferred to Vietnam. In 1973 he received the CIA's Medal of Merit, the Agency's second highest award. In 1975, he was promoted to the CIA's Chief of Station and National Security Council coordinator, managing covert activities during the first years of Angola's bloody civil war. After two years he resigned, a 13-year CIA veteran determined to reveal the truth about the Agency's role in the Third World. Since that time, he has worked tirelessly to expose the criminal activities of the CIA particularly and US foreign policy in general.

176. Stockwell, John, 'The CIA and the Gulf War', speech delivered at Louden Nelson Community Center, Santa Cruz, California, 20 February 1991, http://www.cia.com/au/serendipity.

177. 'Developments in the Middle East', Hearing before the Sub-committee on Europe and the Middle East of the House Committee on Foreign Affairs, 31 July 1990, p. 14.

178. Fisk, Robert, 'Saddam Hussein: The last great tyrant', *The Independent*, 30 December 2000.

179. Waas, Murray, 'Who Lost Kuwait? How the Bush Administration Bungled its Way to War in the Gulf', *Village Voice*, 22 January 1991, p. 30.

180. *New York Daily News*, 29 September 1991.

181. 'Setting the American Trap for Hussein', *International Herald Tribune*, 11 March 1991.

182. H. Res. 86, 21 February 1991, included in the printed report: ISBN 0-944-624-15-4.

183. Clark, Ramsey, *The Fire This Time*, op. cit., p. 37, p. 12.

184. Zunes, Stephen, 'The Gulf War: Eight Myths', Special Report, *Foreign Policy in Focus*, January 2001.

185. Bennis, Phyllis, 'And They Called It Peace: US Policy on Iraq', Iraq: A Decade of Devastation, *Middle East Report* 215, Summer 2000.

186. EIU Report, *Iraq: Country Report 1995–96*, Economist Intelligence Unit, London, 1996.

187. ICRC Report, *Iraq: A Decade of Sanctions*, International Committee of the Red Cross, December 1999.

188. CESR Report, *UN Sanctioned Suffering*, Center for Economic and Social Rights, New York, May 1996, http://www.cesr.org.

189. Schoenman, Ralph, *Iraq and Kuwait: A History Suppressed*, Veritas Press, Santa Barbara, CA, pp. 11–12; *New York Review of Books*, 16 January 1992, p. 51.

190. Zunes, Stephen, 'The Gulf War: Eight Myths', op. cit.

191. Cited in Tyler, Patrick, 'US Strategy Plan Calls for Insuring No Rivals Develop', *New York Times*, 8 March 1992.

192. Peterson, Scott, 'In war, some facts less factual', *Christian Science*

Monitor, 6 September 2002, http://www.csmonitor.com/2002/ 0906/p01s02-wosc.html. My thanks to John Leonard for forwarding me the last two references.

193. *New York Times*, 9 August 1990.
194. *New York Times*, 22 August 1990.
195. Zunes, 'The Gulf War: Eight Myths', op. cit.
196. Parry, Robert, 'The Peace Feeler That Was', *The Nation*, 15 April 1991, pp. 480–2; *Newsweek*, 10 September 1990; *Los Angeles Times*, 20 October 1990.
197. Royce, Knut, 'Middle East crisis secret offer: Iraq sent pullout deal to US', *Newsday*, 29 August 1990.
198. *Newsweek*, 10 September 1990.
199. 'Iraq offers deal to quit Kuwait', *Newsday*, 3 January 1991; 'Rumours of a deal emerge', *International Herald Tribunal*, 4 January 1991.
200. See Curtis, *The Ambiguities of Power*, op. cit., pp. 194–6.
201. Emery, Michael, *Village Voice*, 5 March 1991.
202. Blum, William, *Killing Hope: US Military and CIA Interventions Since World War II*, Common Courage Press, Monroe, Maine, 1995, Chapter 52: Iraq 1990–91 – Desert Holocaust.
203. Ibid.
204. *Los Angeles Times*, 3 August 1990; *Washington Post*, 3 August 1990.
205. *Washington Post*, 10 August 1990.
206. *Los Angeles Times*, 2 October 1990.
207. *The Gallup Poll, Public Opinion 1989*, Wilmington, DE, 1990; *Wall Street Journal*, 21 November 1990.
208. *The Gallup Poll, Public Opinion 1991*, Wilmington, DE, 1992.
209. *New York Times*, 23 September 1990.
210. Dreyfuss, Robert, 'The Thirty Year Itch', op. cit.
211. US General Accounting Office, Cruise Missiles: Proven Capability Should Affect Aircraft and Force Structure Requirements, 04/20/95, GAO/NSIAD–95–116. Cited in Abunimah, Ali, letter to National Public Radio News, 25 January 1999, http:// www.abunimah.org/nprletters/nprindex.html.
212. Blum, William, *Killing Hope*, op. cit., Chapter 52.
213. MEW Report, *Needless deaths in the Gulf War: Civilian casualties during the air campaign and violations of the laws of war*, Middle East Watch (Human Rights Watch), New York, 1991, p. 133.
214. 'Killing is killing – not kindness', *New Statesman and Society*, 17 January 1992.
215. 'Gulf War "will haunt Iraqi children forever"', *The Guardian*, 23 October 1991.
216. MEW Report, *Needless deaths in the Gulf War*, op. cit., pp. 201–24; *The Los Angeles Times*, 31 January 1991, 3 February 1991.
217. MEW Report, op. cit., p. 128–47. Also see Clark, Ramsey, *The Fire This Time*, op. cit., pp. 70–72.

218. *The Gulf War and its Aftermath*, The 1992 Information Please Almanac, Boston, 1992, p. 974.

219. Clark, *The Fire This Time*, op. cit., pp. 70–72; Martin, Miriam, Gulf Peace Team, Interviews submitted to Clark Commission, Sati-Castek-Martin, 1992.

220. Marcy, Sam, 'Damage to the infrastructure: civil defense: the Amariyah bomb shelter', in Clark, Ramsey, (ed.), *Challenge to Genocide: Let Iraq Live*, International Action Center, New York, September 1998.

221. IAC Press Release, 'Did the US Intentionally Bomb Civilians in Basra, Iraq?', International Action Center, New York, 26 January 1999; Becker, Brian, 'Pentagon admits bombing Iraqi civilians', Workers World News Service, 4 February 1999.

222. Boyle, Francis A., 'International War Crimes: The Search for Justice', op. cit.

223. Clark, Ramsey, et. al, *War Crimes: A Report on United States War Crimes Against Iraq*, Commission of Inquiry for the International War Crimes Tribunal, New York, ISBN 0-944624-15-4.

224. *The Gulf War and its Aftermath*, The 1992 Information Please Almanac, Boston, 1992, p. 974.

225. *Washington Post*, 23 June 1991.

226. Chomsky, Noam, *Deterring Democracy*, Vintage, London, 1992.

227. See HRW Report, *Weapons Transfers and Violations of the Laws of War in Turkey*, Human Rights Watch, New York, November 1995; HRW Report, *Forced Displacement of Ethnic Kurds from Southeastern Turkey*, Human Rights Watch, New York, October 1994.

228. Ibid.

229. US House of Representatives, Select Committee on Intelligence, 19 January 1976 (Pike Report). Cited in *Village Voice,* 16 February 1976. Also see Safire, William, *Safire's Washington,* New York, Times Books, 1980, p. 333.

230. al-Khalil, Samir, *Republic of Fear: The Inside Story of Saddam's Iraq*, University of California Press, Berkeley, 1989, p. 23.

231. IAC Press Release, 'Did the US Intentionally Bomb Civilians in Basra, Iraq?', op. cit.; Becker, Brian, 'Pentagon admits bombing Iraqi civilians', op. cit.

232. For instance, *Newsweek* (3 September 1990) reports Bush's approval, right from the outset, of a CIA plan to overthrow Saddam. See Chomsky, *Deterring Democracy*, op. cit. Afterword.

233. Friedman, Thomas, *New York Times*, 7 July 1991. Credit to Chomsky's *Deterring Democracy* for his analysis of this report.

234. International Development Select Committee, 'The Future of Sanctions', 10 February 2000, http://www.publications.parliament.uk/pa/cm199900/cmselect/cmintdev/67/6707.htm.

235. Dickie, John, *'Special' No More – Anglo-American Relations: Rhetoric and Reality*, Weidenfeld & Nicolson, London, 1993, pp. 201–2.

236. Cited in Curtis, *The Great Deception*, op. cit., p. 177.

237. US Defense Intelligence Agency, 'Iraq Water Treatment Vulnerabilities', 22 January 1991. Available on Pentagon website, http://www.gulflink.osd.mil. Cited in Nagy, Thomas J., 'The Secret Behind the Sanctions: How the US Intentionally Destroyed Iraq's Water Supply', *The Progressive*, September 2001. Also available at http://www.globalresearch.ca/articles/NAG108A.html.

238. US Defense Intelligence Agency, 'Disease Information', 22 January 1991. Available on Pentagon website, http://www.gulflink.osd.mil. Cited in Nagy, Thomas J., 'The Secret Behind the Sanctions', op. cit.

239. US Defense Intelligence Agency, 'Disease Outbreaks in Iraq', 21 February 1991. Available on Pentagon website, http://www.gulflink.osd.mil. Cited in Nagy, Thomas J., 'The Secret Behind the Sanctions', op. cit.

240. US Defense Intelligence Agency, 'Medical Problems in Iraq', 15 March 1991. Available on Pentagon website, http://www.gulflink.osd.mil. Cited in Nagy, Thomas J., 'The Secret Behind the Sanctions', op. cit.

241. US Defense Intelligence Agency, 'Status of Disease at Refugee Camps', May 1991. Available on Pentagon website, http://www.gulflink.osd.mil. Cited in Nagy, Thomas J., 'The Secret Behind the Sanctions', op. cit.

242. US Defense Intelligence Agency, 'Health Conditions in Iraq', June 1991. Available on Pentagon website, http://www.gulflink.osd.mil. Cited in Nagy, Thomas J., 'The Secret Behind the Sanctions', op. cit.

243. Ibid.

244. Graham-Brown, Sarah, 'Economic sanctions and the future of Iraq', Centre for the Advancement of Arab-British Understanding (CAABU), Briefing on Iraq for British Parliamentarians, London, 29 February 2000, http://www.caabu.org/press/briefings/economic_sanctions.html.

245. Ibid.

246. International Development Select Committee, 'The Future of Sanctions', op. cit.

247. Graham-Brown, Sarah, 'Economic sanctions and the future of Iraq', op. cit.

248. Concluding observations of the Human Rights Committee: Iraq. 19/11/97. CCPR/C/79/Add.84., http://www.unhchr.ch/tbs/doc.nsf/MasterFrameView/4c6e0bf385b5c8f6802565530050e6b5?Opendocument.

249. Concluding observations of the Committee on the Rights of the

Child: Iraq, October 1998. CRC/C/15/Add.94,
http://www.unhchr.ch/tbs/doc.nsf/(Symbol)/
CRC.C.15.Add.94.En?OpenDocument.

250. Report of the second panel established pursuant to the note by the president of the Security Council of 30 January 1999 (S/1999/100), concerning the current humanitarian situation in Iraq, http://www.un.org/Depts/oip/panelrep.html.

251. Report can be viewed at http://www.cam.ac.uk/societies/casi/info/undocs/sanct31.pdf.

252. United Nations Sub-Commission on the Promotion and Protection of Human Rights, 'Humanitarian Situation of the Iraqi People', 18 August 2000 [E/CN.4/Sub.2/2000/L.32].

253. Cited online at Voices in the Wilderness UK, March 2002, http://www.viwuk.freeserve.co.uk.

254. *Philadelphia Enquirer*, 1 April 1999.

255. McDowell, Rick, 'Genocide Against Iraq', *Catholic Worker Magazine*, January/February 1998.

256. UN figures cited by Dennis Halliday, former director of UN humanitarian operations in Iraq, in Cohen, Dara, 'Halliday lectures on the impact of economic sanctions', *Brown Daily Herald*, 15 November 1999, http://www.browndailyherald.com/stories.cfm?S=2&ID=681. There have been various attempts by apologists for the sanctions regime to deny the validity of UN figures on deaths by sanctions in Iraq. British journalist John Sweeney, for example, argues that: 'In 1999 Unicef, in cooperation with the Iraqi Government, made a retrospective projection of 500,000 excess child deaths in the 1990s. The projection is open to question. It was based on data from within a regime that tortures children with impunity. All but one of the researchers used by Unicef were employees of the Ministry of Health, according to The Lancet.' (Sweeney, John, 'How Saddam "Staged" Fake Baby Funerals', *The Observer*, 23 June 2002.) It is true that the Iraqi Government's own figures almost certainly are incorrect. However, UNICEF's figures are known to be largely reliable since the entire survey including the processes of data collection and analysis were thoroughly monitored and overseen by UNICEF. Former UN official Hans von Sponeck has explained further: 'Sweeney's article is exactly the kind of journalism that is Orwellian, double-speak. No doubt, the Iraq Government has manipulated data to suit its own purposes. Everyone of the protagonists unfortunately does this. A journalist should not. UNICEF has used large numbers of international researchers and applied sophisticated methods to get these important figures. Yes, the Ministry of Health personnel cooperated with UNICEF but ultimately it was UNICEF and UNICEF alone which carried out the data analysis exactly because they did not want to politicize their work... This article is a very serious misrepresentation'

(Media Lens Alert, 'John Sweeney of *The Observer* and the BBC on Iraq', Media Lens, 24 June 2002, http://www.medialens.org). Sponeck also noted in a response to Sweeney that: 'Unfortunately it is very difficult to get any statistics on Iraq which are as rigorously researched as would professionally be desirable. This includes the available mortality figures. You are, however, very wrong in your assessment of the UNICEF analysis. UNICEF, of course, cooperated with the Government but methodology of analysis and the findings is UNICEF's. A large team of UNICEF professionals subjected the data to rigorous review to avoid what you have not avoided and that is a politicization of statistical material.' (Media Lens Alert, 'John Sweeney Responds on Mass Death in Iraq', Media Lens, 28 June 2002.) For detailed elaboration of UNICEF's methodology see 'UNICEF: Questions and Answers for the Iraq Child Mortality Survey', UNICEF: Relief-Web, 16 August 1999, available at http://www.cam.ac.uk/societies/casi/info/unicef/000816qa.html. It is worth adding that *The Lancet*, which Sweeney implies rubbished the UNICEF survey, endorsed it as a thorough and reliable analysis: 'Assessment of data quality... Achieving high quality data was a primary goal and several steps were taken to ensure that the data collected would yield reliable estimates of childhood mortality... The quality of data was undertaken by an independent panel which reviewed both the procedures used and the quality of various aspects of data. No problems were detected.' (Ali, Mohamed M., and Shah, Iqbal H., 'Sanctions and childhood mortality in Iraq', *The Lancet*, 27 May 2000, Vol. 355, No. 9218.)

257. Garfield, Richard, 'Morbidity and Mortality Among Iraqi Children from 1990 Through 1998: Assessing the Impact of the Gulf War and Economic Sanctions', Colombia University, New York, March 1999, available at http://www.cam.ac.uk/societies/casi/info/garfield/dr-garfield.html.

258. Mueller, John, and Mueller, Karl, 'The Methodology of Mass Destruction: Assessing Threats in the New World Order', *Journal of Strategic Studies*, Vol. 23, No. 1, 2000, pp. 163–87.

259. UNICEF, 1995, http://leb.net/IAC/unicef.html.

260. UN Food and Agricultural Organization, September 1995.

261. World Health Organization (WHO), March 1996.

262. UNICEF, October 1996, gopher://gopher.unicef.org/00/.cefdat/.prgva96/.prgva35.

263. UNICEF and World Food Program (WFP), May 1997, available on the Internet at gopher://gopher.unicef.org/00/.cefdat/.prgva97/.prgva11.

264. UNICEF, November 1997, http://unicef.org/newsline/97pr60.htm.

265. UNICEF, April 1998, http://leb.net/IAC/UNICEF1998.html.

266. UN Report on the Current Humanitarian Situation in Iraq [S/

1999/356], submitted to the Security Council, March 1999, http://www.un.org/Debts/oip/panelrep.html.

267. McDowell, Rick, 'Genocide Against Iraq', op. cit.
268. UN Report on the Current Humanitarian Situation in Iraq [S/1999/356], op. cit.
269. Ibid.
270. McDowell, Rick, 'Genocide Against Iraq', op. cit.
271. UN Report on the Current Humanitarian Situation in Iraq [S/1999/356], op. cit.
272. Ibid.
273. Cited in Lennon, Shunna, 'Sanctions, Genocide and War Crimes', Paper presented to the International Law Association, New Zealand, 29 February 2000, available at ZNet, http://www.zmag.org
274. Gonsalves, Sean, 'Hussein and the Hoodwinks', *Cape Cod Times*, June 2001.
275. Mutawi, Abdullah, 'Iraq and the Corruption of Human Rights Discourse', *Middle East International*, London, 11 February 2000.
276. UN Report on the Current Humanitarian Situation in Iraq, [S/1999/356], op. cit.
277. Ibid.
278. See McDowell, op. cit.
279. http://www.un.org/Depts/ oip/reports/phase8_180.html.
280. http://www.un.org/News/briefings/docs/2000/20001019.myatbriefing.doc.html.
281. http://www.un.org/Docs/sc/reports/2000/520e.pdf.
282. World Health Organization (WHO), February 1997.
283. UNICEF, November 1997, http://unicef.org/newsline/97pr60.htm.
284. UNICEF, April 1998, http://leb.net/IAC/UNICEF1998.html.
285. Reuters, 31 March 1999. Also see Gustafson, Erik, 'US Oil Industry and Congress Attack Oil-for-Food Program in Iraq', Monthly Report of the Education for Peace in Iraq Center (EPIC), March 1999.
286. Cited in Pilger, John, 'Squeezed to death', *The Guardian*, 4 March 2000.
287. UNICEF Child and Maternal Mortality Survey 1999, Preliminary Report; UNICEF Press Release, 12 August 1999; Halliday cited in Abuminah, Ali, Letter to National Public Radio (NPR), 30 December 1998, http://www.abuminah.org/nprletters/nprindex.html.
288. Dennis Halliday in an interview with David Edwards, 'Half a Million Children Under Five are Dead and Dying in Iraq – Who is Responsible?', ZNet, March 2000, http://www.zmag.org.
289. Stone, Michael, Letter to *The Independent*, 18 December 1998.
290. World Summary, 'UN aid official quits', *The Times*, 15 February

2000, p. 16. Note that the miniscule *Times* report also adds the following redundant qualification, that von Sponeck 'has been criticized by America and Britain for being lenient with Iraq'. The qualification is meaningless, for what is meant by 'America and Britain'? What is of course meant is that elements in the political leadership of these two countries 'criticized' the former senior UN aid official, 'for being lenient with Iraq'. The charge is nonsensical because the political leadership is in no position to know the facts on the ground in Iraq to the same level as the most senior UN aid official in the country, who has spent 17 months there fulfilling the duties of his post. Who is in a better position to understand the distribution of supplies in Iraq? The most senior UN aid official on the ground – not to mention his predecessor? Or Clinton and Blair sitting in their offices?

291. Agence France Presse, 16 February 2000.

292. Cited in Arnove, Anthony, 'Iraq: Smart Sanctions and the US Propaganda War', ZNet Commentary, 21 May 2002, http://www.zmag.org.

293. Cited in Pilger, John, *The New Rulers of the World*, Verso, London, 2002, p. 59.

294. UNICEF Child and Maternal Mortality Survey 1999, Preliminary Report; UNICEF Press Release, 12 August 1999; letter to the *New York Times* by Professor Richard Garfield, 13 August 1999; 'The Suffering of Innocents', *Washington Post*, August 17, 1999; sources evaluated by Education for Peace in Iraq Center (EPIC), http://leb.net/epic/News/index.html. The Western political fabrications were to such an extent that it was even alleged, as EPIC reports, that: 'Kuwaiti authorities stopped a ship containing baby powder, bottles, and other products coming from Iraq. The State Department immediately alleged that Saddam Hussein was selling products, including baby formula, bought under the Oil-for-Food program to get rich instead of using them to feed his people. It was later revealed that there was no baby formula or food of any kind on the ship, and that the ship was returning goods bought under the program because they were of substandard quality.' Gulf War veteran and Director of EPIC observes: 'The US Administration is evading responsibility for its part in the deaths of half a million children under sanctions by obscuring evidence about the real problems with the Oil-for-Food program, problems which have been documented and confirmed by various UN agencies and independent experts.' (See EPIC url cited above.)

295. Cited in Pilger, John, 'Iraq: yet again they are lying to us', *New Statesman*, 20 March 2000.

296. Dennis Halliday in an interview with David Edwards, 'Half a Million Children are Dead and Dying in Iraq – Who is Responsible?', op. cit.

297. *New Statesman*, 22 January 2001.
298. Herring, Eric, 'Between Iraq and a Hard Place: A Critique of the British Government's Narrative on UN Economic Sanctions', *Review of International Studies*, January 2002, Vol. 28, No. 1, pp. 39–56. Draft version published in September 1999, Department of Politics, University of Bristol, http://www.firethistime.org/herring.htm.
299. Ibid.
300. Ibid.
301. Sloan, Sara, 'Sanctions, Covert Action, Destabilization and Bombings: US Plan to Overthrow the Government of Iraq', International Action Center, New York, 23 August 1999.
302. *60 minutes*, 12 May 1996.
303. International Development Select Committee, 'The Future of Sanctions', op. cit.
304. US/UN sanctions list, Voices in the Wilderness, Chicago; Davidson, Elias, 'A List of Prohibited Items into Iraq', Iraq Action Coalition, 22 December 1997, http://www.iraqaction/list.html#sb. Also see Simons, Geoff, *The Scourging of Iraq*, St Martin's Press.
305. From transcript of Dennis Halliday's speech, 'Why I Resigned My UN Post in Protest of Sanctions', at Havard University in Cambridge, Massachusetts, November 1998. Transcript recorded by Chris Nicholson of the Campaign for the Iraqi People.
306. Cited in Pilger, John, 'Squeezed to death', op. cit.
307. Scott Ritter in an interview with CBN, 30 March 1999.
308. Clinton cited in Husseini, Sam, 'Twisted Policy on Iraq', Institute for Public Accuracy, January 1999. This position was echoed by Britain. 'We must nail the absurd claim,' declared British Foreign Secretary Robin Cook, 'that sanctions are responsible for the suffering of the Iraqi people.' (Cited in Pilger, John, *New Statesman*, 20 March 2000.)
309. Robert M. Gates cited in Gates, Pickering, 'US Sanctions Threat Takes UN by Surprise', *Los Angeles Times*, 9 May 1991.
310. Albright cited in *Washington Post*, 26 January 1999.
311. *Washington Post*, 28 January 1999.
312. *New York Times*, 25 September 1999.
313. *New Statesman*, 22 January 2001.
314. International Conference on Nutrition, World Declaration on Nutrition, FAO/WHO, 1992.
315. Constitution of WHO, 1946.
316. Protocol 1 Additional to the Geneva Conventions – 1977, Part IV, Section 1, Chapter III, Article 54.
317. UN General Assembly Resolution 44/215, 22 December 1989.
318. Mutawi, Abdullah, 'Iraq and the Corruption of Human Rights Discourse', *Middle East International*, London, 11 February 2000.

319. IAC Press Release, 'Ramsey Clark: Charges Against US, British and UN leaders', International Court On Crimes Against Humanity Committed by the UN Security Council on Iraq, Madrid, 16–17 November 1996, http://www.iacenter.org/warcrime/charges.htm. Those charged with 'genocide, crimes against humanity, the use of a weapon of mass destruction and other crimes specified' are: 'The United States of America, President Bill Clinton, Secretary of State Warren Christopher, Secretary of Defense William Perry, US Ambassador to the United Nations, Madeleine Albright, State Department Spokesman, Nicholas Burns, the United Kingdom Prime Minister John Major; aided and abetted by United Nations Secretary General Boutros Boutros Ghali, Rolf Ekeus, Chairman of UN Special Commission on Iraq, and each Member Nation of the Security Council and its UN Ambassador from 1991 to date that failed to act affirmatively to relieve death and suffering caused by United Nations Sanctions against the People of Iraq; and others to be named.' As Ramsey Clark notes, the US 'blames Saddam Hussein and Iraq for the effects [on the Iraqi people], most recently arguing that if Saddam stopped spending billions on his military machine and palaces for the elite, he could afford to feed his people. But only a fool would offer or believe such propaganda. If Iraq is spending billions on the military, then the sanctions are obviously not working. Malnutrition didn't exist in Iraq before the sanctions. If Saddam Hussein is building palaces, he intends to stay. Meanwhile, an entire nation is suffering. Hundreds are dying daily and millions are threatened in Iraq, because of US-compelled impoverishment.' (Clark, Ramsey, *The Fire This Time: US War Crimes in the Gulf*, Thunder's Mouth Press, New York, p. 10.) See Lennon, Shunna, 'Sanctions, Genocide and War Crimes', paper presented to the International Law Association, New Zealand, 29 February 2000, available at ZNet, http://www.zmag.org, for a devastating legal analysis of the sanctions.

320. Childers, Erskine, 'United Nations Mechanisms for Intervention and Prospects for Reform', paper presented to the Life and Peace Institute, Sweden, May 1992, pp. 7–8.

321. See Chomsky, Noam, *Deterring Democracy*, Vintage, London, 1992, Afterword, Segment 4/14.

322. Tachell, Peter, 'West Papua's guerilla war', Observer Foreign News Service, 22 August 1979.

323. Ahmed, Nafeez Mosaddeq, 'Indonesia, East Timor and the Western Powers: A Case Study of the Role of Western Foreign Policy in Conflict Creation and Peace Sabotage', Institute for Policy Research and Development, Brighton, December 2001, http://www.globalresearch.org/view_article.php?aid=781428659.

324. 'What Really Happened in Iraq?', *The Coastal Post*, November 1996.

325. *The Times*, 25 September 1998; cited in Masud, Enver, 'Israel's Willing Executioners', The Wisdom Fund, Arlington, 11 November 1998, http://www.twf.org, and in Masud, Enver, 'Should US Bomb Israel's Chemical, Biological Plant', ibid., 1 October 1998. Also see Margolis, Eric, 'Israel's Covert Nuclear Program', *Toronto Sun*, 2 June 2000.

326. Steinbach, John, 'Nuke Nation: Israel's Weapons of Mass Destruction', *Covert Action Quarterly*, April/June 2001.

327. Cook, Johnathan, 'Vale of tears', *Al-Ahram Weekly*, Cairo, 5–11 April 2001, No. 528.

328. Zinn, Howard, 'Iraq Bombing "Another Lie"', ZNet, December 1998, http://www.zmag.org; also available at the Office of the Americas (OAS), http://www.officeoftheamericas.org.

329. Mesler, Bill, (Mesler is a member of the Investigative Fund of the Nation Institute), 'The Nerve Gas Club', *The Nation*, 29 June 1998.

330. See Lindsay-Poland, John, 'The United States tested mustard gas on its own troops in Panama – and left a mess behind', *The Progressive*, December 1998.

331. Bukowski, G., Lopez, D. A., and McGhee, F. M., *Uranium Battlefields Home and Abroad: depleted Uranium use by US Department of Defense*, p. 6; Doucet, I., 'Depleted Uranium, sick soldiers and dead children?', *Global Security*, Winter 1993.

332. Hoskins, Eric, 'Making the desert glow', *New York Times*, 21 January 1993.

333. Cohen, Nick, 'Radioactive waste left in Gulf by Allies', *The Independent*, 10 November 1991.

334. Doucet, I., 'Depleted Uranium, sick soldiers and dead children?', *Global Security*, Winter 1993.

335. BBC News, 'Depleted Uranium Ban Demanded', 17 December 1999.

336. Wilson, Billy, 'Thousands of Gulf veterans are dying', *The Journal* (London), 9 April 2000.

337. Hoskins, Eric, 'Making the desert glow', *New York Times*, 21 January 1993.

338. Common Courage Press, 'More on depleted uranium', Email Political Literacy Course, 7 April 2000, http://www.commoncouragepress.com. For extensive documentation of the reality of Gulf War syndrome, see http://www.gulfwarvets.com.

339. *Sunday Herald*, 7 June 2001.

340. Army Environmental Policy Institute, *Health and Environmental Consequences of Depleted Uranium Use in the US Army*, June 1995.

341. US General Accounting Office, *Operation Desert Storm: Army Not Adequately Prepared to Deal With Depleted Uranium Contamination*, January 1993 (GAO/NSIAD-93-90).

342. AMMCOM, *Kinetic Energy Penetrator Long Term Strategy Study*, Danesi, July 1990, Appendix D.

343. Excerpts from the July 1990 Science and Applications International Corporation report: 'Kinetic Energy Penetrator Environment and Health Considerations', as included in Appendix D – US Army Armaments, Munitions and Chemical Command report: 'Kinetic Energy Penetrator Long Term Strategy Study, July 1990'.

344. Lt. Col. M. V. Ziehmn, Los Alamos National Laboratory memorandum, 1 March 1991.

345. See especially Depleted Uranium Education Project, *Depleted Uranium – Metal of Dishonor: How the Pentagon Radiates Soldiers and Civilians with DU Weapons*, International Action Center, New York, May 1997. Also see the book by Dr Siegwart Horst-Gunther, President of the International Yellow Cross, *Uranium Projectiles – Severely Maimed Soldiers, Deformed Babies, Dying Children*, Ahriman Verlag; this book is a documentary record of DU ammunition after-effects compiled between 1993 and 1995.

346. Arbuthnot, Felicity, and Mackay, Neil, 'Allies "told in 1991 of uranium cancer risks"', *Sunday Herald*, 7 January 2001.

347. Rokke, Doug, 'Depleted Uranium and its effects on Iraq', in CASI, *Sanctions on Iraq: background, consequences, strategies*, Proceedings of the Conference hosted by Campaign Against Sanctions on Iraq (CASI), Cambridge, 13–14 November 1999.

348. Pilger, John, 'Iraq: The great cover-up', *New Statesman*, 22 January 2001.

349. Rokke, Doug, 'Depleted Uranium and its effects on Iraq', op. cit.

350. *Sunday Herald*, 7 June 2001.

351. *New Statesman*, 22 January 2001.

352. Ibid.

353. 'Shifting Priorities: UNMOVIC and the Future of Inspections in Iraq: An Interview with Ambassador Rolf Ekeus', *Arms Control Today*, Arms Control Association, Washington, DC, March 2000.

354. Interview with Scott Ritter, *New Internationalist*, September 1999, No. 316.

355. Cited in Pilger, John, 'Disarming Iraq', http://pilger.carlton.com/iraq/weapons. Also see AMW Media Resources, 'The Myth of "Evidence" of Iraq's Weapons of Mass Destruction', Arab Media Watch, http://www.arabmediawatch.com/resources.htm.

356. 'Assessing Saddam's Likely Arms Stash', CBS News, 7 September 2002, http://www.cbsnews.com/stories/2002/09/07/attack/main521170.shtml.

357. Interview with Scott Ritter in *Al-Hayyat*, 31 March 1999.

358. Ritter, Scott, *Arms Control Today*, June 2000.

359. Scott Ritter cited in Pilger, John, 'Squeezed to death', op. cit.

360. Interview with Raymond Zalinskas by Bob Edwards, National Public Radio (NPR), Morning edition, 13 February 1998; Masri,

Rania, 'Half Truths and Weaponry', Iraq Action Coalition, August 1998, http://iraqaction.org/womd.htm.

361. Reese, Charley, 'Nothing to do with weapons, everything to do with oil prices', *Orlando Sentinel*, 9 November 1997.

362. *The Guardian*, 15 March 2002, p. 16.

363. Zunes, Stephen, 'The Gulf War: Eight Myths', *Foreign Policy In Focus: Special Report*, January 2001.

364. 'Anticipating Inspections: UNMOVIC Readies Itself for Iraq', *Arms Control Today*, July/August 2000, Vol. 30, No. 6, http://www.armscontrol.org/ACT/julaug00/blixjulaug.html.

365. Bennis, Phyllis, 'Powell's Dubious Case for War', *Foreign Policy In Focus*, 5 February 2003, http://www.fpif.org/commentary/2003/0302powell.html.

366. Said, Edward, 'Apocalypse Now', Znet, http://www.zmag.org. First published in Arabic in *Al-Hayyat*, London, and in English, *Al-Ahram Weekly*, Cairo.

367. UNSCOM Report, 15 December 1998, http://www.un.org/Depts/unscom/s98-1172.htm.

368. UNSCOM Report, 6 October 1997, Annex I, para.33, http://www.un.org/Depts/unscom/sres97-774.htm.

369. UN Security Council Panel report, 27 March 1999, para.14, http://www.un.org/Depts/unmovic/documents/Amorim%20Report.htm.

370. UNSCOM report, 15 December 1998, Annex I, penultimate paragraph, http://www.un.org/Depts/unscom/s98-1172.htm.

371. UNSCOM report, 22 November 1997, para.5, http://www.un.org/Depts/unscom/s97-922.htm.

372. Ibid., para.12.

373. UN Security Council Panel report, 17 March 1999, para. 23, http://www.un.org/Depts/unmovic/documents/Amorim%20Report.htm.

374. UN report, 22 November 1997, para.7, http://www.un.org/Depts/unscom/s97-922.htm.

375. UNSCOM Report, 6 October 1997, para.123, http://www.un.org/Depts/unscom/sres97-774.htm.

376. UN Security Council Report, 27 March 1999, para. 17, http://www.un.org/Depts/unmovic/documents/Amorim%20Report.htm.

377. CRS Issue Brief for Congress, 'Iraq: Compliance, Sanctions, and US Policy', Congressional Research Service, Library of Congress, 29 November 2001, p. 6, http://www.fas.org/man/crs/IB92117.pdf.

378. Ritter, Scott, 'The Case for Iraq's Qualitative Disarmament', *Arms Control Today*, Arms Control Association, Washington, DC, June 2002, http://www.armscontrol.org/act/2000_06/iraqjun.asp.

379. *The Guardian*, 5 March 2002.

380. Ritter, Scott, 'The Case for Iraq's Qualitative Disarmament', op. cit.

381. Gonsalves, Sean, 'Scott Ritter on Iraq', *Cape Cod Times*, 7 March 2000.

382. Vice-President Dick Cheney on 26 August 2002 stated that Kamel's story 'should serve as a reminder to all that we often learned more as the result of defections than we learned from the inspection regime itself'. President Bush stated on 7 October 2002 that: 'In 1995, after several years of deceit by the Iraqi regime, the head of Iraq's military industries defected. It was then that the regime was forced to admit that it had produced more than 30,000 liters of anthrax and other deadly biological agents. The inspectors, however, concluded that Iraq had likely produced two to four times that amount. This is a massive stockpile of biological weapons that has never been accounted for, and capable of killing millions.' On 5 February 2003, Colin Powell stated to the UN Security Council that: 'It took years for Iraq to finally admit that it had produced four tons of the deadly nerve agent, VX. A single drop of VX on the skin will kill in minutes. Four tons. The admission only came out after inspectors collected documentation as a result of the defection of Hussein Kamal, Saddam Hussein's late son-in-law.' Prime Minister Tony Blair stated to the House of Commons on 25 February 2003 that: 'It was only four years later, after the defection of Saddam's son-in-law to Jordan, that the offensive biological weapons and the full extent of the nuclear program were discovered.'

383. *Newsweek*, 24 February 2003.

384. Rangawala, Glen, 'Review of Hussein Kamel's Interview with UNSCOM of 22 August 1995', *Middle East Reference*, 27 February 2003, http://middleeastreference.org.uk/kamel.html.

385. Barry, John, 'The Defector's Secrets', *Newsweek*, 3 March 2003, http://www.msnbc.com/news/876128.asp..

386. Sponeck, Hans, and Halliday, Denis, 'A "New" Iraq Policy: What About International Law and Compassion?' Citizens Concerned for the People of Iraq (CCPI), Seattle, 29 May 2001, http://www.scn.org/ccpi/sponeck-halliday.html.

387. Cited in Albert, Michael, 'Impeachable Offense: Clinton as (Desert) Fox in the Henhouse', ZNet, December 1998, http://www.zmag.org.

388. Routledge, Paul, *Daily Mirror*, 18 December 1998.

389. Ritter, Scott, *Endgame*, Simon & Schuster, New York, 1999, pp. 199–200.

390. Zunes, Stephen, 'The Gulf War: Eight Myths', *Foreign Policy In Focus: Special Report*, January 2001.

391. *New York Times*, 17 December 1998. Also see the UN's own chronology at http://www.un.org/Depts/unscom/Chronology/chronologyframe.htm.

392. Butler, Richard, *Saddam Defiant*, 2000.

393. *The Economist*, 9 January 1999.
394. IAC Briefing, 'Lies, Fraud, Deceit – a Response from the Anti-war Forces to Clinton's Bombing of Iraq', International Action Center, New York, 1998.
395. *Washington Post*, 18 December 1998.
396. IAC Briefing, 'Lies, Fraud, Deceit – a Response from the Anti-war Forces to Clinton's Bombing of Iraq', op. cit.
397. Associated Press, 17 December 1998.
398. Scarborough, Richard, *Washington Times*, 17 December 1998.
399. *Washington Post*, 16 December 1998, 26 January 1999.
400. Ritter cited in *New York Post*, 17 December 1998. Research Director at the Preamble Center in Washington, DC, Mark Weisbrot, had observed of the impeachment factor: 'President Clinton's decision to bomb Iraq on the eve of the impeachment vote gives a whole new meaning to the word "transparency". The circumstantial evidence of a connection between the two events is awfully strong: a vote by the House to impeach was almost certain, and this was his only way out. And the President offered no convincing explanation for why an attack that has been threatened for years could not wait even another couple of days. In addition to the timing, the open-ended nature of the President's attack is very suspicious. When will it end? If he keeps it going until January 6, when the new Congress takes office, the impeachment resolution of the House Judiciary Committee would die.' (Weisbrot, Mark, 'President Clinton Finds a Way to Avoid Impeachment', ZNet, December 1998, http://www.zmag.org.)
401. Petras, James, 'Who's Lying to Who in the Gulf?', December 1998, ZNet, http://www.zmag.org.
402. *Washington Post*, 29 September 1998.
403. BBC News, 3 November 1998.
404. Boyer, Peter J., *New Yorker*, 9 November 1998.
405. CST, 9 PM, 11 November 1998. Also see Masud, Enver, 'Israel's Willing Executioners', op. cit.
406. *Washington Post*, 6 January 1998. Also see 'Annan "Alarmed" by UNSCOM, US Relationship', The News Channel, 6 January 1998, http://www.akhbar.com.
407. Interview with Scott Ritter on the NBC Today Show, 17 December 1998.
408. IPA Press Release, 'Iraq Sanctions: What's the Policy?', Institute for Public Accuracy, Washington, DC, 13 November 1998, http://www.accuracy.org/press.htm.
409. Ritter, Scott, *Endgame*, p. 201; cited in 'Quotes from Scott Ritter', Iraq Action Coalition, http://iraqaction.org.
410. The public was given promises on 16 December 1998 by the likes of Robin Cook that such extreme military action was justified because it would without any doubt succeed in leaving Saddam's weapons of mass destruction 'ineffectual'. Yet this was contrary to

another claim of the Western powers that they did not even know the details and locations of Saddam's weapons. The US/UK claim that they wished to destroy Saddam's weapons was therefore incoherent; Clinton stated that the US/UK allies were bombing because Saddam was failing to cooperate with the UNSCOM in revealing his allegedly hidden weapons. The aim of the bombing was to destroy the weapons that UNSCOM had allegedly failed to find and destroy. This, however, brings up the following question: how could Clinton and Blair plan an operation to destroy Saddam's weapons with full confidence in the success of this operation, when they simultaneously claimed to have no firm knowledge of these same weapons? The whole conception is utterly self-refuting. Either one knows where the weapons are, in which case the UN inspections worked and one can destroy them in confidence – meaning that there is no need to arbitrarily bomb the whole country – or one does not know where the weapons are, in which case arbitrarily bombing the country with no clear idea of where the weapons are is not going to achieve anything at all with even the slightest degree of certainty, rendering the whole operation entirely futile.

411. *Washington Post*, 16 November 1998.
412. CNN, 28 December 1999.
413. Agence France Presse,15 December 1999.
414. *Boston Globe*, 7 January 1999.
415. Fisk, Robert, 'Exposed: Britain and America's merciless secret blitz on Iraq', *The Independent*, 21 February 1999.
416. 'No-Fly Zones on Northern and Southern Iraq: US and British planes have been striking Iraq almost daily since December 1998', Iraq Action Coaltion, 27 May 1999, http://iraqaction.org/ decbomb.html. The report is based on reports from Western news agencies, including AP, AFP, CNN and Reuters.
417. Sloan, Sara, *Workers World*, 16 December 1999.
418. Pilger, John, 'Squeezed to death', op. cit.
419. *The Times*, June 2000.
420. Armsby, Gery, 'US/Britain Bomb Civilian Targets in Iran', International Action Center, 22 August 2000, http://www.iacenter.org/sanact.htm.
421. *The Guardian*, 4 March 2000. It is worth noting Pilger's exceptional documentary aired on British television, *Paying the Price: The Killing of the Children of Iraq*, ITV Carlton, 6 March 2000, in which the Anglo-American war on Iraq was uncompromisingly exposed.
422. Pilger, John, 'The Secret War: Iraq War Already Underway', *The Mirror*, 20 December 2002, available at http://www.globalpolicy.org/security/issues/iraq/nofly/2002/ 1220secret.htm.
423. Ibish, Hussein, letter published in *USA Today*, 28 January 1999 .
424. Pilger, John, 'The Secret War: Iraq War Already Underway', op. cit.

425. Graham-Brown, Sarah, 'No-Fly Zones: Rhetoric and Real Intentions', MERIP Press Information Note, Middle East Research and Information Project, 20 February 2001.

426. Ibid.

427. Pilger, John, 'The Secret War,' op. cit.

428. Cited in Bunch, William, 'Invading Iraq Not a New Idea for Bush Clique', *Philadelphia Daily News*, 27 January 2003, http://www.philly.com/mld/dailynews/2003/01/27/news/local/5025024.htm.

429. Ibid.

430. Ibid.

431. Rose, David, and Vulliamy, Ed, *The Observer*, 14 October 2002, http://www.observer.co.uk/international/story/0,6903,573893,00.html.

432. Sobieraj, Sandra, 'White House Mail Sorters Anthrax-free', Associated Press, 24 October 2001, http://www.phillyburbs.com/terror/news/1024beth.htm.

433. JW Press Release, 'The Government is Lying about the Full Extent and Source of Anthrax Attacks: Evidence Mounts that White House and Federal Agencies are Covering Up Key Information', Judicial Watch, Washington, DC, 24 October 2001, http://www.judicialwatch.org/1060.shtml.

434. For some general discussion of the Patriot Act and other measures imposed by the Bush administration curtailing civil rights and liberties, see Ahmed, Nafeez Mosaddeq, *The War on Freedom: How and Why America was Attacked, September 11, 2001*, Tree of Life/Media Messenger Books, Joshua Tree, CA, 2002.

435. CNN, 'FBI Tests Leahy Anthrax Letter', 18 November 2001, http://www.cnn.com/2001/HEALTH/conditions/11/18/anthrax.letter.

436. Lancaster, John, 'Anti-terrorism Bill Hits Snag on the Hill: Dispute Between Senate Democrats, White House Threatens Committee Approval', *Washington Post*, 3 October 2001.

437. 'Chronology of Anthrax Events', *South-Florida Sun Sentinel*, December 2001, http://www.sun-sentinel.com/sfl-1013anthraxchronology.story.

438. Broad, William J., et. al., 'Anthrax Probe Hampered by FBI Blunders', *New York Times*, 9 November 2001; 'Chronology of Anthrax Events', op. cit.

439. Rosen, James, et. al., 'Bush Signs Anti-terror Bill', FOX News, 26 October 2001.

440. Altimari, Dave, 'Anthrax Killer Outlasting the Hunters', *Hartford Courant*, 7 September 2002, http://www.ctnow.com/hc-911anthrax.artsep07.story.

441. Reuters, 'US Expert Said Behind Anthrax Mails', 29 November 2001.

442. Weiss, Rick, and Schmidt, Susan, 'Capitol Hill Anthrax Matches

Army's Stocks', *Washington Post*, 16 December 2001,
http://www.washingtonpost.com/ac2/
wp-dyn?pagename=article&node=&contentId=
A49502-2001Dec15&notFound=true.

443. Dee, Joseph, 'Anthrax Suspect ID'd', *Trenton Times*, 19 February 2002, http://www.nj.com/mercer/times/index.ssf?/mercer/times/02-19-IZAR1IUB.html. Also see BBC Newsnight, 'Anthrax attacks', 14 March 2002, http://news.bbc.co.uk/hi/english/audiovideo/programs/newsnight/archive/newsid_1873000/1873368.stm

444. A detailed account drawing on several press reports is Martin, Patrick, 'FBI knows anthrax mailer but won't make an arrest, US scientist charges', World Socialist Web Site (WSWS), 25 February 2002, http://www.wsws.org/articles/2002/feb2002/anth-f25.shtml. Also see Rosenberg, Barbara Hatch, 'Analysis of the Anthrax Attacks', Federation of American Scientists, September 2002,
http://www.fas.org/bwc/news/anthraxreport.htm.

445. Madsen, Wayne, 'Anthrax and the Agency: Thinking the Unthinkable', *Counterpunch*, 8–9 April 2002,
http://www.counterpunch.org/madsenanthrax.html.

446. Ibid. Madsen cites a 4 April report by ABC News investigative reporter Brian Ross broadcast on ABC World News Tonight.

447. Ibid.

448. JW Press Release, FBI and Bush Administration Sued Over Anthrax Documents, 7 June 2002, http://www.judicialwatch.org/1967.shtml.

449. Lowry, Richard, 'End Iraq', *National Review*, 15 October 2001, http://www.nationalreview.com/15oct01/lowry101501.shtml.

450. *The Times*, 16 February 2002, p. 19.

451. *The Guardian*, 6 May 2002.

452. Cockburn, Andrew and Patrick, *Out of the Ashes: The Resurrection of Saddam Hussein*, HarperCollins, 1999, p. 37.

453. *The Observer*, 17 November 2002, p. 20.

454. *Sunday Telegraph*, 17 March 2002, p. 15.

455. *Newsweek*, 25 March 2002.

456. Krugman, Paul, 'The Martial Plan', *New York Times*, 21 February 2003, http://www.nytimes.com/2003/02/21/opinion/21KRUG.html?ex=1046832072&ei=1&en=b9794179c1952ba0.

457. Cockburn, Patrick, 'Kurdish leaders enraged by "undemocratic" American plan to occupy Iraq', *The Independent*, 17 February 2003, http://news.independent.co.uk/low_res/story.jsp?story=379060&host=3&dir=508.

458. Buncombe, Andrew, 'US sees "someone like Jimmy Carter" to oversee administration after overthrow of Saddam', *The Independent*, 13 February 2003.

459. *Washington Post*, 17 January 2003.

460. Bruce, Ian, 'General Franks "to run Iraq after war"', *The Herald*, 24 February 2002.
461. 'Full US Control Planned for Iraq', *Washington Post*, 21 February 2003.
462. 'US reveals post-war carve-up', *The Age*, 9 March 2003.
463. 'Promised: Autonomy for British Command, Post War Assets in Iraq', DEBKA-Net-Weekly, 7–12 March 2003, http://www.debka.com/article.php?aid=401.
464. *The Observer*, 17 November 2002.
465. *Time Magazine*, 13 May 2002.
466. Hersh, Seymour, *New Yorker*, 24 December 2001, p. 63.
467. See Rai's ARROW Anti-War Briefings at http://www.j-n-v.org/ARROW_briefings.htm, which formed the basis for his book *War Plan Iraq: Ten Reasons Against War on Iraq*, Verso, London, 2002.
468. *The Times*, 16 February 2002.
469. *The Observer*, 8 December 2002.
470. *The Telegraph*, 17 January 2003.
471. *The Guardian*, 17 January 2003. Also see *The Observer*, 19 January 2003.
472. *The Telegraph*, 17 January 2003.
473. *The Telegraph*, 18 January 2003.
474. *The Independent*, 18 January 2003. Credit to Rai for alerting me to some of the above reports.
475. Pitt, William Rivers, 'Flawed Report: Iraqi Warheads Found', *Dissident Voice*, 17 January 2003, http://www.dissidentvoice.org/Articles/Pitt_CNN.htm.
476. *Sunday Telegraph*, 19 January 2003.
477. *The Times*, *The Guardian*, 20 January 2003.
478. *Los Angeles Times*, 13 February 2003.
479. Associated Press, 'Disputed Iraq Missiles Look to Have Been Previously Declared', 13 February 2003.
480. *Los Angeles Times*, 13 February 2003.
481. Associated Press, 'Blix: No Weapons of Mass Destruction', 14 February 2003.
482. Associated Press, 'Blix Says Iraq "Substantially Disarming"', 7 March 2003.
483. Warrick, Joby, 'Some Evidence on Iraq Called Fake', *Washington Post*, 8 March 2003, http://www.washingtonpost.com/wp-dyn/articles/A59403-2003Mar7.html.
484. 'Dossier cited by Powell called a "sham"', *The Nation*, 24 February 2003. Also see Rangawala's detailed point-by-point deconstruction of the Powell briefing, 'Claims and evaluations in Powell's statement to the Security Council of 5 February 2003', *Middle East Reference*, February 2003, http://middleeastreference.org.uk/powell030205.html.
485. See Rangawala, Glen, 'Claims and evaluations of Iraq's pro-

scribed weapons', *Middle East Reference*, 25 February 2003, http://middleeastreference.org.uk/iraqweapons.html.

486. IAC Statement, 'International Action Centre Statement on US-Iraq crisis: Until Sanctions are Lifted the Crisis Will Continue', International Action Center, New York, 15 November 1998.

487. Zunes, Stephen, 'The Gulf War: Eight Myths', Special Report, *Foreign Policy in Focus*, January 2001.

488. Bennis, Phyllis, 'And They Called It Peace: US Policy on Iraq', Iraq: A Decade of Devastation, *Middle East Report*, 215, Summer 2000.

489. Schoenman, Ralph, *Iraq and Kuwait: A History Suppressed*, Veritas Press, Santa Barbara, CA, pp. 11–12; *New York Review of Books*, 16 January 1992, p. 51.

490. Paul, James A., 'Iraq: the Struggle for Oil', Global Policy Forum, August 2002 (revised December 2002), http://www.globalpolicy.org/security/oil/2002/08jim.htm. Also see 'Iraq Country Analysis Brief', Energy Information Administration, Washington, DC, February 2003, http://www.eia.doe.gov/emeu/cabs/iraq.html.

491. Testimony of General Anthony C. Zinni, Senate Armed Services Committee, 13 April 1999.

492. Associated Press dispatch reporting on US Defense Secretary William Cohen's Seattle speech, 18 February 1999. Since it is Western oil interests that have such a huge stake in Western policy here, it should be remembered that the policy will change in accord with the market. Recently there have been trends tending to make it more profitable to prevent oil prices from increasing further, and to lower them. This may result in Iraqi oil being permitted to enter the global market again. Thus, if the market so desires, no doubt Iraqi oil will begin being gobbled up anew by Western corporations in conditions in which lower oil prices are particularly attractive.

493. Islam, Faisal, and Walsh, Nick Paton, 'US buys up Iraqi oil to stave off crisis', *The Guardian*, 26 January 2003, http://www.guardian.co.uk/Iraq/Story/0,2763,882518,00.html.

494. Ibid.

495. Campbell, Colin J., 'Peak Oil: An Outlook on Crude Oil Depletion', Mbendi Energy News, February 2002, http://www.mbendi.co.za/indy/oilg/p0070.htm.

496. Dfieffer, Dave Allen, 'Is the Empire About Oil?' *From The Wilderness*, 8 August 2002, http://www.fromthewilderness.com/free/ww3/080802_oil_empire.html.

497. Duncan, Richard C., 'The Peak of World Oil Production and the Road to the Olduvai Gorge', presented at Summit 2000, Geological Society of America, Nevada, 13 November 2000, http://dieoff.com/page224.htm.

498. Campbell, Colin J., 'Peak Oil: An Outlook on Crude Oil Depletion', op. cit.

499. Monbiot, George, 'In the Crocodile's Mouth', *The Guardian*, 5 November 2002; Mackay, Neil, 'Official: US oil at the heart of Iraq crisis', *Sunday Herald*, 6 October 2002, http://www.sundayherald.com/print28285; Mackay, Neil, 'The West's battle for oil', *Sunday Herald*, http://www.sundayherald.com/28224. For full text see Report of an Independent Task Force, *Strategic Energy Policy Challenges For The 21st Century*, James A. Baker III Institute for Public Policy/Council on Foreign Relations, April 2001, available online at the Baker Institute website, http://www.rice.edu/projects/baker/Pubs/workingpapers/cfrbipp_energy/energytf.htm.

500. Cited in Clark, William, 'The Real Reasons for the Upcoming War with Iraq: A Macroeconomic and Geostrategic Analysis of the Unspoken Truth', Independent Media Center, January 2003. An extensively documented study of the oil currency issue is available at http://www.ratical.org/ratville/CAH/RRiraqWar.html.

501. Hebert, H. Josef, 'Oil inventories at critical low', *The Mercury News*, 14 February 2003, http://www.bayarea.com/mld/mercurynews/business/5171415.htm.

502. Islam, Faisal, and Walsh, Nick Paton, 'US buys up Iraqi oil to stave off crisis', op. cit.

503. Collier, Robert, 'Oil firms wait as Iraq crisis unfolds', *San Francisco Chronicle*, 29 September 2002.

504. *Current History*, March 2002.

505. *New Statesman*, 20 March 2000.

506. Dreyfuss, Robert, 'The Thirty Year Itch', op. cit.

507. Ibid.

508. Ibid.

509. Spinney, Chuck, 'Is Egypt in Play and Why is it the Prize?' *Defense and the National Interest*, 16 August 2002, http://www.d-n-i.net/fcs/comments/c457.htm.

510. Dreyfuss, Robert, 'The Thirty Year Itch', op. cit.

511. Arieff, Irwin, 'UN Sees 500,000 Iraqi Casualties at Start of War', Reuters, 7 January 2003. Available at http://www.commondreams.org/headlines03/0107-09.htm.

512. Leopold, Evylyn, 'Prospects dim for UN resolution on war with Iraq', Reuters, 14 March 2003.

512. Bright, Martin, et. al., 'Britons Left in Jail Amid Fears That Saudi Arabia Could Fall to al-Qaeda', *The Observer*, 28 July 2002.

514. Boudreaux, Richard, and Hendren, John, 'US halts pursuit of Turkish bases, warns on incursion', *Los Angeles Times*, 15 March 2003.

515. Osnos, Evan, 'Moderate Arabs Shudder, Denounce US as Gulf "Bully"', *Chicago Tribune*, 22 January 2003.

516. Ikenberry, G. John, 'America's Imperial Ambition', *Foreign Affairs*, September/October 2002, Vol. 81, No. 5.

517. Ramonet, Ignacio, 'Servile States', *Le Monde diplomatique*, October 2002.

518. Mowlam, Mo, 'The real goal is the seizure of Saudi oilfields', *The Guardian*, 5 September 2002, http://www.guardian.co.uk/Iraq/Story/0,2763,786332,00.html.

519. Goldenberg, Suzanne, 'Sharon eyes option of large-scale military offensive', *The Guardian*, 9 May 2002.

520. Van Creveld, Martin, *The Telegraph*, 28 April 2002.

521. Hersh, Seymour, *The Samson Option: Israel's Nuclear Arsenal and American Foreign Policy*, Random House, New York, 1991, p. 319, 19. Also see Shahak, Israel, *Open Secrets: Israeli Nuclear and Foreign Policies*, Pluto Press, London, 1997, p. 2, 37–8, 150: 'The wish for peace, so often assumed as the Israeli aim, is not in my view a principle of Israeli policy, while the wish to extend Israeli domination and influence is ... Israel is preparing for a war, nuclear if need be, for the sake of averting domestic change not to its liking, if it occurs in some or any Middle Eastern states ... Israel clearly prepares itself to seek overtly a hegemony over the entire Middle East ... without hesitating to use for the purpose all means available, including nuclear ones ... Israel's insistence on the independent use of its nuclear weapons can be seen as the foundation on which Israeli grand strategy rests ... The prospect of Gush Emunim, or some secular right-wing Israeli fanatics, or some of the delirious Israeli Army generals, seizing control of Israeli nuclear weapons ... cannot be precluded ... [W]hile Israeli Jewish society undergoes a steady polarization, the Israeli security system increasingly relies on the recruitment of cohorts from the ranks of the extreme right.'

522. Shahak, Israel, *Jewish History, Jewish Religion: The Weight of Three Thousand Years*, Pluto Press, London, 1997, p. 9.

523. Samet, Gideon, 'Secrets, Smoke and Lies', *Ha'aretz*, 22 March 2002.

524. Stratfor, 'Uniting Jordan and Iraq Might be Prime Post-War Strategy', 30 September 2002, http://www.stratfor.com/fib/fib_view.php?ID=206509.

525. Friedman, George, 'The Region After Iraq', Stratfor Weekly, 5 February 2003.

526. Klein, Joe, *Time Magazine*, 5 February 2003.

527. IASPS Research Paper in Strategy, 'Coping with Crumbling States: A Western and Israeli Balance of Power Strategy for the Levant', Institute for Advanced Strategic and Political Studies, Jerusalem/Washington, DC, 1996, http://www.iasps.org.il/strat2.htm.

528. Christison, Kathleen and Bill, 'The Bush Administration's Dual Loyalties: A Rose By Any Other Name', *Counter Punch*, 13 December 2003, http://www.counterpunch.org/christison1213.html.

529. Sale, Richard, and Morris, Nicholas M., 'War talk sweeps city', United Press International, 11 February 2003; reprinted in *Washington Times*, 12 February 2003, http://www.washtimes.com/upi-breaking/20030211-065953-3776r.htm.
530. Ibid.
531. Ibid.
532. Agence France Presse, 'Turkey to send forces into N. Iraq in coordination with US', 26 March 2003.
533. Sale, Richard, and Morris, Nicholas M., 'War talk sweeps city', op. cit.
534. Ibid.
535. *Washington Post*, 6 August 2002.
536. Haass, Richard N., 'Imperial America', paper at the Atlanta Conference, 11 November 2000, available at the Brookings Institution, http://www.brook.edu/dybdocroot/views/articles/haass/2000imperial.htm.
537. Wallerstein, Immanuel, 'The Eagle Has Crash Landed', *Foreign Policy*, July/August 2002, http://www.foreignpolicy.com/issue_julyaug_2002/wallerstein.html.
538. Buncombe, Andrew, 'Top US military planner fears a "likely" repeat of Somalia bloodbath', *The Independent*, 15 March 2003, http://news.independent.co.uk/world/middle_east/story.jsp?story=387234.
539. See for example Ahmed, Nafeez M., 'The Impending Abyss: A Comprehensive Assessment of the Past and Future Trajectory of the Israel-Palestine Conflict', Institute for Policy Research and Development, Brighton, July 2002, http://globalresearch.org/view_article.php?aid=551455571. Featured by JustPeace, TheGlobalSite, University of Sussex, http://www.theglobalsite.ac.uk/justpeace/israel-palestine.htm.
540. Friedman, George, 'The Region After Iraq', op. cit.
541. Capra, Fritjof, *The Turning Point: Science, Society and the Rising Culture*, HarperCollins, London, 1983, pp. 443-5.
542. Capra, Fritjof, 'A Systematic Analysis of International Terrorism', Institute for Policy Research and Development, Brighton, 2001, http://globalresearch.org/view_article.php?aid=522779705.
543. Rossi, James M., 'Book Review: Globalization and its Discontents', *Human Nature Review*, 9 July 2002, Vol. 2, No. 293-6, http://human-nature.com/nibbs/02/stiglitz.html. See Stiglitz, Joseph, *Globalization and its Discontents*, W. W. Norton & Co., 2002.
544. Capra, Fritjof, 'A Systematic Analysis of International Terrorism', op. cit.
545. See McMurtry, John, *Value Wars: The Global Market Versus the Life Economy*, Pluto Press, London, 2002. Also see Capra, *The Turning Point*, op. cit., for what is probably the best overall analysis of the multiple world crises that have been developing over the years to

date. Capra does more than analyse; he offers a comprehensive series of social, personal, institutional and ideological solutions based on a broad survey of existing research, and derived from the latest scientific findings.

546. BBC News, 'US will liberate Iraq, says Bush,' 3 January 2003, http://news.bbc.co.uk/2/hi/middle_east/2625981.stm.

547. Interview with Kate Adie, Phillip Knightley, Chris Hedges and Connor Brady, Sunday Show, RTE Radio1, 9 March 2003.

548. RWB Press Release, 'Reporters Without Borders accuses US military of deliberately firing at journalists', Reporters Without Borders, 8 April 2003, http://www.rsf.org/article.php3?id_article=5975.

549. Fisk, Robert, 'Is there some element in the US military which wants to take out journalists?', *The Independent*, 9 April 2003, http://argument.independent.co.uk/commentators/story.jsp?story=395412.

550. Al-Ghalib, Essam, 'Western Journalists Beaten, Starved by Americans,' *Arab News*, Jeddah, 3 April 2003. Al-Ghalib, a seasoned war correspondent who was reporting from Baghdad, experienced the harassment of non-embedded journalists in Iraq by US forces directly. See his 'US military police are acting as "censors" in this war', *Arab News*, 7 April 2003. Al-Ghalib's reports are available online at http://www.arabnews.com/War/Essam.asp.

551. Morley, Jefferson, 'The Origins of "Shock and Awe" ', *Washington Post*, 21 March 2003, http://www.washingtonpost.com/ac2/wp-dyn?pagename=article&node=&contentId=A5948-2003Mar21&notFound=true. CBS News also confirmed that 'Shock and Awe' was the basis for the 2003 war plan in Iraq (see note below).

552. Ullman, Harlan K. and Wade, James P., *Shock and Awe: Achieving Rapid Dominance*, National Defence University Press, Washington DC, December 1996. Available online at the US Department of Defence's Command and Control Research Program, http://www.dodccrp.org/shockIndex.html.

553. Ibid.

554. CBS Evening News, 'Iraq Faces Massive Missile Barrage', 24 January 2003, http://www.cbsnews.com/stories/2003/01/24/eveningnews/main537928.shtml.

555. Peterson, Scott, 'US mulls air strategies in Iraq', *Christian Science Monitor*, 30 January 2003, http://www.csmonitor.com/2003/0130/p06s01-woiq.htm.

556. Mokhiber, Russell, 'Ari & I: White House Press Briefing with Ari Fleischer, Wednesday, February 19, 2003 – 12:15 PM', Common Dreams News Center, 19 February 2003, http://www.commondreams.org/headlines03/0219-10.htm.

557. Transcript of interview with Ambassador Joseph Wilson by Chris Matthews, Hardball, MS-NBC, 25 February 2003.

558. Bunch, William, 'US Plan for Saddam: Shock and Awe', *Philadelphia Daily News*, 26 February 2003.

559. Roy, Arundhati, 'Mesopotamia. Babylon. The Tigris and Euphrates', *The Guardian*, 2 April 2003, http://www.guardian.co.uk/Iraq/Story/0,2763,927849,00.html.

560. Peachey, Paul, 'Baghdad doctors overwhelmed by arrival of 100 patients an hour', *The Independent*, 7 April 2003.

561. Associated Press, 'Red Cross: Iraq Wounded Too High to Count', 6 April 2003.

562. Reuters, 'ICRC says medical system all but collapsed', 11 April 2003.

563. Canadian Press, 'Red Cross Horrified by Number of Dead Civilians', 3 April 2003, http://www.ctv.ca/servlet/ArticleNews/story/CTVNews/1049413227648_10/?hub=SpecialEvent3.

564. Iraq Body Count, viewed 17 June 2003, http://www.iraqbodycount.net. Also see Steele, Jonathan, 'Body Counts', *The Guardian*, 28 May 2003.

565. Jeffery, Simon, 'We may have killed 10,000 civilians, researchers say', *The Guardian*, 13 June 2003. See IBC Report. *Counting the Human Costs: A Survey of Projects Counting Civilians Killed by the War in Iraq*, Iraq Body Count, 12 June 2003, http://www.iraqbodycount.net/editorial_june1203.htm.

566. Ford, Peter, 'Surveys pointing to high civilian death toll in Iraq', *Christian Science Monitor*, 22 May 2003, available at http://www.ccmep.org/2003_articles/Iraq/052203_surveys_pointing_to_high_civilian_death_toll.htm.

567. Kaplan, Fred, 'How many dead Iraqis? Guessing about collateral damage', *Slate*, 25 February 2003, http://slate.msn.com/id/2079264.

568. 'CIA's Golden Victory: US Bribed Iraqi Military Leaders', *Daily Express*, 18 April 2003.

569. Ahmad, Kamal, 'Hoon backs ex-Saddam loyalists to build nation', *The Observer*, 13 April 2003.

570. Goldenberg, Suzanne, 'Ba'athists slip quietly back in control', *The Guardian*, 21 April 2003.

571. Peterson, Scott, et. al., 'Amid chaos, Baghdad frustration rises', *Christian Science Monitor*, 14 April 2003.

572. Morris Stephen and Norton-Taylor, Richard, 'British-appointed Basra chief exposed as former Ba'athist', *The Guardian*, 12 April 2003.

573. Croft, Adrian, 'Protests Meet US-Led Talks on Iraq', Reuters, 15 April 2003.

574. Pasmantier, Deborah, 'Mosul shootings over-shadow US-led talks', Agence France Presse, 16 April 2003.

575. BBC News, 'US Admits Mosul Killings', 16 April 2003.

576. Pasmantier, Deborah, op. cit.

577. Graham, Bob, 'I just pulled the trigger', Evening Standard, 19 June 2003,
http://www.thisislondon.com/news/articles/5402104.
578. Cummins, Chip, 'US Probes its Iraq-Oil Rights', Wall Street Journal, 29 January 2003.
579. Stevenson, Richard, 'Bush Sees Limited Role for UN in Iraq', New York Times, 8 April 2003.
580. New York Times, 17 May 2003.
581. Documents declassified by US Army Corps of Engineers,
http://www.hq.usace.army.mil/cepa/iraq/factsheet.htm.   Cited
in Leopold, Jason, 'Secret November Deal Iraq's Oil: Halliburton and the Pentagon', Counterpunch, 14 May 2003,
http://www.counterpunch.org/leopold05142003.html
582. Leopold, Jason, op. cit.
583. Agence France Presse, 'Iraq War Planned Long in Advance; Banned Arms Not the Priority: Blix', 9 April 2003.
584. The Independent, 20 April 2003,
http://argument.independent.co.uk/
leading_articles/story.jsp?story=398837.
585. Gilfeather, Paul, 'UN watchdog slams intelligence tip-offs', The Mirror, 7 June 2003.
586. Associated Press, 'Blix suspects Iraq may have had no weapons of mass destruction', 23 May 2003.
587. Scheer, Robert, 'How their big lie came to be', The Nation, 3 June 2003, http://www.thenation.com/
doc.mhtml?i=20030616&s=scheer20030603.
588. Lumpkin, John J., 'Ex-Official: Evidence Distorted for War', Associated Press, 7 June 2003.
589. Strobel, Warren P. and Landay, Jonathan S., 'Some administration officials expressing misgivings on Iraq', Knight-Ridder Tribune News, 8 October 2002, http://www.chron.com/cs/CDA/
printstory.hts/nation/1607676.
590. Mackay, Neil, 'Revealed: the secret cabal which spun for Blair', Sunday Herald, 8 June 2003, http://www.sundayherald.com/
34491.
591. Ibid.
592. Krugman, Paul, 'Standard Operating Procedure', New York Times, 3 June 2003, http://www.pkarchive.org/column/060303.html.
593. Gomez, Edward M., 'Blair grilled over missing WMDs', San Francisco Chronicle, 5 June 2003, http://www.sfgate.com/
columnists/worldviews.
594. Ibid.
595. Dean, John W., 'Missing Weapons of Mass Destruction: Is Lying About the Reason for War an Impeachable Offense', Find Law's Legal Commentaries, 6 June 2003, http://writ.news.findlaw.com/
dean/20030606.html. Dean is former Counsel to the President of the United States.

Index

NAFEEZ MOSADDEQ AHMED is an author, human rights activist, and political analyst specializing in the study of conflicts. Born in London, England in 1978 of Bangladeshi parents, he is Executive Director of the Institute for Policy Research and Development, an independent, interdisciplinary think-tank (www.globalresearch.org). Ahmed was a researcher at the Islamic Human Rights Commission (IHRC), a UN-affiliated NGO. He was also an IHRC delegate to the United Nations World Conference Against Racism in 2001, where he delivered a paper on the Israel-Palestine conflict. He is the author of a variety of reports on human rights practices, as well as a best-selling book, *The War on Freedom*, published in English, German and Italian.

Ahmed's work on the history and development of conflict in Afghanistan has been recommended as a resource by leading universities, including Harvard and California State. He was recently named a Global Expert on War, Peace and International Affairs by the Freedom Network of the Henry Hazlitt Foundation in Chicago, and is a member of TRANSCEND, the international network of scholars specializing in peace and conflict resolution. His archive of political analyses, published on the Web by the Media Monitors Network, has been nominated a Cool Site on the Netscape Open Directory Project. Ahmed appears regularly on North American radio shows as an expert on US foreign policy. He lives in Brighton, England, with his wife and daughter.

By the same author:

The War on Freedom, How and Why America Was Attacked,
  September 11, 2001

If you have enjoyed *Behind the War on Terror,* you might enjoy other

BOOKS TO BUILD A NEW SOCIETY

Our books provide positive solutions for people who want
to make a difference. We specialize in:

• **Conscientious Commerce • Progressive Leadership**
• **Sustainable Living • Ecological Design and Planning**
• **Natural Building & Appropriate Technology • New Forestry**
• **Educational and Parenting Resources • Environment and Justice**
• **Resistance and Community • Nonviolence**

New Society Publishers

ENVIRONMENTAL BENEFITS STATEMENT

New Society Publishers has chosen to produce this book on New Leaf EcoBook 100, recycled paper made with 100% post consumer waste, processed chlorine free, and old growth free.

For every 5,000 books printed, New Society saves the following resources:[1]

32	Trees
2,919	Pounds of Solid Waste
3,211	Gallons of Water
4,189	Kilowatt Hours of Electricity
5,306	Pounds of Greenhouse Gases
23	Pounds of HAPs, VOCs, and AOX Combined
8	Cubic Yards of Landfill Space

[1]Environmental benefits are calculated based on research done by the Environmental Defense Fund and other members of the Paper Task Force who study the environmental impacts of the paper industry.

For more information on this environmental benefits statement, or to inquire about environmentally friendly papers, please contact New Leaf Paper – info@newleafpaper.com Tel: 888 • 989 • 5323.

For a full list of NSP's titles, please call **1-800-567-6772** *or check out our web site at:*

www.newsociety.com

NEW SOCIETY PUBLISHERS